INTREPID

Japan

David McElhinney

Hardie Grant

EXPLORE

Intrepid

WHAT MAKES AN INTREPID GUIDE

Intrepid, for us, means being adventurous, brave and, above all, curious. Whether you're trekking through remote countryside or trying a new-to-you dish, these kinds of experiences allow us to reach beyond our everyday to learn something new and connect with people and places.

Intrepid Guides are for the intrepid traveller – those who want to see the world in meaningful and memorable ways, rather than just push through a to-do list.

Each guide highlights places, activities and experiences that make a country special and allow us to connect to these destinations and gain life-long memories and broaden our perspective.

The contents of this guide align with everything that drives Intrepid Travel and Hardie Grant Explore – chasing adventure in new (to us) places while getting to know the people who call them home and supporting their communities along the way.

INTREPID

Japan

*INTRODUCING INTREPID TRAVEL

As the world's largest purpose-led adventure travel company, Intrepid Travel has been taking travellers around the globe since 1989.

On hundreds of trips in over 100 countries, Intrepid brings small groups of like-minded travellers together with a locally based leader. Intrepid itineraries weave the highlights into the hard-to-forget moments in hard-to-find places. From homestays to Indigenous community-led experiences, between the hidden noodle bars and backstreet bodegas, Intrepid experiences are built to keep the economic benefits of travel where they belong.

It all stems from a simple mission: create positive change through the joy of travel. As a B Corp, Intrepid is committed to balancing purpose and profit by operating equitably, sustainably and transparently. The Intrepid Foundation, established in 2002, gives travellers a way to give back to the places they've visited by supporting organisations around the world; that are making a difference in their communities.

At Intrepid, travel is about more than just seeing the world, it's about experiencing it and sparking connections with Intrepid people wherever you go.

Learn more at intrepidtravel.com.

INTRODUCTION

I often get asked why I moved to Japan. The barkeep as he pours me a tumbler of whisky. The journeyman saxophonist, keen to practice his English, wondering what twist of fate led me to an underground music club in a Tokyo suburb. The locals eyeing me with curiosity at a railway station in an anonymous stretch of nowhere, or the tour guide trying to fathom why some schmuck from Belfast is writing about her homeland. It's a fair question, I suppose, but I don't really have an answer. There was little calculus involved; it was a spontaneous decision if not a random one. A better question, and one that is more pertinent to the book you now hold, is: why did you decide to stay?

I stayed for the cities that never sleep and the gardens whose beauty is profound beyond measure. For the convenience stores that never close and the jazz cafes that rarely open. For the bars that exist in the most unlikely of places and the umami broths that turn eating into a form of divine exultation. For the ladies who pick up street litter with chopsticks, and for the artists who yearn for a world of beauty beyond their reach. For the mountain trails that harken back to old Japan, to the Age of the Gods, long before postwar construction projects had drowned the land in concrete. For warm sake and cold soba and temperate autumns. For the unequivocal truth that the deeper one's knowledge of Japan goes, the wider its mysteries become.

There are questions that will never be sufficiently answered and things I'll never comprehend. But if this is an attempt at interpretation, I best go from the start.

David McElhinney

JAPAN

Capital city: Tokyo

There are 4 main islands –
Hokkaido, Honshu, Shikoku,
Kyushu – and a further
14,000 smaller ones

Japan is divided into
47 prefectures

HOKKAIDŌ

Asahikawa • Kitami
▲ *Asahi-dake*
Sapporo • Obihiro
• Tomakomai • Kushiro

SEA OF JAPAN/
EAST SEA

• Muroran

• Hakodate

Aomori •
Hirosaki • • Hachinohe

Akita • Morioka •

Sakata •
Tsuruoka • Sendai •
Yamagata •
Niigata • • Fukushima
Nagaoka •
HONSHŪ • Iwaki
Kanazawa •
• Nagano • Mito
Fukui • Kōfu **TŌKYŌ** ◉
Matsue •
Tottori • Nagoya ▲ *Fuji*
Kyōto •
Hiroshima • Ōsaka ◉ • Hamamatsu
Kitakyūshū • • Wakayama
Fukuoka • *SHIKOKU*
Ōita • Kōchi •
Nagasaki • *KYŪSHŪ*

IZU-SHOTŌ

NORTH

PACIFIC

OCEAN

• Miyazaki
Kagoshima •
▲ *Sakurajima*

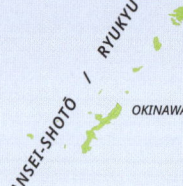

NANSEI-SHOTŌ / RYUKYU ISLANDS

OKINAWA

N

THE BASICS

History

Even when tackling Japanese history in chronological fashion, it quickly reveals itself to be vast, confounding and complex, filled with Machiavellian rulers cunning as foxes, effete court nobles drunk on opulence, warlords who thirsted for blood and lust and samurai whose sense of honour was only trumped by their callous disregard for the gift of life.

At least we have some help with parsing it all. Japanese history is neatly split into *jidai*, or periods – though some overlapping dates muddle things – dictated by technological shifts, changes in agriculture or the sociopolitical state of the nation.

Early History

The first settlers arrived in Japan sometime during the Paleolithic Age – around 30,000 years ago, based on the oldest human remains – crossing over land bridges connected to Korea in the south and Siberia in the north. The first named historical period is the Jomon, usually dated from 14,000 to 300 BCE, when the Japanese archipelago was populated by tribes of semi-sedentary hunter-gatherers. What is known about them comes from pottery fragments, archaeological artefacts and prehistoric art, giving some indication as to the tools, materials, rituals and organisation prevalent in their societies. We know they used cannabis fibres for crafting, as well as hunted (now-extinct) bison, stored acorns, nuts and berries for sustenance during winter, even engaged in trade with fellow tribes and created *jomon*, or 'cord-marked', ceramics from which the period takes its name.

Next came the Yayoi (300 BCE to 250 CE), Kofun (250 to 538) and Asuka (538 to 710) periods, during which agriculture and metallurgy progressed, dynastic clans started claiming ownership of land and the introduction of Chinese art and religion gave shape to a proto-national culture.

Japan's histories were transmitted through an oral tradition before kanji, classical Chinese script, was adopted around the fifth century. The most famous texts, the *Kojiki* (Records of Ancient Matters) and *Nihon Shoki* (Chronicles of Japan), were written in the early eighth century, from which historians have pieced together the preceding dark ages. Rife with mythology and doubtless embellished to appease the emperor, these texts detail the Shinto Age of the Gods and the history of the imperial family going back to Emperor Jimmu, a supposed descendant of the sun goddess, Amaterasu, who ascended to the throne in 660 BCE. Jimmu's existence is a subject of debate, but if the story has a kernel of truth, it makes Japan's imperial family the world's oldest continuous hereditary monarchy. This arrival of recorded history also means Japan's story becomes clearer from the 700s onwards.

Nara Period (710–794)

The Nara period is when Japan started to resemble the country we know today. It established its first permanent capital in Heijo-kyo, present-day Nara, in 710, modelled after the Chinese Tang Dynasty's capital of Chang'an. Heijo-kyo soon grew into one of the great wonders of the age. Temples like Todaiji, one of the largest wooden structures ever built (it required 900 hectares/2223 acres of forest and nearly bankrupted the empire), were constructed to evince the emperor's power and prestige. The *Kojiki* and *Nihon Shoki* kickstarted the Japanese literary tradition, land and taxation systems were introduced and Buddhism and Shinto began to merge into a still-thriving relationship known as *shinbutsu-shugo*.

Heian Period (794-1185)

The capital was moved to Heian-kyo (now Kyoto), where it would remain for 1000 years. The powerful Fujiwara family took control, governing the empire as regents and chancellors, while aristocrats from across the land were lured to Heian-kyo by tales of beauty and revelry, leaving control of their estates to administrators. This is sometimes known as the Golden Age of Japan, when the *kuge* (court nobles) were at such a remove from war and politics they spent most of their time engaged in rituals and ceremonies, writing poetry and painting, learning Chinese history and bedding each other's spouses and concubines – eventually sowing discontent among their panoply of heirs. This dovetailed with the rise of the female literati, mysterious women hidden behind silken screens and pounds of makeup, that were educated in the ways of *waka* poetry and calligraphy. They left us with accounts of court life that have remained essential works in Japan's literary canon, like *The Pillow Book* by Sei Shonagon and Murasaki Shikibu's *The Tale of Genji*, widely regarded as the world's first-ever novel.

Kamakura Period (1185–1333)

Following the Genpei War between the great Heike and Genji Clans, the first shogunate established power in Kamakura in 1192, from where the shogun Minamoto Yoritomo would rule the empire. The emperor was demoted to a symbolic figurehead and the samurai emerged, a duty-bound class of warriors employed by the *daimyo* (lords) who ruled in the provinces. It was a time of politicking, with shady elites pulling strings from the shadows, that has provided historians with plenty of debating material. But 1274 to 1281 might be the most famous years of the Kamakura period, when the Mongol leader Kublai Khan set out to invade Japan twice, amassing as many as 15,000 ships to cross the East China Sea on his second expedition. While Japan used various inventive counter tactics to ward off the Khan's armada, on *both* occasions a typhoon struck the killer blow. In fact, marine archaeologists have estimated gusts blew close to 200km/h (124mph) during the second Mongol assault, quickly turning the ships into flotsam and debris. Japan had won, not just with courage and honour, but with the help of nature itself, with the intervention of the gods. The typhoon was thus christened *kamikaze*, or divine wind, a term with which the world became all too familiar during World War II.

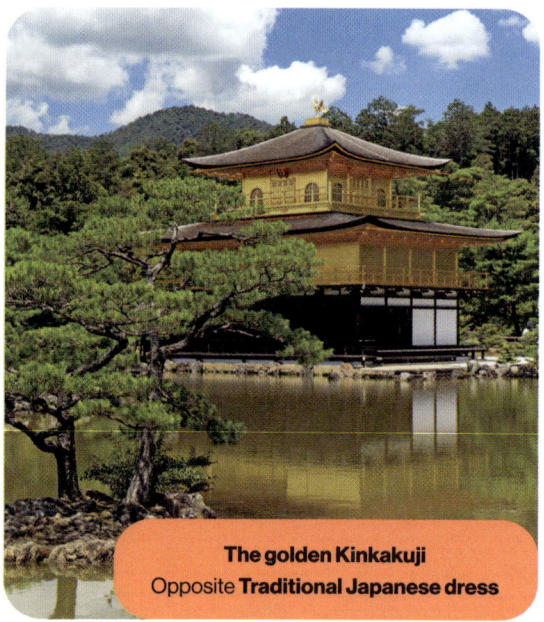

The golden Kinkakuji
Opposite **Traditional Japanese dress**

Sengoku 'Warring States' Era (1467–1615)

The Sengoku era is one of the bloodiest and most fascinating in Japanese history. Technically straddling the Muromachi (1333 to 1573) and Azuchi-Momoyama (1573 to 1615) periods, it has a narrative plucked from the pages of a George RR Martin compendium. The imperial family had not ruled for 400 years and the shogunate, having lost its authority in the wake of the internecine Onin War (1467 to 1477), was busy squabbling over who should be its new leader. This created a power vacuum and ambitious *daimyo* sought to fill it. They erected huge castles in their domains (*see* p. 176) and waged war on their neighbours with frightening alacrity. After 150 years of conflict and backstabbing, three successive men, Japan's Great Unifiers, slowly brought the chaos to an end: Oda Nobunaga, a young, battle-hungry warlord who conquered one-third of Japan; Toyotomi Hideyoshi, a low-born subordinate of Nobunaga who continued his predecessor's conquests; and Tokugawa Ieyasu, who united the empire in 1600 and had crushed any remaining insurgencies by 1615.

Edo Period (1603–1868)

The Edo period (*see* p. 196) saw the end of war and the beginning of peace. Tokugawa Ieyasu established a new shogunate in Edo (now Tokyo), a city on the Kanto Plain that would soon grow into the most populated urban area in the world, with more than one million inhabitants by the 1720s. The shogun exercised military discipline on the citizenry, creating a social order of four divisions – samurai, farmers, artisans, merchants – that dictated most aspects of an individual's life. But perhaps counterintuitively, this lead to a boom in art and culture that hadn't been seen since the days of the *kuge* nobles, with *ukiyo-e* (woodblock prints), hanging scroll paintings, performing arts, ceramics, *kinpaku* (goldleaf) ornaments and delicate lacquerware spreading throughout the country and becoming part of daily life. With Christianity gaining a foothold in the Shimabara Peninsula and Dutch and Chinese traders floating around the wharves of Nagasaki (*see* p. 186), the Shogunate began restricting foreign access to Japan to quell outside influence. That is, until Commodore Matthew Calbraith Perry dropped anchor in Edo Bay in 1853. The era of feudalism was over, Japan was entering the new world and it would never be the same again.

Meiji Period (1868–1912)

This period began with the Meiji Restoration, which returned power to the emperor after seven centuries of shogunal rule and saw Japan shift towards a constitutional monarchy, mirroring the systems of Western Europe. Emperor Meiji moved to Edo, renamed it Tokyo, meaning 'Eastern Capital', and declared it the seat of the nation. The outside world had been banned from entering Japan for more than 200 years – an official policy known as Sakoku – and now diplomats, emissaries, scholars, entrepreneurs and writers were flooding in en masse. Some came chasing a fortune, some were intent on spreading the word of god, others were lured by the overly romanticised descriptions of Japan that were characteristic of the age. Whatever their motive, these mostly Western travellers brought with them new fashions, technologies, engineering knowledge, military tactics and industrialisation. While many saw this as progress, some viewed the assimilation as an affront to traditional Japanese sensibilities. Increasing industrialisation also emboldened the more militaristic wings of the newly formed government. Japan soon waged a successful war on Russia, invaded China, annexed part of the Korean Peninsula and was slowly but surely marching towards allying itself with Nazi Germany in the 1940s.

Wartime Japan (1930s and '40s)

Japan had been in expansion mode since the beginning of the century, and many would argue this led it into World War II. In standard Western interpretations, Japan's most infamous act was the bombing of Pearl Harbour in 1941, though the Imperial Japanese Military also massacred up to 300,000 people in Nanking and turned huge swathes of Southeast Asia into a concentration camp known as the Burma Death Railway. Allied forces rained fire on Japanese cities, with one particular air raid in Tokyo killing 100,000 and injuring up to one million. A travesty by any metric, but one that's been reduced to a historical footnote because of the atomic bombs that flattened Hiroshima (see p. 182) and Nagasaki in August 1945, effectively bringing the war to an end.

Japan was devastated. Every major city, bar Kyoto (see p. 252), had been razed.

Famine, disease and squalor were rife. National coffers were empty, the remaining members of the military were committing *seppuku* (ritual disembowelment) or engaging in mass suicides and the most prominent politicians were soon to be tried for war crimes. The US and other Allied forces occupied Japan until 1952, rewriting its constitution to enshrine secularism, freedom of speech and women's suffrage and, somewhat controversially, forever renounce war as a sovereign right of the nation.

The 'Economic Miracle' Years (1952–2000)

Few would have predicted in 1945 that within a generation Japan would have the second largest economy in the world. US support and economic reforms in the 1950s set Japan on the right track, but the 1964 Tokyo Olympics represented its re-entry into the global community. In the lead-up to the games, Japan opened its first Shinkansen route between Tokyo and Osaka, constructed a high-tech sewage system, cleaned rivers and water channels, built 100km (62 miles) of superhighways and erected 10,000 new office and residential buildings in the capital. A new slate of policies spurred a national drive towards manufacturing and exports, focusing on automobiles, transistors, optical instruments, heavy industries and materials. Japanese companies became the envy of the West, with treatises on Japan Inc. strategies found on bookshop shelves from London to LA. Decadence and materialism reigned supreme. It was the era of city pop and Japanese New Wave cinema, of the soaring yen and lavish spending on luxury goods. Nintendo and Sega were battling for supremacy in the burgeoning console gaming market, while consumer electronics made the likes of Toshiba, Panasonic and

Kabukicho, one of Tokyo's best entertainment districts

Sharp household names. The events of these decades became known as the 'Japanese Economic Miracle'. It was all too big to fail, until the reality of overinflated stock prices and careless investing caused the bubble to collapse, plunging Japan into recession in the early 1990s and creating a generation of disaffected youths known as the Lost Generation.

21st-Century Japan

Whether Japan has recovered from its late-20th-century economic malaise depends on the economist you consult, and any conversation will be rife with terms like deflation, stagnant wages, negative interest rates and bold monetary easing. But it's undeniable that the country has reasserted itself in the collective imagination of humankind. Japan has exerted an insatiable soft power pull in the 21st century, especially in our hyperconnected age where nothing is further away than the click of a button. Manga, anime and Japanese video games, once viewed as the exclusive preserve of otaku (*see* p. 240), have become the go-to form of entertainment for millions of people overseas. In 2023, Studio Ghibli hit *The Boy and the Heron* became the first original anime title to top the North American box office chart, earning $12.8 million on its opening weekend. Meanwhile, recent games by Japanese developers, like *Elden Ring* and *Zelda: Tears of the Kingdom*, have sold in excess of 20 million units, placing them among the best-selling games of all time. Likewise, Japanese literature is now flooding into international bookshops – gone are the days when Haruki Murakami was the only writer one could find in translation – with the likes of Sayaka Murata, Kenji Miyazawa and Yoko Ogawa getting their due. Japanese

cuisine (*see* p. 8) has become such an object of adulation in the foodie world that to slurp ramen in Tokyo (*see* p. 74) or sample the fare at a local fish market (*see* p. 70) is akin to a pilgrimage. Words like okonomiyaki (*see* p. 79) and omotenashi have entered the Oxford English Dictionary, and even arcane practices such as tea ceremony, zazen meditation (*see* p. 282) and Noh theatre are familiar to people with only passing interests in Japan. Whether this translates into another economic boom is a matter of opinion. But as a product, a brand, Japan has never been in higher demand.

Geography

Both in mind and matter, Japan is an island country. It was born 15 to 20 million years ago when tectonic movements decoupled it from the Eurasian continent, creating the Sea of Japan and a long, thin archipelago floating in the North Pacific. It comprises 14,125 islands, by the most recent count, four of which – Honshū, Hokkaido, Kyūshū, Shikoku – are collectively referred to as 'the mainland', distinguishing them from the many smaller, remote and uninhabited islands within Japan's national borders.

It's hard to believe now, but Japan was once quite flat. Converging and colliding plates then warped the land into steep mountain ranges running along the spine of the mainland. Compared to the Himalayas, the Andes or even the Rockies, Japan's mountains aren't particularly soaring, but they cover around 70 per cent of the country's landmass and are home to some of the snowiest climes on earth. The snow dumped on the Japan Alps and the Hidaka Mountains in winter is both voluminous and exceptionally powdery – just ask the skiers and snowboarders swarming to Japan's slopes each year with dreams of experiencing the fabled 'Japow' (*see* p. 152).

While the seasons (*see* p. 20) are quite distinct, this depends on where you are. Japan is approximately 3000km (1864 miles) from top to tail and covers 25 degrees of latitude, with the subtropics of Okinawa and Yakushima (*see* p. 39) at one extreme and the boreal forests of the Shiretoko Peninsula (*see* p. 48) at the other.

Tectonics

Japan's unusual geographic position, on the confluence of four plate boundaries – the Eurasian, Philippine, Pacific, North American – makes it a hotbed of volcanic and seismic activity.

Lying on the western edge of the Pacific Ring of Fire, Japan contains around 10 per cent of the world's volcanoes. The most famous, 3776m (12,388ft) Mount Fuji (*see* p. 158), has been dormant since 1707, but some are still highly active. Sakurajima smokes constantly and experiences multiple minor eruptions each week, while an underwater volcano near Ogasawara (*see* p. 2) birthed a new island in the autumn of 2023. Cataclysmic eruptions are not common, but when Mount Ontake erupted in 2014, killing more than 60 people, it was a reminder that volcanoes can, and do, strike with little warning.

The archipelago also receives around 1500 earthquakes a year. Mercifully, most are too mild to be felt, but you don't have to delve deep into the archives to see how destructive they can be. The Great Kanto Earthquake of 1923 ravaged Tokyo and Yokohama, setting the two primarily wooden cities ablaze and killing as many as 140,000. The Great Hanshin Earthquake of 1995 caused 6000 deaths, rendered a further 45,000 homeless and damaged the city of Kobe to the tune of US$100 billion. The shadow of 2011, the Great East Japan Earthquake, still looms large over the country. A mammoth magnitude-9.0 earthquake displaced ocean water above the Pacific Plate and sent tsunami waves the size of a 12-storey building hurtling towards the Tohoku (*see* p. 42) coastline at 800km/h (500mph). Around 20,000 people lost their lives and the waves triggered a triple core meltdown at the Fukushima Daiichi Nuclear Power Plant, the effects of which will be debated for years to come. Even today, some of the evacuees remain displaced or are living in temporary housing.

The Green Archipelago

All that violent tectonic activity – never mind regular summer typhoons and their attendant flood risks – makes Japan sound like a foreboding place. But there's a reason people settled here: it was unmistakably fertile. One of the old names for Japan, 'Midori no Retto', means the 'Green Archipelago', and for thousands of years Japan was covered in virgin forests of beech, oak, cypress, cedar and red and black pine. The Jomon tribes would have been surrounded by a land of plenty: good sources of protein in the woods, rivers, sea and sky, and numerous edible plants and fungi. Japanese butterbur, rakkyo (shallots), asatsuki (chives), sansho (Japanese mountain pepper), wasabi and myoga (ginger) are all indigenous, as are maitake, shiitake, enoki, hiratake and matsutake mushrooms. Chinese travellers then introduced yuzu, ume, persimmon, rice and various other fruits and vegetables into the local diet.

As the Japanese became domesticated, farming on whatever tracts of flat land they could find, they started building their monuments and cities with wood. Partly because there was so much of it available and partly because stone couldn't be trusted to withstand the frequent temblors. They hacked and slashed through the glorious raw materials nature had provided, giving rise to a logging industry that continues to this day. Only 40 per cent of Japan's remaining woodland is primaeval, with industrial cedar and pine plantations making up the rest. This monoculture is a frequent source of consternation among hikers and has developed into an ecological timebomb, spiking hay fever levels so aggressively that the national government has formulated policies to reduce annual pollen dispersion. A lot of the damage is irreversible, but national parks (*see* p. 48) and organisations like the Most Beautiful Villages in Japan (*see* p. 32) have offered some protection to the old-growth forests and remaining areas of scenic beauty.

All Roads Lead to Tokyo

Japan is divided into nine informal geographic regions – Hokkaido, Tohoku, Kanto, Chubu, Kansai, Chugoku, Shikoku, Kyūshū, Okinawa – and 47 prefectures, serving as the main units of local government. But there's no denying the country still revolves around Tokyo. A third of Japan's 120 million or so inhabitants live in the Greater Tokyo Area, making it the world's most populous megacity despite Japan's overall demographic decline. Tokyo is the national centre of finance, commerce and trade, and a global hub of gaming and entertainment, contemporary art (*see* p. 200), cocktail mixology (*see* p. 110) and innovative cuisine (*see* p. 93). It has more than 100 universities and colleges, the second most Fortune Global 500 companies worldwide and a GDP that outstrips many major economies.

And yet it makes little sense. For one, it's clean, safe, almost crimeless and has a transport system that leaves no room for improvement – things which shouldn't be true in a city of this size. It also feels entirely accidental, or as Donald Richie phrased it, not so much contrived as naturally grown. The Imperial Palace is a sort of loose midpoint from which the rest unfurls, but even then, some think of Shibuya or Shinjuku or Ginza or Akihabara or Roppongi as de-facto city centres, while Nihonbashi is technically the city's Point Zero (where Japan's five major trade routes once converged). Tokyo blends into Kanagawa in the south and Saitama, Chiba and Ibaraki in the north; prefectures from where sleep-deprived

people flood into the capital's office blocks each day. Running out of land in the east didn't stop the expansion. Ginza was once on a peninsula and Tokyo Bay was literally a bay until significant land reclamation efforts in the post-Edo period. There was more space in the west and it, too, was put to use. From Tokyo Station to Ome is 50 unbroken kilometres (31 miles) of concrete, and even after that, a mountain chain still separates you from the prefectural border.

The point being: Tokyo is too vast to really get your head around and too dynamic to chart in any meaningful way. The lack of street names, an abstruse address system, the density and verticality of the buildings and the constant redevelopment strike you like a bout of amnesia. Things are often not where you remembered them – in fact, you're not sure if they were ever there at all. But with that comes the mystery and spontaneity and endless exploration that makes Tokyo a joy to get lost in, a jumbled megalopolis that is so much more than the sum of its ever-changing parts.

Culture and Language

I've already touched on the beginnings of Japanese culture – the eras in which it arose, the milieus that allowed it to flourish – and it is discussed further in Art & Culture (*see* p. 191). But suffice it to say that much of what we think of as traditionally Japanese – calligraphy, paper crafting, ceramics, landscape gardening (*see* p. 246) – originated in China before developing its own signature. Under the influence of Zen Buddhism, Japan's design sensibility became the aesthetic of minimalism, where the use of space was paramount, colours were subdued, tones

Enjoying a meal in Shinjuku
Opposite **Arashiyama's famed Bamboo Grove**

Japanese writing class
Opposite **One of Japan's many sweet culinary delights**

were soft and abstract symbolism conveyed the beauty of ephemera or polarities in nature. These days, we see a lot more maximalism – in anime and Japanese role-playing games, in street fashion and kawaii accessories, in the artworks of Takashi Murakami and in Japanese website design – but it feels like an act of rebellion against something deeply ingrained in the national psyche.

Linguistics

Japan's writing system is also a (mostly) Chinese import, though pronunciations and readings of the kanji characters usually differ from the originals. There are tens of thousands of these characters in existence, and one ought to know the 2136 *joyo* (common-use) kanji to read a newspaper. It is learning by attrition, and many budding students of Japanese sail through hiragana and katakana – simple phonetic writing scripts – before kanji lessons bludgeon them back to earth.

Japanese is a linguistic isolate, most closely related to the old Ryukyuan tongues that were once spoken around Okinawa. From an English-speaking perspective its grammar is not just back to front but also inside out and upside down. Add to that context and nuance, different conjugations and words depending on how polite you want (or are expected) to be and subtle changes in intonation. Nevertheless, Japan's English proficiency level is among the lowest in Asia, so it's worth remembering a few handy phrases.

– **Good morning** o-ha-yo go-sa-i-ma-su
– **Good day** kon-ni-chi-wa
– **Good evening** kon-ban-wa
– **Excuse me** su-mi-ma-sen
– **Thank you very much** a-ri-ga-to go-sa-i-ma-su
– **Okay** dai-jo-bu de-su
– **How much is it?** i-ku-ra de-su ka?
– **Can I have the bill please?** o-ka-i-ke-i o o-ne-ga-i-shi-ma-su
– **Two beers please** na-ma bi-ru o fu-ta-tsu ku-da-sai
– **Before a meal** i-ta-da-ki-ma-su
– **After a meal** go-chi-so-sa-ma-de-shi-ta
– **Delicious** o-ii-shi-de-su

Though it might sound like a crass joke, if you're unsure of a word in Japanese, just say it in Japanese-accented English and sometimes you'll be understood – it's a trick I've been using for seven years. This is because borrowed words, rendered in katakana script, are becoming more ingrained in the Japanese vernacular. Examples include *ko-hi* (coffee), *ho-te-ru* (hotel), *su-ma-ho* (smartphone), *su-po-tsu* (sports), *tei-bu-ru* (table), and the unforgettable *ma-ku-do-na-ru-do* (McDonald's).

Travelling in Japan

Getting Around

Japan has one of the best, most efficient transport networks in the world. The Shinkansen, or bullet train, webs the country, hitting most of the major cities in Kyūshū, Honshū and the southern part of Hokkaido. Not only is it always on time, but it runs with startling frequency. There are dozens of high-speed trains between Tokyo and Shin-Osaka Stations each day, covering the 550km (342-mile) distance in around two-and-a-half hours.

Flying is so easy in Japan it makes you wonder why airports the world over make such a hash of it. Arriving at the security line 30 minutes before a domestic flight is standard practice.

Renting a car is the best way to explore less connected areas of the country, especially in Hokkaido, Shikoku or remote islands off the coast of the mainland, where public transport is less frequent.

Currency and Money

Japan's currency is the yen, and it is known to fluctuate. Looking at a graph of yen–dollar exchange rates is like looking at a Japanese mountain range. The exchange rate was ¥234 to US$1 in 1984, ¥106 to US$1 in 2004, and ¥160 to US$1 in 2024. Economists are rarely in agreement about where it will go next. But at the time of writing, it's considered excellent value for overseas travellers, which has been one factor in the post-pandemic tourism boom.

Japan, contrary to popular belief, is not the most technologically advanced of nations, and many smaller and independent businesses are still cash-based, especially in the countryside. The pandemic did contribute to increased digitisation of business infrastructure, so card readers have become more commonplace, and in rare instances, restaurants or bars have gone totally cash-free. But it's always worth having physical money in your pocket.

The train to Yudanaka

It's also worth bearing in mind that Japan does not have a tipping culture. I've been chased down the street by exasperated restaurant staff for leaving a couple hundred yen on the table. The logic states that hospitality workers are paid commensurately for their work, so salary shortfalls need not be passed on to the consumer. Knowing Japan's paltry minimum wage, I have my reservations about that. Nevertheless, tipping is still viewed as a foreign concept.

Disaster Preparedness

For all the natural disasters Japan receives, it's fastidiously prepared to deal with them. Strict seismic-standard regulations have been in the legislature since 1981, with subsequent refinements, to ensure new structures are earthquake resistant. Seawalls and tetrapods cover large stretches of coastline to nullify destructive waves. Emergency warnings are delivered to the public via loudspeakers installed on streets and in parks and train stations. And there are plenty of apps you can download, like the JTA Warning App, which provides disaster alerts and evacuation information.

Overtourism and Ethical Tourism in Japan

Barely a day goes by in Japan's travel industry when you don't hear the terms 'overtourism' and 'regional revitalisation', and both emerged as ever-present themes during the writing of this book.

From 2012 to 2019, Japan underwent unprecedented tourism growth, with a record 32 million inbound visitors the year before Covid brought international travel to a halt. There was much lip service paid during the pandemic years about better tourism management once the borders reopened. But then they did, and it was back to business as usual: no limits on visitor numbers at museums, no booking systems or time slots for historic sites and limited conservation fees in popular, biodiverse regions. It seems a quaint, egalitarian approach until you stand cheek-by-jowl in the baking sun, slowly trudging towards a hilltop temple, sweating like a condemned man and getting poked in the eye with errant umbrellas. It's a complete obliteration of the atmosphere and serenity such a place should evoke, but people slog as though tourism is a duty.

Some authorities have tried to push back. Iriomote, an island off Okinawa, now accepts a maximum of 2000 visitors per day. In Kyoto's Gion district, certain areas are now closed off to the public after tourists have been treating the resident geisha like animals in a zoo. And anyone hoping to climb Mount Fuji's Yoshida Trail now has to pay ¥2000 for the pleasure. Steps in the right direction, for sure, but they're half-baked and far too insipid to combat overtourism – how the Yamasahi government came to the Fuji evaluation, which is equivalent to the cost of a couple of craft beers, is anybody's guess.

I get it, nobody wants to go to the Vatican and skip on the Sistine Chapel. What's important is setting your expectations and understanding that Japan as a whole isn't overtouristed, but some towns, cities and neighbourhoods are, and by no means are you obliged to visit them.

So what can you do? For a start, consider travelling outside the peak spring and autumn tourism seasons. June and July can get a little muggy and August is fiercely hot, but winter can be beautiful, with snow blanketing the mountains in the north and west, lots of sunny blue skies, and plenty of *onsen* (see p. 26) bathing opportunities.

The easiest way to avoid tourists, though, is to go where they are not. The Golden Route, encompassing Tokyo, Fuji-Hakone, Kyoto, Osaka and sometimes Hiroshima, is the go-to itinerary for most first-timers. But there are destinations across Japan that provide a more nuanced view of the country: Shimane Prefecture (*see* p. 120), Niyodogawa in Kochi (*see* p. 108), Kyotango (*see* p. 88), the Michinoku Coastal Trail (*see* p. 42) or Eiheiji Temple (*see* p. 257).

This is where regional revitalisation comes in. Japan's rural population is in freefall. Some villages have already disappeared and others are hot on their heels – more than 800 municipalities are predicted to vanish in the two decades between 2020 and 2040. Some see tourism, rightly or wrongly, as the panacea to fix their economic-depopulation woes and are making concerted efforts to attract inbound visitors. The trend of *albergo diffuso*, or diffused hotels (*see* p. 262), has taken root in rural Japan, turning ageing townscapes into chic accommodations. A festival on the Oga Peninsula (*see* p. 126) is keeping one of Japan's most obscure traditions alive while bringing in much-needed economic stimulus. Activities like surfing in Kuroshio (*see* p. 166), diving in Amami and Okinawa (*see* p. 60), and walking the Shikoku Pilgrimage (*see* p. 286) or the Kumano Kodo (*see* p. 34) are also luring travellers into parts of the country that need them most. But these are the exceptions, not the norms.

A Japanese tourism professor recently told me that 'travel should be a happy industry'. While I agree with the sentiment, it also comes with some responsibility. What we do with that responsibility is ultimately up to us.

The busy streets of Tokyo

BEST OF JAPAN

A NATIONAL PARK FOR EACH SEASON

Spring

Ogasawara National Park

The Ogasawara Island chain, also known as the Bonin Islands, is technically within the administrative limits of Tokyo, yet it lies 1000km (620 miles) off the coast of mainland Japan. Travellers make the day-long ferry journey here to snorkel, scuba dive, hike the undulating forest trails and keep their eyes peeled for rare and endemic species. One such creature, the humpback whale, is often sighted in the spring when mothers retreat towards the shoreline to bear their calves in the safety of shallow waters. It's also a more temperate, albeit rainier, time of year, before the mercury and humidity start nudging towards uncomfortable levels in the height of summer.

OGASAWARA SHOTŌ
(OGASAWARA ARCHIPELAGO)

Mukojima Rettō

Yomejima

Nishi-no-shima

Ogasawara Visitor Centre

Chichijima Rettō

PHILIPPINE SEA

Hahajima Rettō

Top **Humpback whales at Ogasawara National Park**

Bottom **The marine life is impressive**

3

SEA OF JAPAN/
EAST SEA

N

Tango Sand Dunes

Ryugu ∧

Kyōtango

Ryujindo ∧

Shin'onsen

Kami

Genbudo Museum

Tottori Sand Dunes Visitor Centre

Iwami

Toyooka

Tottori

HONSHŪ

Summer

San'inkaigan National Park

The San'inkaigan National Park stretches along 75km (46 miles) of the Sea of Japan coastline. Among its jumble of basaltic cliffs, cave networks, reefs and bays, you'll find what's known as the 'Tottori Desert'. Obviously, this is a misnomer, but it is telling. Strong coastal winds, tidal currents and fine sediments deposited by the Sendai River have formed a 16km (10-mile) dune system, the largest of its kind in the country. Standing atop one of the 50m (164ft) dunes, in the country's least populous prefecture, sun beating down upon the vast sea of sand, it's easy to feel at a complete remove from urban Japan – it takes some convincing that Tottori City is only 6km (3.7 miles) away. Though some of the dunes have been reclaimed,

mostly through postwar afforestation projects, many creatures still call the area home. On summer nights, visitors gather to see wild foxes and *tanuki* (raccoon dogs), both crafty creatures in local folklore, and gaze at the star-flecked firmament above.

Tottori Desert

Autumn

Bandai-Asahi National Park

Straddling three prefectures in northern Japan – Yamagata, Niigata and Fukushima – Bandai-Asahi National Park is perhaps best known for its esoteric yamabushi (mountain monks). Members of the 1400-year-old Shugendo sect, who are sympathetic to both Buddhist teachings and Shinto mountain worship, walk the stone steps and mossy trails of the Dewa Sanzan, or three mountains of Dewa, as part of their daily ascetic rituals.

In the Fukushima section of the park, a volcanic eruption in 1888 resulted in a catastrophic mudslide, redirecting rivers and burying hundreds of square kilometres of forest under lakes and marshland. A walking trail winds through this area, circumnavigating a series of extraterrestrial-looking volcanic lakes – the goshikinuma – signatures of nature's violent past. They are prepossessing any time of year, but particularly when surrounded by autumnal foliage.

Top **Shiretoko National Park**

Bottom **Yamabushi (mountain monks) roam Bandai-Asahi National Park**

Winter

Shiretoko National Park

If you were to set sail from the tip of Shiretoko National Park and head north, you'd hit land somewhere in the wilds of Siberia, perhaps around Okhotsk. Spanning a blade-shaped peninsula in Hokkaido, Shiretoko signifies the end of Japan's world – and the scenery is a constant reminder. Standing on cliffs shaped by volcanic eruptions in winter, a mosaic of drift ice stretches and creaks across the sea as thick-feathered Steller's sea eagles glide across cloudless skies and divebomb towards prey. Take an icebreaker ferry tour, bulldozing its way through the frozen seawater, or clip on snowshoes and follow the tracks of Ezo deer and red foxes, perforating the snows. You are very much at nature's mercy here, so travelling with a guide is recommended.

SEA OF OKHOTSK

Shishiiwa Rock

Uīnupuri ▲ *Medaki and Odaki Falls*

Poromoi-dake ▲

HOKKAIDŌ

Shiretoko-dake ▲

Tokkarimui-dake ▲

Shiretoko Goko Lakes

Rusa Field House

PACIFIC

Furepe-no-taki

Utoro

Rausu-dake ▲

Shiretoko Pass

OCEAN

Chinishibetsu-dake ▲

Rausu Visitor Centre

Kumagoe-no-taki

Rausu

Onnebetsu-dake ▲

BEYOND SUSHI AND RAMEN

Yakiniku

Yakiniku literally means 'grilled meat,' but *yakiniku* restaurants specialise in wagyu (Japanese beef), cooked over charcoal at diners' tables. The quality of the wagyu is categorised using a grading system that assesses yield – how much meat exists on the cow compared to body weight – and the marbling, texture, firmness and brightness. Good wagyu has a sumptuous, buttery texture; a popular urban myth suggested this was because farmers massaged the cows in butter and serenaded them with classical music. Actually, they just keep them well fed and indolent, ensuring they live stress-free lifestyles. Doubtless, you'll have heard of Kobe beef, but Matsusaka Ushi and Ohmi beef are equally prized wagyu brands in Japan.

Tempura

When Portuguese missionaries landed in Japan in the 16th century, they brought with them a strange cooking method: coating food in flour, then frying it. Over the subsequent centuries, Japanese chefs refined this technique, creating the light, lumpy batter that has become synonymous with Japanese cuisine. It's best enjoyed as *tendon* (tempura-battered protein and veg served on a bowl of steamed rice) or as an accompaniment to soba noodles.

Kaiseki Ryori

When we think of the esoteric refinement of Japanese food, kaiseki ryori is likely the style of cuisine that comes to mind. The term refers to elaborate, multi-course repasts – often served in ryokan (traditional inns) – that showcase various methods of food preparation. *Kaiseki* chefs have carte blanche for creating the menu, but a typical degustation includes soup, sashimi,

a boiled dish, a grilled dish, a steamed dish, a vinegared dish and a deep-fried dish.

Shojin Ryori

Shojin ryori, the food of Zen monks (who abstain from eating animal protein), is a vegan-vegetarian alternative to kaiseki ryori. Where kaiseki is grand and indulgent, shojin ryori is all about culinary austerity. Seasonal vegetables, mountain plants and the natural flavour of the produce are of key importance because Zen practitioners believe they bring balance to mind and body.

Shabu Shabu and Sukiyaki

Both sukiyaki and shabu shabu are types of nabemono, or hotpot dishes. Authorities claim the dishes are entirely different, but both involve chucking vegetables, fungi and protein into a simmering broth. The difference being, shabu shabu broths are lighter, the pots heat up more quickly and the meat is supposed to be taken out as soon as it changes

colour. Incidentally, the name *shabu shabu* is onomatopoeic, coming from the swishing sound as vegetables are stirred in the pot.

Japanese Curry Rice

Japan's surprise national dish, curry rice, is said to be eaten by most members of the population at least once a week. A combination of sticky, short-grain rice and a thick, brown curry sauce, it's often served with tonkatsu (breaded pork) or vegetables. The Coco Curry Ichibanya chain, a high-street staple, has grown into a national institution.

Wagashi

Traditional Japanese confections, called wagashi, are usually made from mochi (pounded rice cakes) and anko (sweet red bean paste) and flavoured with matcha, black sugar or sakura petals. Among the most popular are daifuku, mochi wrapped around an anko filling, and namagashi, seasonal mochi-based sweets served during a tea ceremony.

JAPAN'S GREAT WALKING ROUTES

The Michinoku Coastal Trail

The 1025km (637-mile) Michinoku Coastal Trail was established in 2019, in part to promote the ongoing recovery of the regions devastated by the 2011 earthquake and tsunami. Tracts of untamed wilderness, towns reclaimed by nature, battered seawalls and magnificent geological features – the Michinoku is a journey through the Japan less travelled.

Hirosaki

Hachinohe

Kuji

Akita

Morioka

Miyako

Yamada

HONSHŪ

Ofunato

Sakata

Minamisanriku

Onagawa

Sendai

NORTH
ATLANTIC
OCEAN

Soma

Fukushima

The Kumano Kodo

The Kumano Kodo, meaning 'the old roads to Kumano', is an ancient pilgrimage route and UNESCO World Heritage Cultural Landscape. A series of undulating mountain trails, the Kodo connects three major Shinto shrines and is rooted in Japan's mythical origin story.

The Kumano Kodo is made up of ancient pilgrimage trails

Opposite **The Shikoku Pilgrimage connects 88 temples**

◎ ŌSAKA

Matsusaka

Taki •

Toba

Ise

Yoshino

Kudoyama

Koya

Wakayama

Kihoku

Owase

Gobō

Kumano

Tanabe

Shingu

Shirahama

Nachikatsuura

Susami

Kushimoto

N

The Shikoku Pilgrimage

Formed in the likeness of a Buddhist mandala, the 1200km (746-mile) Shikoku Pilgrimage connects 88 temples that pay homage to the great monk Kukai, also known as Kobo Daishi. It is a test of endurance and mettle, offering those who complete it a shot at nirvana and passage to the Pure Land.

TOKYO AFTER DARK

It's no surprise that so many storytellers find inspiration in Tokyo at night. Gaspar Noé's *Enter the Void*, Sophia Coppola's *Lost in Translation*, Haruki Murakami's *After Dark*, Yaro Abe's *Midnight Diner* – all harness the cinematic power of the Japanese capital when the fluorescent lights flicker to life and this paradoxical urban environment, lurid and electrifying, ethereal and soporific, engages your senses on every level. You may embrace your inner night owl when in Tokyo because there's plenty to keep you entertained after dark.

Top **Tokyo is known for its vibrant night life**
Bottom **The brightly lit Rikugien**

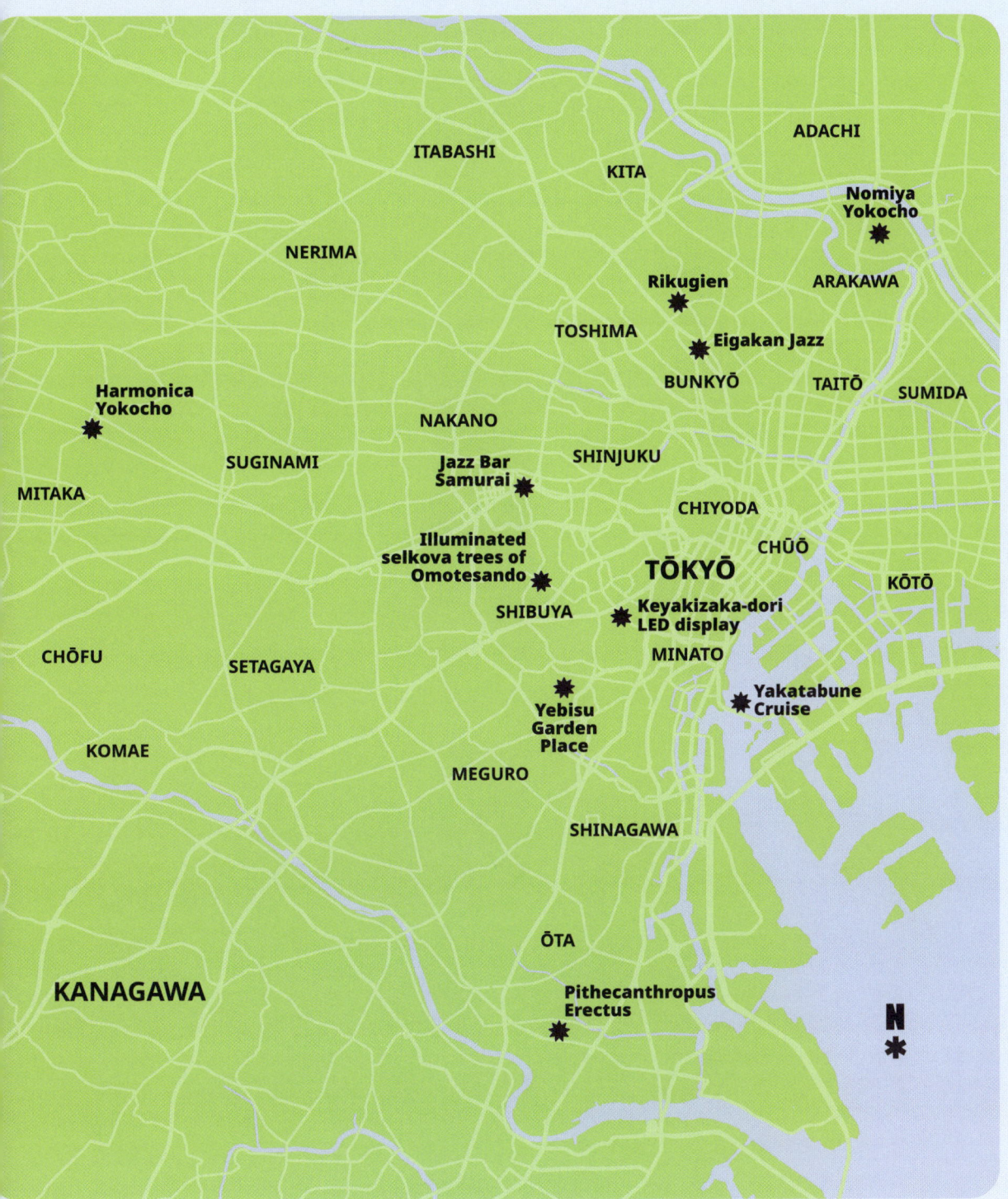

ITABASHI

ADACHI

KITA

Nomiya Yokocho
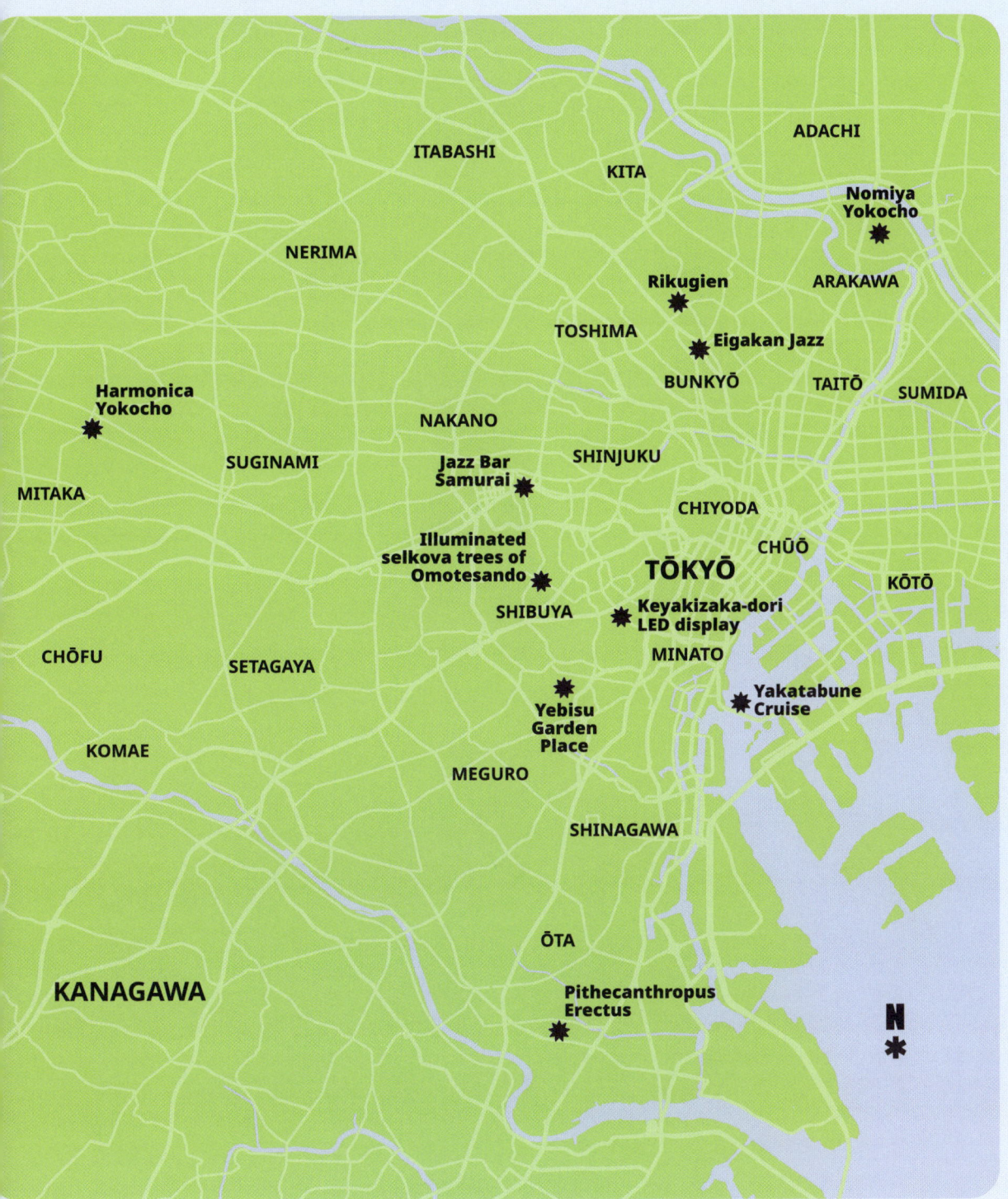

NERIMA

Rikugien

ARAKAWA

TOSHIMA

Eigakan Jazz

BUNKYŌ

TAITŌ

SUMIDA

Harmonica Yokocho

NAKANO

SHINJUKU

SUGINAMI

Jazz Bar Samurai

MITAKA

CHIYODA

CHŪŌ

KŌTŌ

TŌKYŌ

Illuminated selkova trees of Omotesando

SHIBUYA

Keyakizaka-dori LED display

CHŌFU

SETAGAYA

MINATO

Yakatabune Cruise

Yebisu Garden Place

KOMAE

MEGURO

SHINAGAWA

KANAGAWA

ŌTA

Pithecanthropus Erectus

N

See a Seasonal Illumination

Throughout the year, parks, trees, streets, department stores, commercial complexes and event plazas are dressed in LED lights, as though in competition to see who can run up the highest electricity bill. Some 'illumination events' are ham-fisted attempts to lure in shoppers and Instagrammers, but others are quite spectacular. The autumn and spring illuminations in Rikugien, a gorgeous feudal-era garden in Bunkyo Ward, are worth the detour. In winter, Roppongi's Keyakizaki-dori LED display, the Christmas lights in Yebisu Garden Place and the illuminated zelkova trees of Omotesando serve to enhance already-sleek corners of the city.

Book a Pleasure Boat Cruise

Yakatabune (pleasure boats) used to course along the Sumida River, peopled by drunk aristocrats and geisha tasked with keeping their cups full and their spirits merry. For a throwback to yesteryear, book a yakatabune dinner cruise – some tours include geisha performances – and get unimpeded views of the Rainbow Bridge and the Tokyo night skyline.

Explore the City's Yokocho

When you picture Tokyo at night, your mind's eye is likely conjuring up a *yokocho*, those steam-choked alleyways crammed with bleeding lights, red paper lanterns, the hubbub of tipsy revellers and the smell of sizzling beef or pork-bone soup. Tokyo's yokocho are numerous, so I wouldn't be too exercised about going to Golden Gai, the most famous, and therefore most overtouristed. Head to Harmonica Yokocho or Nomiya Yokocho instead.

Sip Whisky in a Jazz Kissa

Granted, it's odd that a musical genre embodying the struggles of 1960s Black America found spiritual succour in Japan. But that is Japan's relationship to jazz in a nutshell. As this relationship blossomed in the postwar years, many young Japanese opened jazz *kissa* (*see* p. 222), communal listening spaces with high-end sound systems, in their local neighbourhoods. Head to a *kissa* after dinner and order a whisky. Favourites in Tokyo include Eigakan, Jazz Bar Samurai and Pithecanthropus Erectus.

End the Night in a Karaoke Parlour

This is both the crescendo and denouement to every great night in Tokyo. Multistorey karaoke parlours are found throughout the city, but for a unique karaoke experience, *see* p. 227.

Looking out at Rainbow Bridge
Opposite **Omoide Yokocho is a busy alleyway known for its street food**

"The forest trails are empty, too, though locals might argue the *kami*, divine spirits, congregate here in great numbers."

NATURE

THE IMPORTANCE OF NATURE AND SEASONS IN JAPANESE CULTURE

◉ AROUND JAPAN

'Our country, as a special mark of favour from the heavenly gods, was begotten by them, and there is thus so immense a difference between Japan and all the other countries of the world as to defy comparison. Ours is a splendid and blessed country, the Land of the Gods beyond any doubt.'

The 19th-century theologian Atsutane Hirata was, it's fair to say, fond of Japanese nature. Living when he did, from 1776 to 1843, Hirata existed in pre-concrete Japan, when even the cities were architectural reflections of the natural world. Taking a break from his Kokugaku (Native Japanese) studies in Edo and venturing into the countryside, he would have stepped into a world of *unkai* (seas of clouds) rolling through steep-sided valleys, dramatic coastlines fringing the vast and unknowable ocean, and pine-choked forests penetrated by the sound of warbling birds and screeching cicadas.

The ukiyo-e (woodblock prints) of Hirata's contemporary, the great Katsushika Hokusai, showed an equal appreciation of Mother Nature. Of course, Hokusai was an impressionist, recreating real-world scenery with dreamlike fidelity and flair. But while he's most famous for depicting Mount Fuji in 36 different ways, there was much more to it than creative chutzpah. Take one look at *Fine Wind, Clear Morning* or *The Great Wave off Kanagawa*, works which have helped immortalise Hokusai, and one thing becomes clear: he agreed with Hirata's assessment. He, too, believed they lived in the Land of the Gods. In fact, it was beyond any doubt.

In modern, post-industrial Japan, one can still find scenes of preternatural beauty. But when you're in Tokyo, or anywhere else in the urban belt that runs along Japan's central eastern coastline all the way to Osaka, there is scarcely a whiff that nature once dominated this fertile archipelago.

People often say that Japan has four distinct seasons, perhaps even five if you count tsuyu (rainy season), and even in urban Japan, they make their presence felt: vibrant ginkgo and momiji (Japanese maple) trees shedding their leaves in autumn or the warm haruichiban wind that wafts through Tokyo's concrete canyons at the start of spring. A keen sensitivity to the seasons has long been used by Japanese artists and storytellers to explore humanity's interdependent connection to the natural world and the transient nature of all living things.

Religious scholars and clergymen understood the importance of nature, too. Shinto, Japan's native polytheistic belief system, puts faith in ancestral spirits that live in every moss-covered rock and prowling nocturnal creature. Whereas Japanese Buddhists believe in the interconnectedness of all things, as though humanity is nature experiencing itself subjectively. There's a reason the most dedicated monks and priesthoods are found deep in the wilderness – in Koyasan or in the Tottori hinterlands, say – where civilisation is but a fleeting notion.

'Because of the power of valley sounds and mountain colours, the Buddha with the great earth and sentient beings simultaneously attains the way,' wrote the 13th-century priest Dogen, 'and countless buddhas become enlightened upon seeing the morning star.'

Spring

The Transience of Nature

Nothing in Japanese culture symbolises the transience of the material world like sakura, or cherry blossoms. Arriving every spring, they bloom, wilt and die, drifting from the trees like floral snow, all within a two-to-three-week period. They may be poignant reminders of mono no aware, the beauty of impermanence, but that doesn't mean they *only* signify a time for morose reflection.

Even Matsuo Basho, the 17th-century father of haiku poetry, witnessed cherry blossoms bringing people together to celebrate life:

Drunk by cherry blossoms
a lady wearing a haori coat
and a sword

Cherry blossom season is a highlight of Japan's spring

Basho captures the idea that cherry blossom season was a time of unlimited possibilities. During hanami (flower-viewing) parties, which may have existed as far back as the eighth century, nobles would gather to admire the sakura, write seasonal poetry and drink a Dionysian amount of rice wine.

This practice has only grown in popularity over the subsequent centuries. Head to a public park in Japan during sakura season, and you'll likely find hordes of tipsy hanami revellers on tarpaulin mats surrounded by half-eaten bento boxes, empty beer cans and falling blossoms. That said, those areas most abundant in cherry trees – Tokyo's Ueno Park or Maruyama Park in Kyoto, for example – now suffer because of their own popularity, where it's common for bleary-eyed souls to arrive at the crack of dawn to claim a picnic spot for the rest of the day.

For the crowd-averse, it's better to seek out roads less travelled. I was fortunate to live in Eifukucho for a couple of years, a Tokyo suburb that rubs shoulders with Wadabori Park, a charming greenspace bisected by the Zenpukuji River, along which hundreds of sakura trees have been planted. While tourists jostled for photos in the busiest parks of downtown Tokyo, I would take in the natural phenomenon at a leisurely pace and had plenty of unoccupied parkland upon which to set up camp for the day.

If there is a trick to maximising the hanami experience, it's as simple as that. Head for regions off the typical tourist trail, or if you can't stray too far from a major city, hop on a train towards a park in a residential neighbourhood. Predicting when the cherry blossoms will arrive has become easier than ever, too. The Japan Meteorological Agency (JMA) has honed the art of sakura forecasting, and for means of comparison, they can rely on official records stretching back to the year 812 CE.

Cherry blossom areas outside major cities:

Yoshino-Kumano National Park, Nara

Mount Yoshino in Nara Prefecture is home to around 30,000 cherry blossoms, the highest concentration of these trees anywhere in Japan.

Kawazu, Shizuoka

The cherry trees in Kawazu on the Izu Peninsula are early bloomers and are generally in full thrust by late February. There's an accompanying sakura festival, with stalls selling seasonal food and local produce, along the Kawazu River throughout the month.

Hirosaki Park, Aomori

The 2600 or so cherry trees at Hirosaki Park bloom in late April. A special pruning technique, adopted from apple tree pruning, means the sakura produce more flowering buds than their more southerly cousins.

Mifuneyama Rakuen, Saga

A sprawling Japanese garden constructed at the foot of a sacred mountain, Mifuneyama Rakuen is particularly prepossessing in spring, when 2000 cherry trees bloom across the grounds.

Niyodo, Kochi

One of Japan's most mountainous prefectures, Kochi, is home to plunging gorges, fantastic rock features and turbulent rivers. Along the Niyodo River in March, cherry trees bloom in their thousands, creating one of the most scenic sakura drives in the country.

Summer

The Season of Death

> Nothing in the cry
> of cicadas suggests they
> are about to die

If you've ever heard a cicada's blood-curdling screech, you may quibble with Basho's aphorism. But it's appropriate nonetheless because if there's one sound I'd most identify with the Japanese summer, it would be cicadas in full arousal. It's not a noise you can escape, either; there are 35 cicada species in Japan, some of which screech at up to 120 decibels, equivalent to a bulldozer or revving motorcycle. And oh, how they love to sing in unison.

Basho's mention of death is also apposite. Summer may be the time when Japan's gardens and forests explode with life – thanks largely to the month-long rainy season – but it's also when the spirits of the dead revisit our material plane. Where the Mexicans have

Dia De Los Muertos and the Hindus have Shraddha, the Japanese have Obon, a mid-August celebration during which families welcome back the travelling souls of their deceased relatives. People may visit their local temple or invite a priest to their home to carry out a ceremony in front of the family butsudan or kamidana (altars). They'll light fires to guide the spirits on their journey or display some seasonal art in the tokonoma (alcove), such as ikebana or bonsai.

Obon is the most significant Buddhist holiday on the calendar, when the membrane between the physical and spiritual worlds is supposedly at its most permeable. And it happens to coincide with the blooming of Buddhism's most iconic plant, the hasu, or lotus flower. Enduring symbols of Eastern mysticism, lotuses feature in the sutras of Jodo (Pure Land) Buddhism, the most prevalent denomination in Japan, and their golden likenesses adorn temple halls throughout the country and the Mausoleum of Great Master Kobo Daishi, where the founder of Shingon Buddhism is entombed.

Growing in muddy water, yet admired for their elegance and beauty, they represent the ability to thrive in the face of hardship.

Hardship is a fitting descriptor for the season as Japanese summers can be difficult. Remembering the dead will always stir conflicting emotions, but the soaring temperatures present their own challenge: 35°C (95°F) days are not uncommon and humidity levels can surpass 80 per cent. People walk around reflexively blurting out 'atsui desu ne' (it's hot, right?), like it's the only phrase left in their vocabulary. They talk about 'getting through' August, as though it were a sickness, and go on holiday to avoid the heat or flee to Hokkaido to remember what a cool breeze feels like. Autumn sits mirage-like in the distance; it looks to be close, but you're not quite sure if it's just the sweat clouding your eyeballs or the perpetual dehydration. But then you hear the call of the higurashi, the cicada that sings as the sun is going down and the day is cooling off, and you realise you're one day closer to autumn after all.

Lanterns light up Yasukuni Shrine to commemorate Mitama Matsuri
Opposite **Rikugien in autumn**

Autumn

Fire and Farewells

Travel writer Pico Iyer described autumn in Japan as the 'season of fire and farewells.' As fiery hues blazed across the hillsides of his residential Nara suburb and nature began its cycle of decay, he reflected on the aesthetic of subtraction, the removal of all that is unnecessary to charge the few things that remain.

But what the *koyo* (autumn leaves) taketh, they also giveth. Because autumn is, for my money, the most visually energising time of year. As the summer heat abates, Japan's deciduous trees – zelkovas, weeping willows, cherry trees, momiji, gingko – represent both the fire and the farewell. The theme of transience is hard to escape: the trees' decline is their glory, and their glory is their decline.

The Japanese daimyo, feudal warlords, appreciated the ephemeral wonder of *koyo*. They were a bloodthirsty bunch, no doubt, but once they stopped slaughtering each other, they turned their attention to crafting supremely stunning gardens. They understood the way of the poet as adroitly as they understood the way of the warrior.

Take Rikugien in Tokyo's Bunkyo Ward as an example. The garden was constructed in 1702 at the behest of the fifth shogun, Tsunayoshi Tokugawa. 'Rikugien' references the six divisions of Chinese poetry, which in Japan became known as waka. Across 20 acres, Rikugien depicts 88 scenes from famous waka poems – 32 of which remain – with landscape features depicting the unity of man and woman and rocks symbolising mountains, birds and the Buddha. Gardens of a similar ilk are littered throughout the country, be it Ritsurin in Takamatsu, Kenrokuen in Kanazawa, Korakuen in Okayama or Kairakuen in Ibaraki. But to see these gardens in autumn, in the throes of decay, is to understand what is meant by *ichi-go ichi-e*, the beauty of a moment that can never be repeated.

For those who have the time and inclination, it's a case of leaves by day, moonlight by night. Because autumn is also a time for admiring the heavens.

Autumn moonlight –
a worm digs silently
into the chestnut.

Tsukimi, or 'moon viewing,' has been a popular pastime for over a thousand years, as a way of thanking the gods for a bountiful harvest. Formerly celebrated on the 15th night of the eighth month of the lunar calendar, tsukimi now falls between September and October. During the festivities, people gather to gaze at the full moon, usually from vantage points like mountain peaks or on the top floor of skyscrapers, and eat tsukimi-dango (moon-shaped mochi cakes) and other seasonal produce, like chestnuts, pumpkins and persimmons. At the hallowed Ise Jingu Shrine in Mie Prefecture, there's an annual tsukimi event emulating the celebratory style of the Heian period, complete with poetry readings and music performances.

Winter

A Story of Ice and Fire

Winter solitude –
in a world of one colour
the sound of wind

Perhaps it is weird, but I've always thought of snow as inherently Japanese. Obviously, I know this not to be true, but why let facts get in the way of ruminations? Japanese artists have done a pretty good job of drilling this into my mind. From the becalmed, almost deferent, winter poetry of Basho to the snowy landscapes captured by Edo-period *ukiyo-e* artists, many used snow as a driving force in their artistic expression.

And there is no shortage of snow in Japan to remind you that winter is here. AccuWeather places four of the world's top-ten snowiest cities in Japan: Akita (seventh), Toyama (third), Sapporo (second) and Aomori (first). Aomori alone receives up to 8m (26ft) of snow per year.

The snow lures a few million people into Japan's ski resorts each year and many more into its rotenburo (outdoor baths). Because of Japan's location on the Pacific Ring of Fire, it's home to 111 active volcanoes, making it a hotbed of geothermal activity, and in turn, one of the world's best countries for reclining in hot springs.

Known locally as *onsen*, there are nearly 30,000 hot spring sources throughout the country. Towns where the sources are concentrated have become bathing pilgrimages, like Beppu, Oita Prefecture, which has 3000 individual springs. The Beppu Tourist Information Centre sells 'spaports' for bathers to collect stamps at each onsen they visit. The journey is complete upon soaking in 88 onsen – mirroring the 88 shrines of the Shikoku pilgrimage – after which one attains the honorary title of 'onsen master.'

Going to an onsen is a form of *hadaka no tsukiai*, or 'naked companionship,' because the baths are usually separated by sex with no textiles allowed. They are also places of sef-administered physiotherapy. Kusatsu

An onsen town in Wakayama

Onsen, a hot spring resort located along an enchanting 350km (217-mile) stretch of highway known as Japan's 'Romantic Road', has the largest flowing water volume of all Japan's hot springs. The water here is also some of the most acidic and mineral-dense, killing harmful pathogens on the skin, reducing inflammation and alleviating muscular and arthritic pain and high blood pressure.

We know that people have been using *onsen* for a long time: they are mentioned in the *Nihon Shoki*, the Chronicles of Japan, which was completed in 720 CE. Shinto adherents saw the geothermal water as divine and used bathing as a method of purification. Buddhists believed it brought good fortune and established temples that made onsen accessible to commoners. Religion aside, when not hunting, procreating or warring, onsen provided a space where people could relax and socialise; the belief was, and still is, that shedding all clothes is tantamount to shedding all conversational pretence.

Best onsen towns to visit:

Ginzan Onsen, Yamagata

This is one of the most cinematic hot spring resorts in the country, drawing aesthetic comparisons to the town in Hayao Miyazaki's 2001 animated masterpiece *Spirited Away*. Submerged in deep snow each winter, the wooden ryokan (traditional inns) lining the Ginzan River are illuminated by Taisho-era streetlamps each evening, while the outdoor baths are surrounded by dense pine forests.

🏮 ginzanonsen.jp

Kinosaki Onsen, Hyogo

Tattoos come with negative connotations in Japan – they're associated with the Yakuza, Japan's largest organised crime syndicate – meaning tattooed visitors are often forbidden from entering *onsen*. But in the 1300-year-old Kinosaki Onsen resort, there are seven tattoo-friendly hot springs, each renowned for its health-giving properties. Some travellers aim to complete the Kinosaki Onsen Meguri, a pilgrimage to all the town's public bathhouses.

🏮 visitkinosaki.com

Nozawa Onsen, Nagano

Best known for its powdered slopes in winter, Nozawa Onsen is a compact, old-world town home to a collection of soto-yu. These free-to-enter bathhouses, maintained by the local community, are frequented by skiers and boarders resting weary limbs.

🏮 nozawa-onsen.com

Dōgo Onsen, Ehime

There is much debate over which *onsen* town is Japan's oldest, but one town with a good claim to the title is Dōgo Onsen, believed to have a 3000-year history as a bathing spot. The main bathhouse, designated an Important National Cultural Property in 1994, has two stone baths: Kami no Yu (Bath of the Gods) and Tama no Yu (Bath of the Spirits).

🏮 dogo.jp/en

Shirahama Onsen, Wakayama

This onsen is ancient enough that it was venerated in the eighth-century *Man'yoshu*, Japan's oldest and most distinguished compilation of waka poetry. With more than 120 hot springs clinging to the coast of the bulbous and craggy Kii Peninsula, travellers come for both its soothing waters and striking geological features.

🏮 shirahama-ryokan.jp/en

Yunomine Onsen

UNDERSTANDING ZEN GARDENS

⦿ KYOTO

I have spent most of the morning trying to find shade. It's stultifyingly humid – the whole of Kyoto feels like the inside of a kettle – and the city's flagstone streets and web of alleyways are choked with groups of tourists walking in the slow, plodding, unpredictable way that groups of tourists do. So it's a good thing Andrew William has asked me to meet him at Keage Station, at the foot of the eastern hills, where there is no impression this city is creaking under the strain of inbound travellers.

Andrew, who runs An Design (andesignkyoto.com), a garden consultancy and tour company, is a soft-spoken encyclopaedia of Zen gardens and Eastern philosophy. As we chat en route to Nanzenji, a Buddhist campus once hosting more than 70 temples, he explains, in as simple terms as the subject allows, the aesthetics of Zen gardens.

There are three main commonalities: *Composition*: the rocks, gravel, moss and pruned trees from which the garden is made; *perspective*: the sense of depth and scale; *framing*: temple walls, sliding doors or wooden gates acting as natural frames, as though the garden were a living painting. Asymmetrical design and balance are musts, blossoms and greenery are sometimes avoided altogether and the garden usually reflects real-world landscapes or depicts lands from ancient Chinese mythology.

All of this is designed to instil a feeling of calm, tranquillity and peace of mind.

'The monks here have been studying Zen and its related aesthetics for centuries,' says Andrew. 'But Japan is not the place of spiritual practice it once was. People are often surprised when I tell them that, but most young people don't contemplate any of this stuff on a day-to-day basis. It's superstition, tradition; going to shrines and temples is a cultural practice rather than a spiritual one.'

Nevertheless, it's small corners of Kyoto like this, a precinct of Nanzenji that really does feel like a living artwork, that convince Andrew this city is still one of the most spiritually profound places in the world.

We enter through a wooden arch and wander around a pond scattered with lotus flowers – a symbol of resilience and enlightenment in Buddhist lore – on our approach to Konchiintoshogu, a shrine dedicated to the first Edo shogun, Tokugawa Ieyasu. But Andrew is more interested in what's in front, a mostly empty space, save for two stone lanterns, a plum and a pine tree.

'This is one of my favourite gardens,' he says. 'It's the simplicity. The plum tree only blooms for 10 days a year; it represents ephemera. Whereas the pine is evergreen, it's associated with eternity.'

The trees bend towards one another, creating an invisible feedback loop between the permanent and impermanent. It is no

happenstance. 'It would be wrong to think of eternity and ephemera as opposites,' says Andrew, 'because one can't exist without the other.'

We then come to Horai, the paradise of the immortals, a dramatic mountain range shrouded in clouds. Though many artists have rendered Horai in the nihonga (Japanese painting) style, here it has been recreated with the forms of nature. A karesansui (dry garden) of miniature stones shaped into wave patterns, far too beautiful to be walked on, and a selection of trees that haven't been grown so much as curated and manicured, all elevated with shakkei (borrowed scenery) from the hills in the background. In the centre of the scene, rocks are arranged in the likeness of a turtle, a creature that swims underwater and embodies life's challenges, and a crane soaring through the clouds, embodying life's successes.

'Really, the turtle and the crane represent *all* polarities,' Andrew says. 'They're complementary forces that bring balance to the world.'

I could spend hours here, viewing this space through every frame and from every angle. Each one adds texture and meaning. To envision a garden like this is one thing, but the repetitious approach required to realise it is another: raking the same patches of gravel day after day, carefully manipulating the pine needles to appear as though they've grown in the wild, plucking weeds and gathering fallen foliage to ensure the garden is kempt.

'What you're looking at is the result of hundreds of years of continuous mental exercise,' says Andrew. 'Maintaining these gardens is itself a form of meditation.'

He asks me to step inside the adjacent temple, to look at sliding doors covered in spiritual motifs. The sun flows in, lightening the panels, but it's the rest of the room to which my eyes are drawn: the ma, the empty space, the auxiliary particle and invisible glue that binds the whole piece together.

'Everything in Zen is about decluttering the mind,' says Andrew. 'So that's what you get in Zen art and gardens, all this space to give the rest meaning.'

UTSUKUSHII MURA: THE MOST BEAUTIFUL VILLAGES IN JAPAN

⊙ **AROUND JAPAN**

Here's an inconvenient truth: many hamlets, villages and small towns in Japan have been smothered in concrete and linked by unsightly motorways, their primaeval forests hacked down for lumber and their glorious mountain ranges strung with transmission towers from stem to stern. This emphasises the importance of Utsukushii Mura, the Association of the Most Beautiful Villages in Japan, a non-profit preservation group that encourages the country's most scenic villages to be independent, protect their natural resources and pass those resources on to future generations.

In 2020, Otama Village in Fukushima Prefecture became a bellwether for the group's ambitions when it resisted government plans to erect a photovoltaic solar panel grid on its land. It was not an anti-green stance, per se; more of an aversion to the industrial scars that have brought many other Japanese rural regions into ruin.

Utsukushii Mura was founded in 2005 by Satoshi Hamada, the former mayor of Biei Town in Hokkaido, and Masahiko Matsuo, then-CEO of snack company Calbee. Hamada grew concerned as the rolling, Shire-like hills surrounding Biei were being levelled to make way for Calbee warehouses, so he contacted Matsuo and found in him a surprise kindred spirit.

Both men believed the patchwork floral displays enveloping the Biei hills in spring and summer were worth protecting, and that the culture, tradition, scenery and history rooted in Japan's small villages and towns would find strength in numbers.

'However, because Japan was in the midst of the 'Great Heisei Merger' [when villages and small towns were amalgamated into larger municipalities], things did not proceed as expected,' says Yoko Tsumagari, a staff member at Utsukushii Mura. 'But seven courageous towns and villages decided to launch the project.'

The organisation now has 64 geographically diverse member villages. Sai Village sits on the tip of Shimokita Peninsula, where archaeological digs have uncovered Jomon-period (14,000 to 300 BCE) pottery artefacts. The most northerly fishing village in Honshū, Sai is buffeted by the turbulent waters of the Tsugaru Strait, with dramatic, fang-like rock features along its coastline. At the opposite end of the archipelago, Tarama, a potato-shaped island village in Okinawa, is surrounded by coral reefs and schools of sea turtles. The island is covered in sugar-cane fields, whose saccharine smells are carried by temperate winds through the village during harvest season.

Some villages are known for their wildlife, like the red-crowned cranes of Tsurui in Hokkaido (Tsurui means 'where cranes live'). Other villages are known for their trees, like the 30,000 cherry blossoms sweeping through Yoshino in Nara Prefecture or the Ou Mountains Green Corridor running through Higashinaruse in Akita.

'Protecting the villages will help to preserve their diverse environments and cultures, the history of Japan's farming and fishing communities and the local ways of life,' says Tsumagari. 'Rural villages are facing challenges like declining and ageing populations. We need to increase 'fans' who share our ideals so that we can increase the number of people travelling to and living in Japan's most beautiful villages.'

◉ utsukushii-mura.jp

Top **Cherry blossoms in Yoshino**
Bottom **Sai, one of the Utsukushii Mura**

WALKING THE KUMANO KODO

◉ **WAKAYAMA**

I have been on all kinds of hikes. Hikes that have meandered through bucolic countryside, hikes that have started with sun and finished with snow, hikes that have pummelled me with rain and wind and swirling fog, making me wish I was sitting in the pub exercising nothing more than the muscles required to bring pint to mouth. But sometimes – and these are the times to hold on to – a hike lands in a Goldilocks zone. There were moments on the Kumano Kodo, the only pilgrimage trail beside the Camino de Santiago in Spain to be designated a UNESCO World Heritage Cultural Landscape, where it felt utterly defining, like there was no other place I could possibly be.

I recall it in snapshots, as though viewing the hike through an old stereoscope. *Click*. Traversing Moja-no-Deai, the Abode of the Dead, where fallen relatives are said to visit the living, shafts of misty light spilling through the trees like sun splitting the windows in a cathedral. *Click*. Threading narrow paths with overhanging ferns and flowering bamboo, lizards skittering across tree stumps and snakes eyeing me with trepidation. *Click*. Cresting a hill after an ascent so gruelling even the poet Fujiwara no Teika was shorn of

his eloquence – 'This route is very rough and difficult,' he scribbled in his diary, doubtless in between gasps for air. 'It is impossible to describe precisely how tough it is.'

Postwar industrial logging efforts mean some of the old-growth forest has been replaced by columns of industrial cedar, the forest orchestra replaced by thrumming chainsaws. It's a little dispiriting, but then you pass chuckling streams and plunging waterfalls and gigantic stones green with age, and you understand why this area has been a site of pilgrimage for more than 1000 years.

The abridged version of the Kumano Kodo's history is this: around 2700 years ago, Emperor Jimmu, the fabled first monarch of Japan, got lost in the dense forests of the Kii Peninsula. Then, on the verge of giving in, a three-legged crow, Yatagarasu, crossed his path and guided him to safety. Buoyed by his stroke of luck, Jimmu attacked his enemies with the rising sun at his back, put them to the sword and founded the empire of Japan.

During the Heian period, when Japan was under a system of feudalism, the court nobles in Kyoto sought spiritual enlightenment and started journeying through the region where Jimmu once lost his way. Trails expanded

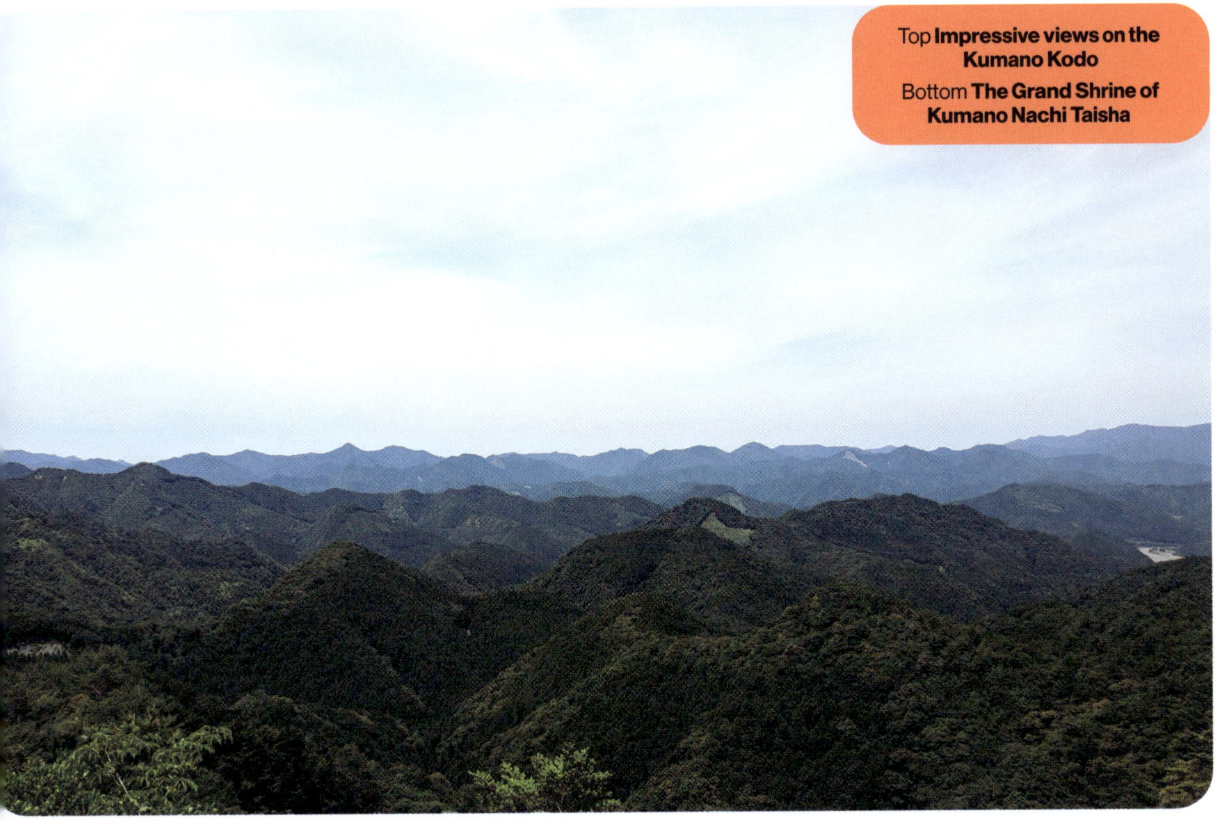

Top **Impressive views on the Kumano Kodo**

Bottom **The Grand Shrine of Kumano Nachi Taisha**

across the mountains, paved with huge cobbles and marked by torii gates, to form a network between Koyasan, the home of Shingon Buddhism, and the Kumano Sanzan (Three Shrines of Kumano), where significant members of the Shinto pantheon reside.

Of all the main trails – Kiiji, Kohechi, Nakahechi, Ohechi, Iseji and Omine Okugake-michi – the Nakahechi remains the most intact and attracts the most pilgrims today. My own walk along the Kodo felt like a pilgrimage of sorts, partly because I shared footsteps and rice wine with Kento Ozaki, a mountain monk who learnt the ways of Shugendo in a small Kumano temple, and partly because the destination felt so immaterial. For long spells, there wasn't so much as a hint of a view or a point to be moving towards. Just metronomic footsteps, one after the other, somehow enlivening my spirit.

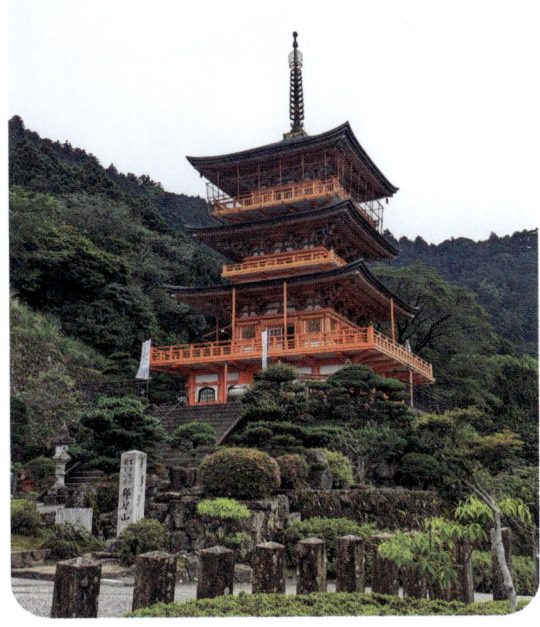

THE JOYS OF SHINRIN-YOKU

Japan has a habit of intellectualising the mundane. Saving money becomes *kakeibo*, the art of mindful spending. Idleness becomes boketto, the art of doing nothing. But what about shinrin-yoku, the art of forest bathing? Is there really more to this craze than just walking in the woods?

'Yes,' says Dr Qing Li, author of *Shinrin-Yoku: The Art and Science of Forest Bathing*. 'Five-sense is a keyword in forest bathing... [It] is a total effect of the five senses: the quiet atmosphere, beautiful scenery, mild climate, good smells, fresh, clean air and the taste of forest fruits.'

Originally from China, Li works as a doctor and clinical professor at Nippon Medical School Hospital in Tokyo, and is widely viewed as the world's foremost expert on shinrin-yoku.

Shinrin-yoku is a simple concept. All you need to do is enter a forest, forgo all technological devices and let your mind drift as your senses tune into the environment. Li insists that you walk slowly and let your body guide your movements; shinrin-yoku is not akin to jogging, trekking or hiking. It's a mode of being, one that helps create a bridge between you and the natural world.

Li says it's also important to make a plan, to view it as therapy. If you have an entire day, stay in the forest for about four hours and walk about 5km (3 miles). If you have just a half day, 2km to 3km (1.25 to 1.9 miles) should suffice. Rest when you are tired, sit for a while and enjoy the scenery, maybe practise yoga or tai chi. Select the forest bathing course based on your aims.

To distance forest bathing from new age, pseudo-scientific wellness treatments, Li and his team have conducted years of research on shinrin-yoku and the aromatic, health-giving compounds emitted by trees. In 2012, he established Forest Medicine as a preventative treatment when the benefits became too manifold to be ignored.

Li emphasises that 'stress' is a key word to understanding those benefits. Stress can induce almost all lifestyle-related diseases, such as cancers, hypertension, depression, cardiovascular diseases, stroke, gastric ulcers, obesity and other eating disorders. Studies have shown shinrin-yoku improves sleep quality, mood, ability to focus and stress levels due to its effect on the nervous system, or more specifically, the psycho-neuro-endocrino-immune network.

In a recent paper, 'New Concept of Forest Medicine', Li explained this in more detail. 'When people practise forest bathing, the brain is relaxed, the parasympathetic nervous system is dominant, the secretion of stress hormones is suppressed, and the immune function is enhanced. An elevated immune response feeds back into the autonomic nervous system to further reduce the stress response.'

Forests occupy 67 per cent of Japan's landscape, and at the time of writing, there are 65 registered forest therapy sites in Japan. At each site, visitors can meet physicians who conduct medical assessments before they enter the woodland trail and again following their walk to monitor any changes. Some sites are in far-flung locales, like Akasawa Natural Recreation Forest in Nagano, the birthplace of forest bathing, and Chizu in Tottori Prefecture. Others are closer to Japan's urban sprawls, like Tokyo's Okutama region or the forests of Atsugi near Yokohama.

The key is that the barrier to entry for shinrin-yoku is low: all you need is access to a forest and the will to embrace the journey ahead of you.

🧭 fo-society.jp/en/forests.html

Cobblestone path on the Nakasendo trail

The mossy Shiratani Unsuikyo

YAKUSHIMA: PROTECTING THE FLOATING FOREST AT THE END OF THE WORLD

⊙ KAGOSHIMA

You may associate the cherry blossom, *momiji* or gingko tree with Japan, but I've always felt *koke* (moss) was the most elemental form in Japanese nature. Its strength is in numbers: turning mundane trees into miniature ecosystems, coating forests in a high-definition sheen and imbuing gardens with wabi-sabi imperfections. Moss is mentioned in the national anthem, 'Kimigayo', and represents rough-hewn beauty and the passage of time in Japanese culture – were the legend of Ozymandias rooted in Japan, his statue wouldn't have been withered by the sands of time, it would have been usurped by moss.

And if moss has a spiritual home, it is the island forest of Yakushima.

Cast 60km (37 miles) adrift of the Kyūshū mainland and shrouded in a perennial mist, Yakushima looks like the sort of place a sage would retreat in search of epiphany, or where a poet would discover their most profound insights. It is a final frontier, so devoid of construction and the general tenor of life on the mainland, you could be convinced it's an independent microstate.

When I join Steve Bell, who runs the YES Yakushima guiding service, to walk the forest's Yakusugi Land trail, he strides purposefully with an umbrella, as all good English outdoorsmen do. Though Bell is worlds away from the hilly Northumbria trails of his youth, I get the sense he's never felt more at home. His enthusiasm for 'the island', as he lovingly refers to Yakushima, is palpable, and never more so than when he's talking about moss.

'Think of this as sperm,' he says, handling a sprig of moss, from which a globule of water is about to fall. 'When it lands on the sex organ of a female moss, they reproduce. There's sex going on everywhere in the forest. The mosses are going at it like rabbits.'

There are around 650 moss species on Yakushima, making the small, subtropical island one of the most concentrated moss ecosystems in the world. Moss serves as the glue that holds the forest together, clinging to the broad trunks of ancient trees and covering gargantuan slabs of granite. In the absence of soil, it provides a platform for seeds to germinate so that every towering conifer is home to dozens of plants that grow on the host tree without stealing its nutrients. This locks the rainforest in a state of perpetual growth, so saturated in green it feels eternal.

'People come for the trees,' Bell adds, as if to put a finer point on it. 'But it's the moss they leave with.'

I haven't come to Yakushima for the trees or the moss this time. At least not exclusively.

I have come to be at a remove from urban Japan, to spend a few days on island time, to be in a place that will give me the space to remember where I am. The tourist crush will be coming soon, but this is Yakushima in early February – the travel off-season – where little of note is happening other than locals milling about in the quiet seaside villages or men in overalls sitting by the roadsides shooting the breeze and smoking cigarettes. Cafes open around lunchtime or they don't open at all. It's difficult to tell if some of the restaurants, bathhouses and lodges are abandoned or just off-duty till the spring.

The forest trails are empty, too, though locals might argue the *kami*, divine spirits, congregate here in great numbers. Folktales speak of magical trees, sacred granite, blood-sucking sprites and a white deer carrying messages from the gods; a land where the material world and the spirit world are interdependent.

As Bell and I walk through the forest, high up in the island's interior, the air is wet and each footstep is amplified by the silence. Animal life is eerily absent. The macaques have retreated towards the more temperate coast, where they can pilfer oranges from disgruntled farmers. There are no buzzing insects – the rushing water sources aren't conducive to laying larvae – so the birds also go elsewhere in search of food.

We stop at a large, hollow stump and Bell tells me the story of Jochiku Tomari, a priest who permitted felling Yakushima's sacred trees after 'holding council with the gods'. The trees – called yakusugi or *cryptomeria japonica* – provided sturdy lumber; the best in Japan, by many accounts. It's a shame, because they're among nature's most grandiose creations, up to 30m (100ft) tall,

thick enough to drive a car through, with trunks knotted and gnarled over millennia. Ageing the trees precisely is difficult, but the most ancient, Jomon Sugi, is thought to be at least 7000 years old, and even the younger yakusugi – the Buddha, Old Long Beard, Heaven's Pillar – far predate Japan's oldest historical records.

But this ecosystem, fine-tuned over an unfathomable expanse of time, could be entering one of its most precarious epochs.

'During Covid, when there were no visitors, I took my kids into the forest three or four times a week, and I could literally see it recover in real time,' says Bell as we sit down for lunch. 'But now, with tourism returning to pre-pandemic levels, we're seeing lasting ecological damage.'

It is a sombre thought, to feel like an interloper. But Bell says it's all about management, perhaps introducing tourist taxes and limiting the numbers of inbound visitors – policies that have been introduced in other biodiverse islands, like the Galapagos – to maintain the health of the forest.

The Yakushima government, however, has proposed plans to build a large airstrip on the island so that travellers can fly directly from Tokyo, and maybe Singapore, Hong Kong, Taiwan and Seoul in the future. The din of jet engines flying over the island and the increased footfall will have repercussions for the flora and fauna. It could disrupt the breeding processes of endangered loggerhead and green turtles or affect the reproductivity of moss and liverworts, both of which are used as forest regulators and indicators of air and water pollution.

A cohort of guides and residents are fighting to halt the new runway, though Bell admits it's a losing battle. It does, however,

give us, as travellers, time to reflect on why we travel. Is it an exercise in checking items off a bucket list? Or do we want to leave a destination better off than when we found it?

'I am a resident here, first and foremost. That's where my concerns come from,' says Bell. 'I'm just suggesting better policies to manage tourism that would benefit everyone, and more importantly, would benefit the forest.'

⊙ yesyakushima.com

WALKING THE MICHINOKU COASTAL TRAIL

◉ **TOHOKU**

Tohoku, the north-eastern section of Honshū, was once known as Michinoku, the 'end of the road'. It was considered a harsh and redoubtable place, offering little sanctuary to travellers. When poet Matsuo Basho ventured there in the late 1600s, he feared he might never return. Victorian explorer Isabella Bird found a 'garden of Eden' as well as communities of poverty, squalor, hunger and disease. Even Alan Booth, traipsing through the north in the 1970s for his seminal travelogue *The Roads to Sata*, encountered strange folk rituals, snow-and-ice-blasted towns and the frequent threat of bears and packs of provincial schoolboys.

Each carved their own track through Tohoku because there was no obvious way to travel it. The Michinoku Coastal Trail now offers a solution. Established in 2019, the 1025km (637-mile) walking route runs along the Pacific Ocean, traversing Aomori, Iwate, Miyagi and Fukushima Prefectures.

Going north to south, the trail begins at Kabushima, an island now connected to the mainland, where tens of thousands of black-tailed gulls roost, mate, nest and fill the air with their feline caws – hence their name in Japanese, umineko, cats of the sea – and finishes in Soma, a city known for little more than its strawberries and central role in Yu Miri's award-winning novel *Tokyo Ueno Station*.

The Michinoku charts one of Japan's most epic stretches of coastline, navigating villages and regions still recovering from the 2011 Tohoku earthquake and tsunami. Civilisation has marched northwards, as has a new chain of gargantuan concrete seawalls, one final attempt to quell nature. But this remains a wild land. Thick evergreen forests and winding woodland trails cling to the bluffs and headlands, alongside echoey, hand-dug caves, pitch-black and dripping, and striated coastal stacks where seafowls stop to dry their wings.

And though the path drifts inland, you cannot escape it: the raw, unflinching power of the sea.

At the beginning of the rainy season, I walked part of the trail in Iwate Prefecture, trudging over undulating paths through impenetrable fog and incessant rainfall in the heart of Japan's bear country. One late afternoon, I descended, alone, into the bowels of the forest. Every rustle in the thick undergrowth caused an adrenaline spike, every soughing tree and note of owlsong closed in around me. I can still smell the wet leaves, hear the mulch of my feet on the matted pine straw, see the thick red trunks rising up through the mist.

I began talking to myself, raving mad, perhaps to ward off ursine intruders, maybe just to keep myself company. A couple of serows quenching their thirst by the river darted off when I stumbled into their path. I was accosted by a wild bird, something large and territorial, believing I was trying to pinch one of its chicklets.

They say this is the real Japan, and I was beginning to sense it. The convenience stores and screeching trains, the pachinko parlours and all-you-can-drink menus, the ostentatious architecture and the fluorescent Tomorrowland – it was all so far away, a parallel universe.

But it's the beach I remember most. The beach in Tanohata with the old seawall, what was left of it anyway. Reinforced concrete, all twisted and bent askew. A ravaged memory of the waves.

Top **Kabushima Shrine**
Bottom **A rocky section of the Michinoku Coastal Trail**

The Michinoku Coastal Trail overlooks the Pacific Ocean

"Despite the sub-zero winters, Hokkaido's ecosystems exhibit great biodiversity."

WILDLIFE

WILDLIFE'S LAST FRONTIER

◉ HOKKAIDO

Hokkaido covers a little over 20 per cent of the Japanese landmass and is the wildest, quarter of the archipelago, with a population density one-fifth the national average. Where civilisation is absent, thick conifer forests, caldera lakes, mountain ranges and wetlands unspool across the landscape.

Despite the sub-zero winters, Hokkaido's ecosystems exhibit great biodiversity; they're home to raptorial seabirds and majestic waders, Northern pikas, Siberian flying squirrels and Yezo sika deer, marine mammals like porpoises, seals and orcas, and even alpine wildflowers and species of snow algae. Many of the species that thrive here are endemic or exist only in Hokkaido and Russia's far east.

The Ussuri brown bear is the symbol of Hokkaido's animal kingdom, known by the indigenous Ainu population as Kimun Kamuy, God of the Mountains. The bears are largely herbivorous, though sometimes they fish in rivers and streams, search in burrows for small mammals or insects and occasionally, seek out bipedal prey. Bear attacks are not common, though they did hit a national record in 2023, in lockstep with Hokkaido's estimated bear population surpassing 12,000, more than double the total in 1990. Ussuri brown bears migrate as hunger and habitat

dictate, but most are concentrated on the Shiretoko Peninsula.

Red-crowned cranes have also come to symbolise the northernmost island of Japan. They were nearly hunted to extinction in the 19th century, and though the population has since rebounded, they're among the rarest cranes in the world. Not only do they move with all the grace and poise you'd expect of a long-legged wading bird, they're also known for their playful mating dance and tremulous, dinosaur-esque squawk which was designated one of the 100 Soundscapes of Japan.

Blakiston's fish owls, another of Hokkaido's endangered avian species, are viewed by the Ainu as protectors of their villages and settlements. They're the largest species of owl in the world, with a wingspan of nearly 2m (6.6ft), and given their size, they need old-growth forests with large trees in order to nest and reproduce. But these have proved challenging to find in an era of deforestation, so the world's Blakiston fish owl population now numbers fewer than 200 individuals, all of which live in eastern Hokkaido and Kunashiri Island.

In light of changing environmental conditions, organisations like the Hokkaido Nature Conservation Society were established to make the relationship between humans and nature more symbiotic. There are also six national parks in Hokkaido – alongside a host of quasi-national parks, geoparks, prefectural natural parks and Ramsar wetlands – which serve as wildlife conservation areas.

Shiretoko, for example, designated a UNESCO World Natural Heritage Site in 2005, is one of the richest integrated ecosystems in the world – defined by the interactions between marine and terrestrial ecosystems – providing a habitat for several threatened species, including seabirds, salmonids and marine mammals like Steller's sea lion and some cetacean species.

In a country that tends to equate construction with progress, it's no surprise that Japan's National Biodiversity Strategy highlights the importance of national parks, habitat preservation and nature restoration projects. If its varied wildlife community is to continue to thrive, it needs all the help it can get.

Top right **Blakiston's fish owl**
Left **Red-crowned crane**
Bottom right **Ussuri brown bear**

THE SPECIES OF JAPAN

◉ AROUND JAPAN

Asiatic Black Bear

These languid creatures, sometimes called 'moon bears', for the crescent-shaped patch under their chins, are the second-largest land animals in Japan (the first is the Ussuri brown bear). Hiking trails in Honshū are littered with signs warning you that you're in black bear habitat, but it is quite rare to encounter one. That said, Japan's moon bear population is growing and its habitat is expanding as nature reclaims abandoned villages.

Cicada

Cicadas screeching is the preeminent sound of the Japanese summer. There are 35 semi (cicada) species in Japan, some of which have the most wonderfully onomatopoeic names, like minminzemi, niiniizemi or tsukutsukuboushi. Semi live throughout Japan, though which species is most prevalent depends on the region.

Grey Heron

Grey herons are found throughout Japan year-round (except in Hokkaido), perched on rowboats, gliding over parks and preening their feathers on riverbanks. Called *aosagi*, they appear in Japanese folktales, often with creepy or negative connotations, and are strongly associated with the supernatural.

Japanese Giant Salamander

A rare creature, but surely the Japanese giant salamander is one of the world's most magnificent amphibians, reaching lengths of up to 1.5m (5ft) and weights of 25kg (55lb). Mostly aquatic and nocturnal, they live in fast-flowing streams and rivers in mountainous areas and are particularly prevalent in Hiroshima's Sandakyo Gorge.

Japanese Macaque

Colloquially known as 'snow monkeys', Japanese macaques are the northernmost primates in the world and the only ones to live in a snowy environment. They are perhaps most famous for bathing in hot springs in northern Honshū each winter, thanks to appearances in several wildlife documentary series. An endemic species, snow monkeys are also found in the more temperate forests of Shikoku and Kyūshū.

Japanese Marten

Japanese martens are inherently Japanese-looking animals, as though they were created by local cartoonists or designed for a kawaii mascot contest. These small, endemic mammals, which are closely related to weasels, sables and other marten species, usually have a creamy or reddish-brown coat and live in broadleaf forests across Japan.

Japanese Pond Turtle

Go to any of the great strolling gardens of Japan and chances are you'll spot a Japanese pond turtle, probably sunning itself on a rock. An endemic species, they are valued for their longevity and are often placed in shrine and temple gardens to imbue visitors with good fortune and healthy lives.

Japanese Red Fox

Kitsune, or Japanese red foxes, can be split into two subspecies: hondokitsune, found in Honshū, Kyūshū and Shikoku; and kitakitsune, found in Hokkaido. Though popular creatures, foxes have been portrayed in conflicting lights in Japanese folklore. Sometimes they appear as messengers of Inari, the god of rice, on other occasions they're mischievous shapeshifters, prone to trickery and deceit.

Japanese Serow

Furry, deer-like creatures, Japanese serows are informally classed as ungulates, or members of the hoofed-mammal family, and they are considered 'living national treasures' of the forests of Japan. This endemic species is often seen wandering through forest clearings alone or in pairs, or drinking from shaded mountain streams.

Tanuki

Tanuki, or Japanese raccoon dogs, are viewed by most Japanese as dastardly creatures. They live in mountains, forests and urban areas, where they occasionally rummage through people's trash. In pop culture they're famously depicted with oversized scrotums, as seen in *tanuki* statues outside liquor shops or in the surreal Studio Ghibli epic *Pom Poko*, ostensibly a child-friendly film in which raccoon dogs use their giant balls as parachutes.

Top to bottom **Tanuki; Japanese red fox; Japanese giant salamander; Asiatic black bear**

Japanese Macaque, also known as 'snow monkeys'

"Residents compost organic waste and separate inorganic waste into 45 categories for reuse or recycling."

RESPONSIBLE TRAVEL

AN EDUCATIONAL PROGRAM IN JAPAN'S FIRST ZERO-WASTE TOWN

◉ TOKUSHIMA

It's not often that a town becomes famous for its rubbish. Forty-five categories of it, to be precise. But that is the unlikely story of Kamikatsu, a municipality of 1400 people spread throughout the mountains of Tokushima Prefecture, which grabbed international headlines for its bid to become Japan's first zero-waste town.

Kamikatsu residents made the zero-waste declaration back in 2003, and by 2021, were recycling more than 80 per cent of their waste, four times the national average. You won't find any dump trucks here. Residents compost organic waste and separate inorganic waste into 45 categories for reuse or recycling. The waste facility, located at Hotel WHY, has become an icon of the town. Shaped like a question mark when viewed from above, Hotel WHY encourages people to ask themselves why they consume and produce waste and how they can mitigate it.

INOW, meaning 'let's go home' in the local dialect, is an educational, experience-based program that asks visitors to Kamikatsu the same questions. But program managers Kana Watando and Sil Van de Velde say it's about more than just waste.

'We focus on "place-making",' says Van de Velde. 'We're working with a community in Kamikatsu that's trying to regenerate and revive its local culture.'

Watando adds that it's important to establish their guests' motivations for coming and what aspects of a sustainable lifestyle they're most interested in, whether it's composting, permaculture, circular business models or creating textiles from felled trees.

'As a base, we always do a tour of the Zero Waste Centre and do our own workshops around waste,' she adds. 'Other experiences, like rice farming, are very seasonal. We organise cooking workshops with local ingredients and bring guests to local people's homes where they can have lunch or tea. People who own businesses in Kamikatsu might also provide lectures and discussions.'

When Watando founded INOW, alongside local chef Terumi Azuma and writer-entrepreneur Linda Ding, it was aimed at people who wanted to travel slowly and experience life in a rural Japanese community. The program now attracts tourism professionals, academics, students, chefs, architects and innovators working in sustainability-focused fields.

At the Japan Travel Awards 2024, a growing industry showcase run by advertising agency Shiitake Creative, INOW won the award for Best Transformative Travel.

'[Transformative] is a word that we gravitated towards with the program,' says Watando. 'By being in a place that has examples of sustainability in non-conventional ways, then maybe guests could reflect on their own values, and maybe those values could change. Whether that's their relationship to waste, their relationship with money or how they think about food.'

Of course, INOW is a two-way street; the program is designed to leave a positive impact on the Kamikatsu community. Guests might maintain terraced rice paddies that ageing farmers are no longer able to or help cultivate and package tea leaves (in recyclable containers) to be shipped across Japan. The program is designed to facilitate relationships that go beyond the transactional.

'When we're doing a workshop with a farmer, for example, we're actually interacting with that person. What is their story? Why are they living here?' says Van de Velde. 'They are not just teachers in the program. We have built that trust with them as friends and fellow community members.'

Neither Watando nor Van de Velde want to romanticise life in Kamikatsu, but they admit there are manifold benefits to a subsistence lifestyle high in the mountains: the connectedness to nature, the togetherness of being in a small community and the lack of stimuli that drive consumer impulses.

Tokushima City might only be an hour drive from Kamikatsu, but when standing on

Farming in Kamikatsu

a mountain precipice or on the wooden deck of a room in Hotel WHY as mist rolls through the steep-sided valleys below, it's hard to believe you're in the same country that throws up high-rise buildings, department stores and fluorescent lights as though the wells were running dry tomorrow.

Such immersion is key to understanding the program's benefits. An INOW experience isn't supposed to be shoehorned into the middle of a beefy, two-week Japan itinerary. It's about approaching life in Kamikatsu slowly and deliberately, as though you were a resident.

'Most research has been done on sustainability, and branding and marketing of tourism, but what happens to the guests afterwards is never really studied,' says Van de Velde. 'The idea is that they come to Kamikatsu to gain a deeper understanding of this place, and ultimately, of their own day-to-day lives.'

🌐 inowkamikatsu.com

SCUBA DIVING TO MAKE A DIFFERENCE

⊙ OKINAWA, KYŪSHŪ

Okinawa Diving Service Lagoon

When coral cultivation began taking off in Okinawa's Onna Village, Shoichi Ikeno had an idea. Why not combine the growing thirst for sustainable tourism with Okinawa's feted scuba culture? This notion soon morphed into Okinawa Diving Service Lagoon, where guests plant coral seedlings and conserve the marine ecosystem while diving or snorkelling among the island's bounty of underwater reefs, arches, domes and tunnels.

'Living coral provides shelter and food for small organisms, and even after they die, they still provide food and shelter and become the foundation for new life,' says Ikeno. 'Because of the abundance of coral reefs in Okinawa, many marine organisms depend on them.'

Though Japan's reefs have suffered due to human and industrial activity, Ikeno says the local coral population has been recovering over the last decade, due in part to aquaculture planting, but mostly because the coral is adapting to its changing environment and withstanding higher water temperatures. But intervention, he says, is key to sustaining this vibrant ecosystem.

'International tourism has become commonplace for people around the world, and anyone can post good spots on social networking sites,' adds Ikeno. 'But overtourism is a problem in many parts of the world and this has led to the deterioration of the local environment. We believe that it is necessary for tourism operators to prepare experiences that allow tourists to experience the natural environment, residents and culture of the destination, and to be close to them and protect them.'

🔗 padi.com/dive-center/japan/okinawa-diving-service-lagoon

ZeroGravity, Amami Islands

Almost 40 years ago, when Junichi Torihata was diving in the Oshima Strait, an area of reefs, caves and diverse schools of fish bisecting the Amami Islands, he stopped for a moment to watch sunlight filtering through the surface. He felt like he was floating in the sky – in zero gravity – and he wanted this experience to be available to all, regardless of one's physical capabilities.

In 2016, he realised his vision, founding an accessible marine sports facility called ZeroGravity. Torihata was focused on totally barrier-free experiences and maintaining the dignity of his customers – two-factors that helped ZeroGravity win the Grand Prix prize at the Japan Travel Awards 2024.

'[Torihata-san] kept searching for a way to create a facility that people with disabilities can truly enjoy,' says Ryota Kurihara, ZeroGravity's manager. 'We developed a boat with a lift as a way for them to dive freely. In addition, we focused on facilities for wheelchair users in our accommodation. We paid special attention to the location of electrical outlets, the size of restrooms and barrier-free access.'

Not only did this open an industry previously viewed as inaccessible, it did so in a region of translucent waters and charming islands encircled by beaches and cloaked in virgin forests. Providing habitat for sea turtles, cuttlefish, ghost crabs and crown-of-thorns starfish, the Amami marine ecosystem is home to approximately 1600 fish species and 400 types of coral.

'It is [also] a special environment for Amami's endemic hoshizorafugu (white-spotted pufferfish), whale watching in winter,' Kurihara says. 'I think that facilities like ZeroGravity will become more and more necessary in the future.'

◈ zerogravity.jp

Amami's Naze Port

Coral cultivation in Okinawa

"What a doner kebab would be in Berlin, or what a slice of pizza might be in New York City, in Tokyo it's a bowl of ramen."

FOOD & DRINK

WASHOKU: THE WAY IS DEEP

⊙ AROUND JAPAN

I am sometimes amazed that when I first arrived in Japan, I thought of Japanese food as 'sushi and ramen and stuff.' But as the Buddhists like to intone, *oku ga fukai* – the way is deep. Or put more simply, there is much to learn before you can fully understand the depth and breadth of a given art – in this case, Japanese cuisine.

I soon realised the pantheon of Japanese food is as varied as any country's, if not more so – just ask the chefs who make the same soba, tempura, yakitori, unagi, agedashi tofu or tuna tataki as their fathers did, and their fathers before them. Go to any prefecture, city or town and there will be a *meibutsu*, a regional speciality, that is typically some kind of food: takoyaki in Osaka, Hakata ramen in Fukuoka, fugu (pufferfish) in Yamaguchi, gyutan (beef tongue) in Sendai or kenoshiru (vegetable soup) in Aomori.

Variety, in this case, breeds excellence. There is, after all, a reason that Tokyo, Kyoto and Osaka are consistently in the top five cities worldwide for most Michelin-starred restaurants. It's no coincidence that *washoku*, Japanese cuisine, was designated as UNESCO Intangible Cultural Heritage in 2013. This is why practices once viewed as Japanese quirks – eating raw fish, prioritising texture, eschewing spices in favour of broths – are now mainstays in the global culinary market.

In *A Simple Art*, Shizuo Tsuji, the godfather of Japanese cooking, noted that Japanese cuisine was deceptively simple, its core ingredients only two: a delicate stock (called dashi) made from konbu (giant kelp) and flakes of dried bonito; and shoyu, Japanese soy sauce.

But out of such simplicity, comes a world of complexity. The key is produce. In ancient times, Japan's four distinct seasons were broken down into 72 microseasons, with such haiku-esque names as takenoko shozu (bamboo shoots sprout) and atsukaze itaru (warm winds blow), which described minute changes in the natural world. They also indicated which produce was shun, or at peak freshness.

The level of freshness informs how a vegetable, protein or fungus should be treated in the cooking process and how best to extract their fumi, or hidden taste-aromas. This is known as subtractive cooking, a foundational element of Japanese cuisine that brings out the inherent flavours in food by using dashi, shoyu, diluted sake or broths to remove the disagreeable bitterness and odours. Subtractive cooking is a minimalist approach, exercising subtlety and refinement. It is representative of the Japanese artistic method writ large: we see it in the spatial metaphor of calligraphy painting, in the blank and liminal spaces in Japanese architecture and in the less-is-more simplicity of ikebana flower arrangements.

This may all sound rather effete, but when you slurp buckwheat noodles dipped in an unassuming tsuyu broth or warm your insides with a bowl of miso soup, you can thank subtractive cooking for the resulting sensations.

Of course, this isn't applied to every dish in Japan. In fact, local soul foods, like savoury okonomiyaki pancakes, kushikatsu (deep-fried meat and veg skewers) and Hokkaido-style soup curry, are about as subtle as a karate chop to the face. But this brings me back to the original point: Japanese cuisine is wildly varied. Indeed, the way is deep.

Top **Fugu (pufferfish)**
Bottom **Preparing takoyaki**

Top **Omakase allows chefs to choose the food served to diners**

Bottom left **A kaiten sushi shop**

Bottom right **Sushi is one of Japan's landmark dishes**

SUSHI: A SYMBOL OF JAPANESE CULINARY CULTURE

◉ AROUND JAPAN

This may sound a tad hyperbolic, but whenever my teeth slide through a piece of high-quality raw *otoro* (fatty tuna), I experience something that goes beyond the senses. It is nourishment for the soul as much as the body. The Japanese tend to think I'm a little pedestrian in my sushi tastes – punting for the familiar tuna and salmon in lieu of more indecipherable sea creatures – but *otoro*, when served correctly, can spark a transcendental experience.

It is reasonable, therefore, to think of the fish as the hero of the dish. But sushi means 'sour rice', and the quality of the rice and the vinegar used to make it also delineates good sushi from bad. In Tokyo's legendary sushi restaurants – think Sukiyabashi Jiro (sushi-jiro.jp) of Netflix fame or three-Michelin-starred Harutaka (ginza-sushi.com/harutaka. html) – chefs can spend years making rice before they so much as touch a piece of seafood.

That's not to say all fish are created equal. Top chefs seek out the highest-quality produce at early-morning markets and pay big bucks for the prize catch. How the fishermen attain the fish is important, too: if the fish is caught in a struggle, it produces cortisol and its muscles contract, hindering the tenderness of the meat.

The best sushi restaurants are omakase, or 'I'll leave it to you', meaning the food is chosen by the chef, who will use their discretion and

intimate knowledge of local food culture to express themselves through the menu. They'll consider which fish are in peak season and how they've been caught; they'll reflect the time of year through colour and presentation; and they'll improvise dishes based on the moods, appetites and dietary requirements of guests. It's all embedded in the hospitality concept of *omotenashi*, knowing what the customer wants or needs before they know themselves.

There are an estimated 30,000 sushi restaurants in Japan. Dining in the most exclusive Michelin-starred haunts is a good way to scythe through a week's wages. In *kaiten* (conveyer belt) sushi shops, cheap, colour-coded plates denoting the price of each dish are fizzed out at factory speed and with industrial efficiency. These latter institutions might not be winning any awards, but the sushi is generally still leagues above your average sushi elsewhere in the world, especially at popular chains like Hanamaru (sushi-hanamaru.com) and Sushi Zanmai (sushizanmai.com).

Other than stumbling upon a sushi shop that looks appetising – which most places do – a good way to find one that suits your budget and location is at Tabelog (tabelog.com/en) or Gurunavi (gurunavi.com), Japan's largest restaurant listing sites.

JAPAN'S GREAT FISH MARKETS

⊙ AROUND JAPAN

Another great way to sample sushi, and seafood of any kind, is in Japan's markets. For 83 years, Tsukiji Market in Tokyo was considered the world's greatest fish market – it was 'Japan's Kitchen' – until many of the wholesalers and fishmongers migrated to the new location at Toyosu. The old ramshackle outer market at Tsukiji is still in operation and looks much as it did in the 1930s. You have to weave through droves of gawking tourists here, but it's worth it for the fist-sized scallops blowtorched in their shells with butter, stalls selling raw tuna that's so texturally moreish you'll likely return for further helpings and small restaurants specialising in kaisendon (sashimi rice bowls) or uni (sea urchin), a creamy, orange-coloured delicacy that carries the faintest notes of the sea.

One of old Tsukiji's main draws was the early-morning tuna auction, where restaurant owners, sushi chefs and food distributors would bid for the day's catch. If you still want to watch this live, you'll have to set your alarm for the crack of dawn and head over to Toyosu. The retailers and sushi shops here, high-quality though they may be, are spread out across 400,000 sq m (4.3 million sq ft) of drab and airy warehouses. But the atmosphere has been improved with an adjacent Edo-inspired complex, Toyosu Senkyaku Banrai, that has 50 restaurants and a public footbath overlooking the bay.

But to think of Japan's fish-market culture only in terms of Tokyo is to do it a great disservice. Almost every coastal city has an asaichi (morning market), with trestle tables full of hulking crustaceans and shellfish, fishmongers filleting fish the size of their torsos and vendors profering all manner of freshly harvested seaweeds and fermented delicacies.

FISH MARKET RECOMMENDATIONS

✱ **Omicho Market, Kanazawa** Enclosed within a warren of shotengai (broad arcade streets), Omicho Market is one of the great markets on the Sea of Japan coast. Kindly local cook Naoko-san also runs cooking classes here, harnessing the flavours of local produce. 🔗 **ohmicho-ichiba.com**

✱ **Wajima Morning Market, Ishikawa** Home to 200 stalls, this market has been running since the Heian period (794–1185), and is back in action after being damaged during the 2024 Noto Earthquake. 🔗 **asaichi.info**

✱ **Minato-no-Asaichi, Higashiizu** In this small town on the Izu Peninsula, the weekend *asaichi* is a great place to try agar jelly noodles soaked in soy sauce or a hotpot called kinmedai kama-meshi, made from rice, snapper and seasonal vegetables. 🔗 **japantravel.navitime. com/en/area/jp/spot/02301-2100124**

✱ **Makishi Public Market, Naha** Head to this market in the capital of the Okinawan archipelago for umi budo, or 'sea grapes', a native seaweed composed of salty, umami-filled spheres. 🔗 **makishi-public-market.jp**

✱ **Hirome Market, Kochi** Hirome Market, in the heart of Kochi City, is encircled by fishmongers, butchers and hole-in-the-wall seafood restaurants. People come for the tuna *tataki*, tuna fillets seared over open flame with the flesh left raw and tender inside. 🔗 **hirome.co.jp**

Fish markets are a great place to sample Japan's seafood

Top **Browsing at Omicho Market**
Bottom **Octopus on display**
Opposite **The bustling Tsukiji Market**

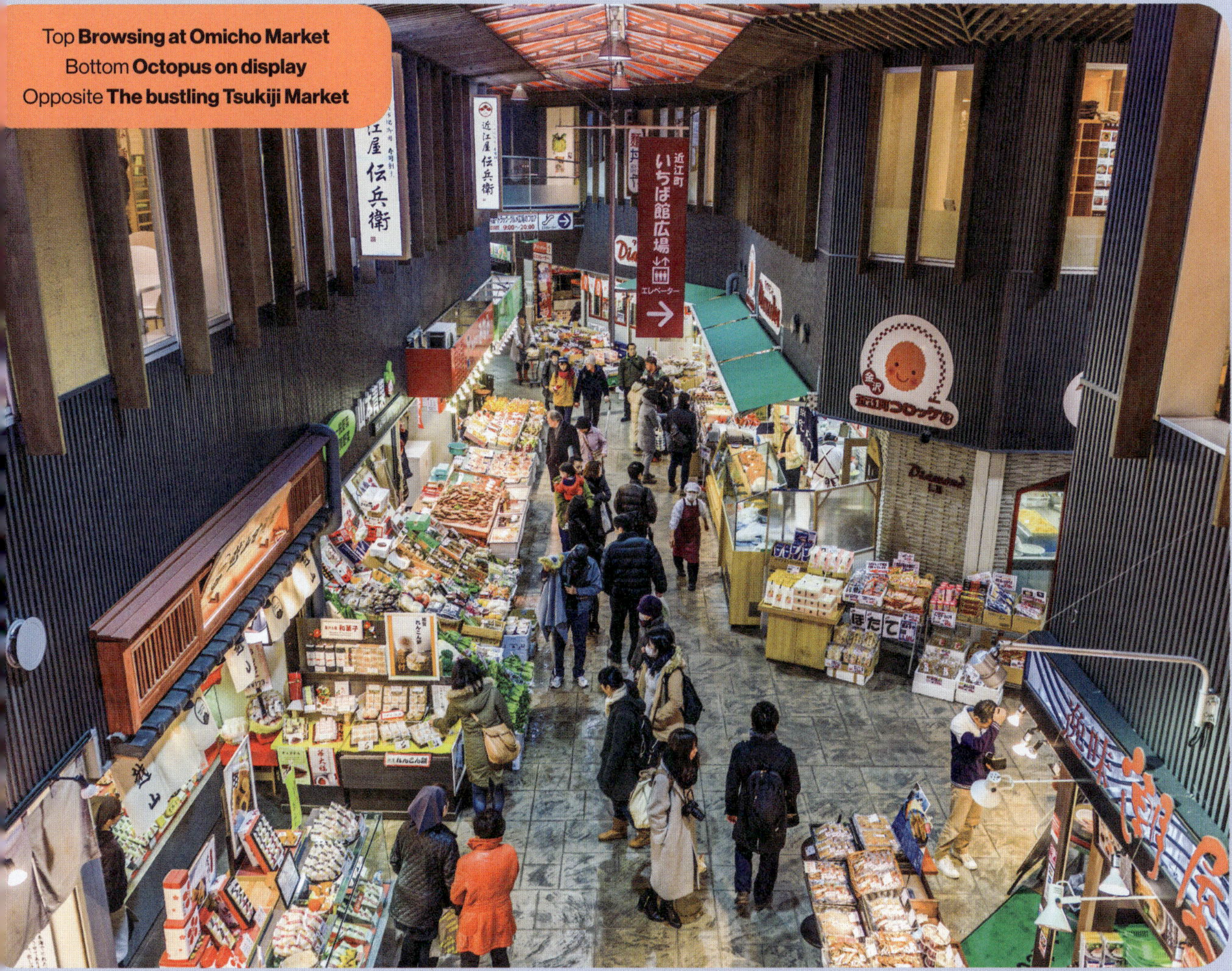

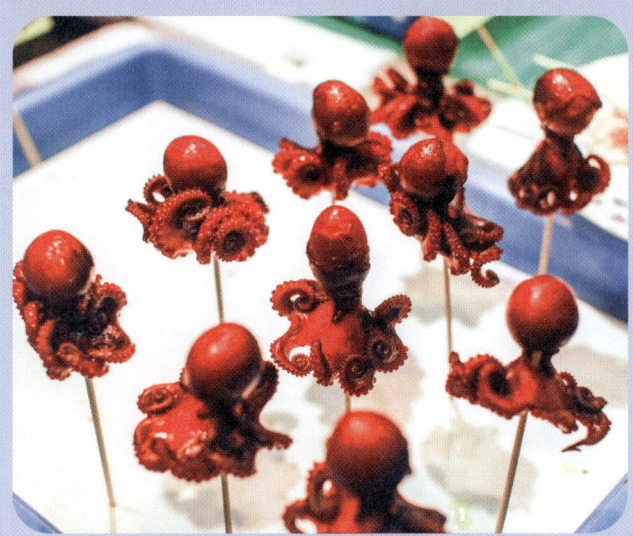

JAPAN'S RAMEN CAPITAL

⊙ TOKYO

Frank Striegl, a Filipino-American born and raised in Tokyo, believes nothing beats a late-night bowl of ramen. And in fairness, there are few better ways to soothe the vocal cords after a night of belting out Meat Loaf in the local karaoke parlour than with a bowl of noodles swimming in hot broth.

'Of course, that isn't the only time I eat ramen,' says Striegl, who runs the 5AM Ramen blog and conducts ramen food tours in the city. 'But what a doner kebab would be in Berlin, or what a slice of pizza might be in New York City, in Tokyo it's a bowl of ramen. If you've been out for several drinks, think of it as a ramen nightcap.'

Ramen has long been an outlier in the Japanese culinary world because of its openness to innovation and change. And in Tokyo, where ramen was born back in 1910, chefs are given licence to throw paint all over the canvas.

'Ramen started out as an experiment, taking Chinese noodle dishes and turning them into something else, and that experimentation that turned into ramen still continues in Tokyo more so than anywhere else,' Striegl says. 'There are always new styles coming out. So, if you want to eat amazing ramen, in Tokyo it's not just the quality, but the variety.'

Striegl, who's just shy of 40, reckons he's eaten in a couple thousand ramen restaurants, which when including repeat visits, amounts to a lot more bowls than his trim figure would suggest. But he has plenty still to try – there could be as many as 7000 individual shops in the Tokyo Metropolitan Area alone, and some would argue there are nearly as many different styles. This raises an obvious question: what defines a bowl of ramen?

'You do see certain things that show up in the bowls regardless of the style, like using soy sauce or miso,' Striegl says. 'When these dishes made their way from China to Japan, they were likely very meaty, so chefs added some Japanese elements, like kelp, dashi, niboshi [dried fish] or katsuobushi [fish flakes]. The noodles should be made from wheat flour, with alkaline water in them, which gives them that extra springiness. And as for toppings, we've got bamboo shoots, pork, spring onions, eggs.'

Though there are technically four main base broths for ramen – tonkotsu (pork bones), shio (salt), shoyu (soy sauce) and miso – categorisation is a little messy. This is further confounded when you consider ramen-adjacent dishes like mazemen (soupless ramen), tsukemen (dipping ramen), hiyashi chuka (cold ramen) or dishes that look like ramen but deviate from traditional Japanese flavour profiles by using chicken mousse, slices of pineapple or parmesan and shredded bacon. And where do fellow noodle dishes like soba and udon fit into the ramen story?

Striegl says they played a fundamental role in ramen's development, inspiring ramen chefs to use dashi to add flavour to the dish. 'Soba and udon are very much the heart and soul of Japan,' he adds. 'Ramen has the heart and soul, too, but with some outside influence.'

As if to emphasise his point about Tokyo's ramen variety, Striegl brings me to a mapo tofu ramen shop in Nakameguro, one of the capital's most fashionable neighbourhoods. As I get started on the dish, I'm glad I haven't eaten breakfast. A thick and gelatinous soup, singing with doubanjiang (fermented chilli bean paste) and Szechuan peppercorns, every slurp goes straight from my mouth to settle in my stomach like cement.

As Striegl wolfs his down, I ask him if he has a favourite shop. Of course, he isn't able to pick. But he says exploring the ramen scene is all about being curious, looking for shops off the main thoroughfares and trying styles you haven't experienced before.

'To say that somewhere with a Michelin star is better than another place is difficult because food is very subjective. What's popular with tourists and what's popular with locals is often very different,' he says. 'It's so easy for us to go on Google and look for the highest-ranked place in the language that we speak, but if you're doing that you're definitely missing out on a lot of great ramen.'

🌀 5amramen.com

WHERE TO EAT OTHER NOODLE DISHES IN JAPAN

* **Soba** These buckwheat noodles, often eaten cold with a tsuyu dipping sauce, are found across Japan. Go to Nagano Prefecture for the best, where the high altitude and terroir are suited to buckwheat cultivation.

* **Udon** These thick noodles made from wheat flour are the meibutsu (regional specialties) in Kagawa Prefecture. Typically, they're eaten as kake udon, a dish of noodles swimming in a mild umami broth.

* **Somen** These noodles are popular in Hyogo Prefecture, particularly in the southwest Harima region. Super thin and smooth, *somen* retains its texture after boiling and is best enjoyed cold with tsuyu.

* **Yakisoba** This stir-fried dish comprises wheat noodles, pork, cabbage, spring onions, beansprouts, carrots and beni shoga (shredded pickled ginger). Cheap and cheerful, you'll find it at festivals throughout Japan.

FRANK'S PICKS FOR RAMEN OUTSIDE TOKYO

* **Sapporo, Hokkaido** This northern city is well known in the ramen scene, thanks to the popularity of Ganso Ramen Yokocho, a narrow alleyway filled with miso ramen shops. But Striegl says Menya Saimi, in Sapporo's Toyohira Ward, 'might serve Japan's best miso ramen.'

* **Yonezawa, Yamagata** The ramen shops in this region favour light broths, using pork, chicken and fish for an umami punch. For Striegl, Hirama is the pick of the bunch, pairing one of the five classic Yonezawa ramen styles with super-light, thin, frizzy noodles.

* **Tsubame, Niigata** In the snowy climes of Niigata Prefecture, locals turn to ramen as a winter warmer dish. Koshu Hanten is Striegl's go-to shop in the area. 'The noodles are thick and heavy,' he says, 'and they do a nice style of *shoyu* ramen with a lot of pork back fat.'

* **Saga Prefecture** This region is a secret big hitter in the ramen scene. The local style is tonkotsu (pork bone), owing to its proximity to Fukuoka, where tonkotsu was born. Striegl recommends Koyokaku in Shimodamachi, which 'has a really rich pork-bone soup, but it's super smooth, with raw egg on top.'

* **Osaka City** Better known for its local soul food, Osaka City is no slouch in the ramen department, either. Striegl is a fan of Chukasoba Uemachi, which is consistently ranked among the country's best ramen shops. The shop's shoyu ramen is 'very simple looking,' he says. 'But there's a lot going on under the hood.'

🌐 5amramen.com/blog/categories/best-ramen-lists

とくいちとみや

特一富屋

二代目
萬来軒
BANRAIKEN SECOND STAGE

熊吉

Sapporo is a ramen hotspot
Opposite **Tonkotsu ramen**

Okonomiyaki

JAPAN'S SOUL FOOD CAPITAL

⊙ OSAKA

People in Osaka don't beat around the bush. In the rough-and-tumble local dialect, known as Osaka-ben, a popular greeting is mokarimakka? It literally means 'are you making good money?' The standard reply is bochi bochi denna, or 'things ain't great.' Such vernacularisms are indicative of the brazen, carefree approach to life in Japan's soul-food capital.

Once, when I was visiting a friend in Osaka, we walked into a coffee shop where the staff and customers were embroiled in the kind of familiar, ball-busting exchange that feels anathema to the formality of Tokyo. My friend turned to me and said, 'People just seem to enjoy life a little bit more here, don't they?'

This is reflected in the food. Osaka's culinary scene isn't entirely devoid of subtlety – the city does have 100-plus Michelin stars – but a night on the town is more likely to involve stumbling down yokocho (alleyways filled with bars and restaurants), drinking nama (draft) beers or nihonshu (rice wine) and wolfing down plates of doteyaki (stewed beef tendon), kushikatsu (deep-fried skewers), butaman (steamed pork buns), okonomiyaki and takoyaki. This is, after all, the city of kuidaore, 'eating oneself bankrupt.'

Okonomiyaki and takoyaki are perhaps most synonymous with Osaka's culinary culture. Okonomiyaki, meaning 'what you like, cooked', is a savoury pancake filled with your choice of ingredients, cooked on a teppan (hot plate) and smothered in richly sweet sauce and topped with mayonnaise and katsuobushi (dried bonito flakes). Though it sounds like the sort of thing you'd throw together on a Sunday morning to obliterate a hangover, some chefs have elevated the dish to a higher plane. Restaurants like the wildly popular Mizuno and Shimizu, both in central Osaka, whip up okonomiyaki with Michelin flair.

Takoyaki is more of a street food, something you might pick up in the Dotonbori neighbourhood as you make your way from one bar to the next. It's made from little pieces of tako (octopus), battered, fried and smothered in the same toppings as its okonomiyaki sibling. Little is left to the imagination with takoyaki. Usually served from hole-in-the-wall shops, you can peer in and watch the chefs cook the octopus on cast-iron griddles with small spherical moulds that give the food its distinctive shape.

TAKOYAKI RECOMMENDATIONS

* **Hanadako** There's a good chance you'll have to queue at this shop underneath Osaka Station, but it's a testament to the quality of the takoyaki on offer.

* **Takohachi** This shop specialises in akashiyaki, a lighter style of takoyaki dipped in broth. **takohachi.jp**

* **Juhachiban** Dotonbori is about as touristy as Osaka gets, but it's worth braving the crowds for Juhachiban. The chefs play on the traditional style by adding ginger, tempura bits and sakura shrimp. **d-sons18.co.jp**

OKONOMIYAKI RECOMMENDATIONS

* **Mizuno** Michelin-star quality okonomiyaki at backpacker prices. Queues guaranteed. **mizuno.gorp.jp**

* **Ajinoya** The seven-decades-old recipe here is heavy on the cabbage, giving it some extra crunch. Best to book in advance. **http://ajinoya-okonomiyaki.com/en**

* **Chigusa** A classic, alleyway okonomiyaki shop, where guests cook the food on a hot plate at their table.

Takoyaki is a popular street food in Osaka

Opposite **Dotonbori** has some of Osaka's best dining spots

YATAI CULTURE

⦿ FUKUOKA

In Fukuoka, the largest city on the island of Kyūshū, you'll find a curious cultural dichotomy. It has a distinctly cosmopolitan air, with Shanghai, Seoul and Taipei all short flights away, and a booming startup culture pioneered by the city's young, camera-hungry mayor Soichiro Takashima. While at the same time, it has stayed true to its working-class roots, with people and a dialect that share the same lack of pretence as free-spirited Osaka.

When Fukuoka locals go out to eat, they're equally at home in a chic teppanyaki restaurant as they are crammed cheek-by-jowl around a yatai, or outdoor food stall, where chefs hurl out bowls of tonkotsu ramen or plates of steamy oden – boiled eggs, shellfish and vegetables stewed in a soy and dashi broth. Though some of the flavours are classically Japanese, yatai food tends not to be subtle. Indeed, it almost certainly appeals to the bolder palates of its East Asian neighbours.

The city's yatai are numerous – estimates usually put the number at more than 100 – but the greatest collection of stalls lines the Naka River on Nakasu Island. Here you'll find yatai draped in plastic wrapping and chefs surrounded by naked bulbs and bubbling pots of broth. On balmy summer evenings, some stalls will set out trestle tables for customers along the riverbank. The lively Tenjin area has some great yatai, too, one of which, Fukuchan-tei, specialises in fugu (pufferfish), a local delicacy.

🌐 gofukuoka.jp/yatai.html

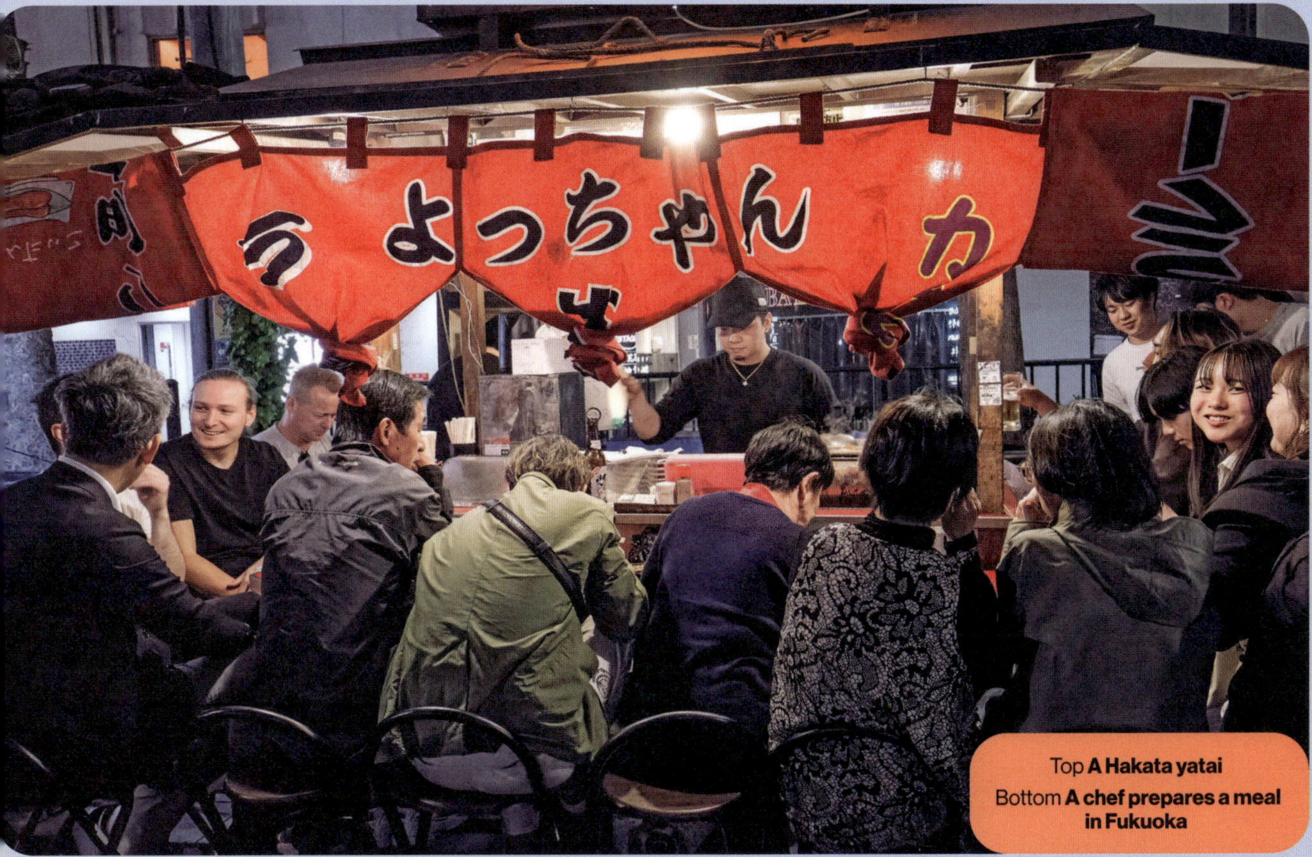

Top **A Hakata yatai**
Bottom **A chef prepares a meal in Fukuoka**

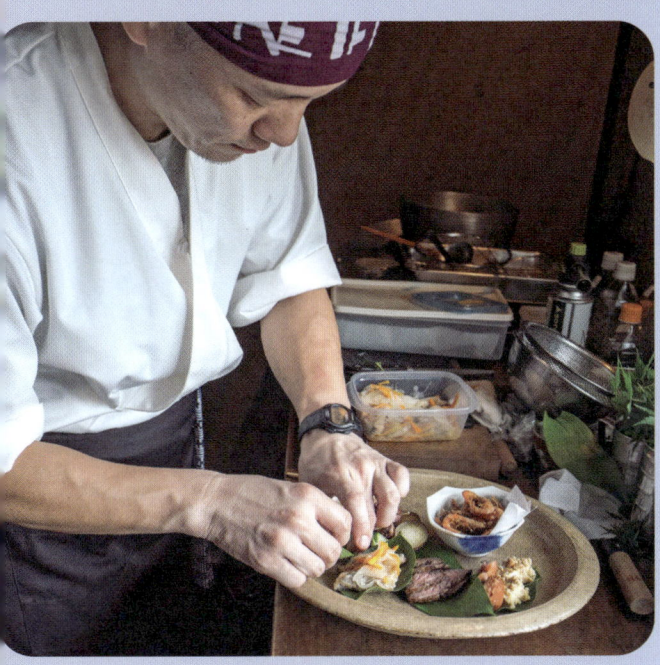

POPULAR IZAKAYA AREAS IN TOKYO

* **Ameyoko** An open-air shopping bazaar in Ueno, full of seafood restaurants and izakaya with outdoor seating.

* **Nomiya Yokocho** Meaning 'Drinking Hole Alley,' Nomiya Yokocho is more popular with students and salarymen than it is with tourists. Some Tokyoites think of it as a ghetto – which I don't see as a pejorative – partly because it's had little renovation since the mid-20th-century Showa period.

* **Harmonica Yokocho** A warren of shaded alleys resembling the reeds of a harmonica, this area in Kichijoji was a flea market in the immediate postwar era. Now it's packed with izakaya, ramen shops and hole-in-the-wall bars.

IZAKAYA NIGHTS

◉ AROUND JAPAN

Glasses clink, chopsticks whirr, steam billows from the open kitchen. Tomato-faced salarymen roar with laughter, one ashtray between them buried under a mound of cigarette butts. The couple beside me glance furtively, sipping their highballs, working up the courage to talk to me in English. A flask of hot sake arrives on the table with a deft bow from the waitress. An otoshi, a small dish served before the rest of the food, lands alongside it. It looks like some kind of seaweed. I shovel it into my mouth with a pair of chopsticks, and bursts of umami dance across my tongue. Ah, the Japanese izakaya.

People often translate izakaya to 'gastropub,' but this feels a little inadequate to me. Gastropub suggests one of those stripped-back, hipster-ish eateries in London or Toronto or New York, where the food is overpriced and the music so loud I start brandishing my decibel metre to the apathetic staff.

An izakaya is where one goes to eat cheap and cheerful food – maybe gyoza dumplings, yakitori (chicken skewers), fried tofu or steamed eggplant. The food and beer are delivered at a pace and often ordered from tabehoudai (all you can eat) or nomihoudai (all you can drink) menus. Typically, the interiors are traditional: wooden beams, *noren* curtains, sliding doors, optional floor seating, sake bottles lining the shelves and lanterns and posters covered in elegant kanji script. Yes, there will be trappings of modernity – an iPad menu here, a toilet with 40 buttons there – but a night in an izakaya is a quintessential Japanese dining experience. Izakaya evolved from the increased habit of communal dining during Japan's prosperous Edo period (1603–1868) and remain among the most important shared spaces in public life.

Most izakaya are multidisciplinary. They might have a specialty on the menu, like basashi (raw horse meat), shabu shabu hotpots or chazuke (hot green tea poured over rice), but variety is one of their principal drawcards. Izakaya are plentiful, too, and often they congregate in yokocho (alleyways) with akachochin (red paper lanterns) indicating the fare inside.

POPULAR IZAKAYA AREAS OUTSIDE OF TOKYO

* **Tenma, Osaka** Located next to Tenjinbashi-suji, the longest shopping street in Japan, Tenma is a great place to eat kushikatsu, or raw-meat delicacies, including horse, duck and chicken.

* **Noge, Yokohama** The vintage izakaya in this lantern-lit, riverside district are popular among students and homeward-bound commuters letting their hair down after a day in the office.

* **Bunka Yokocho, Sendai** Few first-timers to Japan head to Sendai. But if you're out for drinks in this vibrant northern city, you'll likely end up in one of the 50 or so izakaya along Bunka Yokocho.

Izakaya are perfect locations for a cheap meal and drink

Previous **A bustling izakaya**

THE SECRET TO LONG LIFE: FERMENTED CUISINE IN TANGO

⊙ **KYOTO**

You may be familiar with the term Blue Zones, popularised by author and longevity expert Dan Beuttner, referring to regions of the world most abundant in centenarians – people over 100 years old. Beuttner travelled to the villages of Sardinia and the islands of Greece, to a sunny suburb in California and to Costa Rica's Nicoya peninsula, in search of the secrets to a long life.

Japan, and particularly Okinawa, was also an object of his research. But the Tango region of Kyoto Prefecture is arguably the longest-lived in the country, with 2.8 times more centenarians than the national average – a 2019 study suggested it was due to elderly residents' superior gut health – so perhaps it's no coincidence the oldest man in history, Jiroemon Kimura, spent his life here, dying in 2013 at the age of 116.

Tango residents say it's all about the food: fresh produce, the quality of mountain water, good rice and most importantly, the fungal mould koji, which contains up to 100 digestion-facilitating enzymes. The peninsula's temperate climate is conducive to growing koji, a vital ingredient in miso, soy sauce, vinegar and sake production.

Junko Hamilton, who was born in Kyoto but spent several years living in Ireland, never imagined she'd end up in the Japanese countryside making miso and running traditional Japanese cooking classes (tabeltable.net/en).

'I wanted to show people how to make Japanese food simply, using umami, which leaves people satisfied, even if they only eat small amounts,' she says. We're sitting in Hamilton's cooking studio in a refurbished farmhouse in Kyotango, as she concocts her appropriately named Mammy Sauce, a combination of soy, mirin, katsuobushi and dried shiitake mushrooms. She hands me a spoonful; I take a sip and convulse with pleasure. 'Four ingredients,' she laughs. 'That's all it is.'

Food has been central to Hamilton's life for as long as she can remember. From age eight, she attended cooking classes for children; by 10, she was preparing meals for the family, and when her mother died seven years later, the cooking responsibilities fell to her and her sister. After she moved to Ireland with her husband and children, cooking Japanese food allowed her to stay close to her roots. 'I've always loved it,' she says. 'Cooking is a joy for me.'

She uses her Mammy Sauce and a homemade kombu mizudashi (a mix of kelp and water) as the base for broths and simmering vegetables. There is little complexity nor fuss in the assortment of dishes Hamilton creates, but each one drives the umami flavours home.

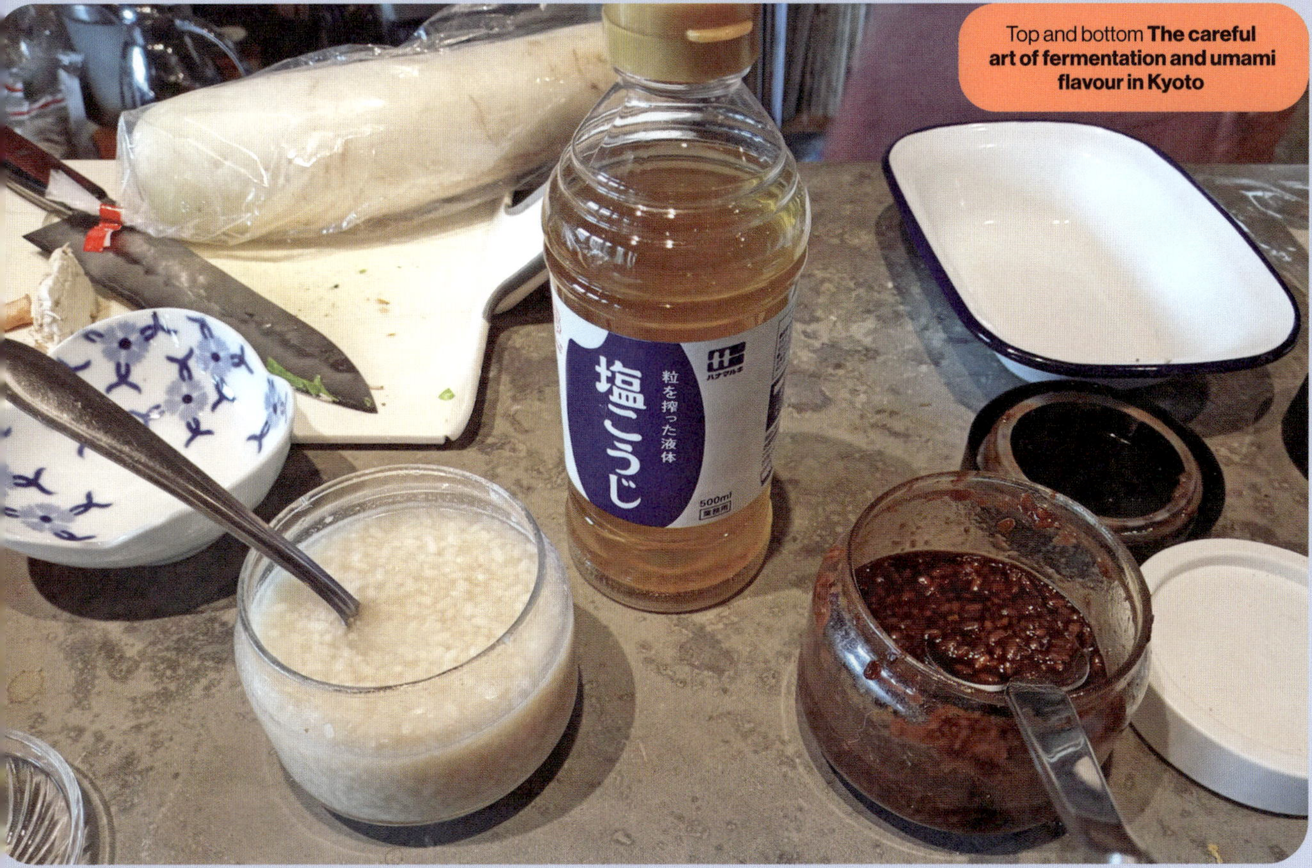

Top and bottom **The careful art of fermentation and umami flavour in Kyoto**

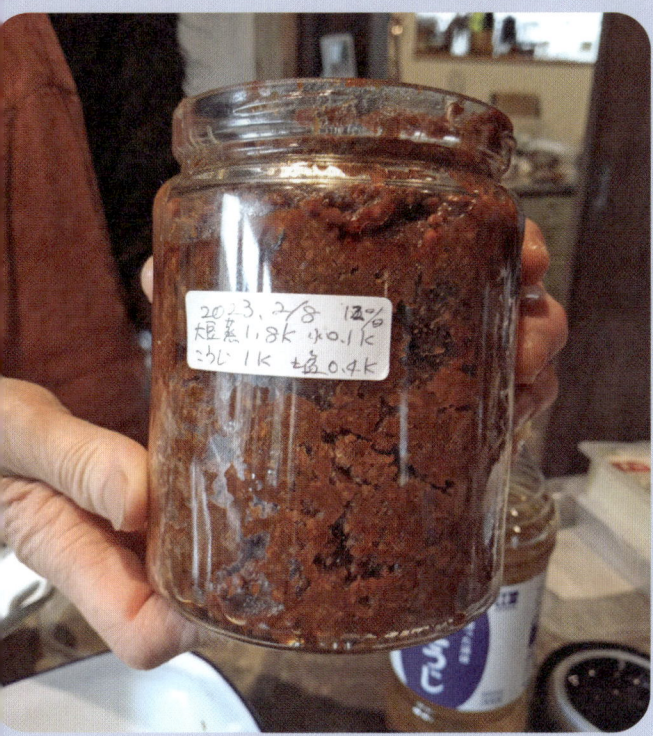

Tofu, mushroom caps and spinach stems with a light dipping sauce. Steamed spinach leaves in sesame paste. Fried butterfish with a salt-koji marinade and grilled chicken in a shoyu-koji sauce. And of course, miso soup, the denouement to every traditional Japanese meal.

The Tango region is full of culinary shokunin (artisans) producing fermented food made with koji, and Hamilton takes me on a tour of the local producers. We sip chilled sake at Yosamusume Shuzo, sample the soy sauce at Onojin Brewery and try what might just be Japan's best rice vinegar at Iio Jozo (iio-jozo.co.jp/en).

We're greeted at Iio Jozo by fourth-generation vinegar maker Tsuyoshi Iio, whose family has been brewing sake and turning it into vinegar using pesticide-free rice since 1893. He shows us around and then sits us down at a long table for the taste test. A vinegary-sweet smell wafts out of the fermentation room and lingers under my nose as Iio hands me a small beaker of rice wine vinegar. 'This is the most popular brand in Japan,' he says. 'Try it.'

I wince, as the sharp, yellowy liquid runs down my throat. He laughs, suggests I have some water and passes me a cup of Iio Jozo's premium vinegar. I sip it, and assess the cup, not quite convinced it's vinegar; there is a mild, comforting sweetness where there ought to be astringency. I tell Iio I could – in fact, I would – drink pints of this. Line them up, bleed the barrels dry.

'If you want to drink vinegar, you should try this one,' he says. He brings out a glass bottle filled with a caramel-coloured liquid. It's infused with sweet potato during the brewing process and Iio says he's been drinking it every day for years. As if to illustrate his point, he pulls out a before-and-after brain scan chart to show the effects. I have no idea what I'm looking at, but I concede that he looks younger than the septuagenarian he claims to be.

Iio says they make a super-premium brand of vinegar, too, aged for 14 years, but there's no chance of trying it. The few bottles remaining are in the hands of Michelin-star sushi chefs and French restaurants, or doubtless, in Iio's private stash.

Jinicho Ono, another fourth-generation producer, puts equal stock in the therapeutic power of his soy sauces. When we arrive at the sloping tile-roofed building that houses his family brewery (onojin.com), he's quick to call for samples. Ono's daughter Eriko, the heiress apparent, places ceramic trays with spoonfuls of soy sauces on the table. One for sashimi and sushi, one for extracting the fumi (taste-aroma) from fresh produce, another that has a refreshing acidity and another fused with dashi to add umami when cooking. It's a soy sauce symphony – words I never thought I'd write – with each composition as complex as the last.

Ono's philosophy is simple: use local ingredients. But if there is a secret, he says, it's the koji. 'People want to live healthier lifestyles,' he adds. 'So, there's been a koji revolution. This region is perfect for it. I think that's why there are so many people here making fermented foods.'

It isn't often that fungal moulds kickstart revolutions, but few things are as alluring as adding extra years to your life. Most longevity experts will attribute the ability to reach 100 to genetics, good sleep, low stress, keeping the brain and body active and eating a variety of foods with medicinal properties. But if the people of Tango are anything to go by, you could do worse than adding koji to your diet.

🜂 kyotobythesea.com

Top **The Kyotango coast**
Bottom **Iio Jozo vinegar**

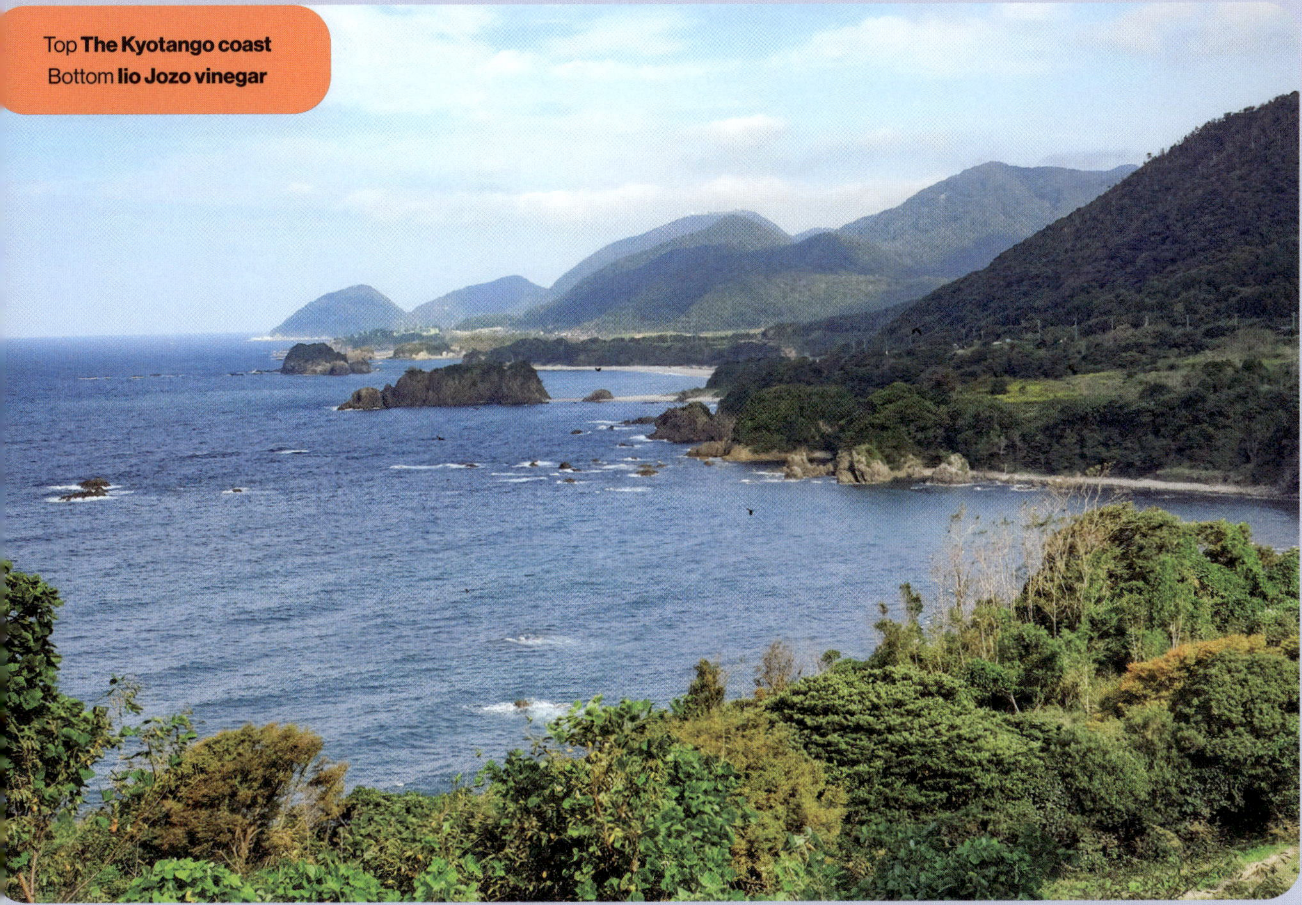

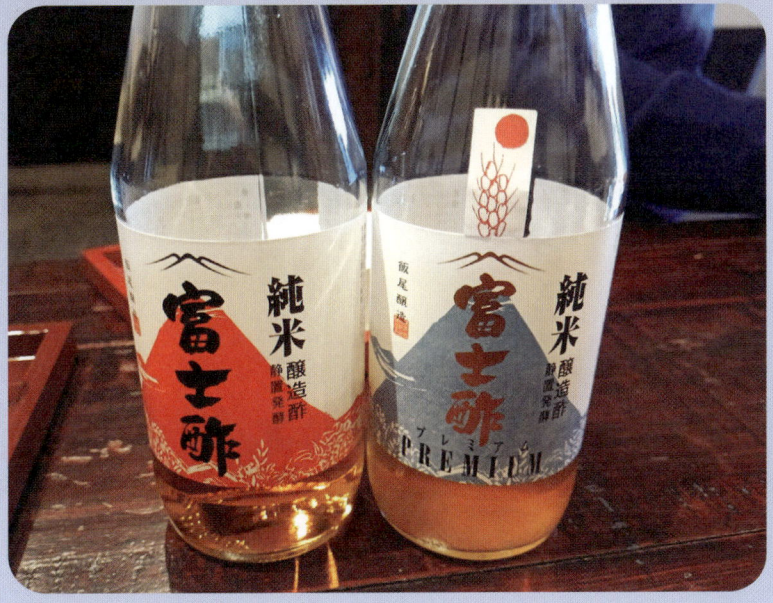

CHEF MARK SEKITA ON THE CAPITAL'S DYNAMIC DINING SCENE

◉ TOKYO

Japan's culinary world has earned a reputation for resisting change. In times past, adapting trusted recipes, applying excessive heat to fresh produce, introducing foreign influences to Japanese food or, god forbid, using the word 'fusion', didn't sit well with culinary traditionalists. High-end dining was viewed as a formal affair, with restaurants cloaked in funereal seriousness and helmed by pedantic chefs more concerned with rules than creating a holistic dining experience.

But change is afoot, and nowhere is this truer than in Tokyo. With around 160,000 restaurants in the capital, there is ample space for bold young chefs and gung-ho visionaries to challenge the status quo and change perceptions of what Japanese food can be.

Just ask Chef Mark Sekita.

'The restaurant scene over the past two or three decades has definitely changed,' he says. 'I think you're seeing a lot more chefs taking locally sourced ingredients that were traditionally found only in Japanese cuisine and turning them into something more innovative.'

The owner and head chef of Mark's Tokyo, a chef's table restaurant in Meguro Ward, Sekita creates a seasonal menu that explores his family roots and lifelong relationship to food.

'We grew up around food. There was always somebody doing something in the kitchen,' says Sekita, who was born in San Francisco to a Japanese chef father and an Italian-American mother who loved to cook. He has fond memories of being put to task in the kitchen as a child and watching his parents create meals for guests.

'My mum used to bring people together during Christmas. She would cook an enormous amount of food, including a lasagna, and she would invite all the Christmas orphans: people who didn't have anywhere to go, or maybe their families lived far away, or they were going through a divorce. We would all celebrate Christmas together, so people could feel like they were with family.'

Sekita didn't realise how much this impacted him until he came to Japan and began spending Christmases away from his home in California. He knew that if he ever had a restaurant of his own, he wanted to recreate that familial atmosphere.

'I think the key word there is "experience". That's why people go back to restaurants,' he says. 'You want people to leave your restaurant feeling like they've just had a big hug. So you create an atmosphere where people feel welcome ... It's the little personal touches: conversing with the guests, asking them why they came in, getting to know them.'

Italian and Japanese cuisine might sound like strange bedfellows, but Sekita plates dishes that harness the best of both culinary cultures. The general flow at Mark's Tokyo is soup, seafood, pasta, meat dish, dessert, with Japanese ingredients working as the undertones. He also uses some of his parents' recipes and other 'little pieces' of his history on the menu. It is cooking as an act of communication, which is something he feels gets lost in larger restaurants.

Sekita is a proponent of supporting local producers – he sources vegetables from the Aoyama Farmers Market and seafood from Toyosu Fish Market – and believes that season should always dictate the menu if you want to bring the best produce to the table. This is borne out of a philosophical approach shared by Japanese and Italian cuisine, both of which are renowned for their simplicity; focusing on basic, seasonal ingredients prepared well.

Clearly, innovative dining doesn't require overcomplicating your menu or throwing out the rulebook. At Mark's Tokyo, Sekita has proved you can respect – even praise – hard-worn conventions while retaining the spirit of experimentation.

'I think the culinary world is all about doing new things with food, and that's what makes it interesting for people to dine out,' he says. 'You're always going to have people who want traditional things, who want traditional sushi, who want traditional kaiseki. But to keep people interested, you need to have that innovation, to have that creativity ... And personally, I don't want to always serve the same stuff. That's boring. To take it to the next level is a challenge that we all strive for.'

⊘ markstokyo.com

Mark's Tokyo
Opposite **Florilege has created a unique dining experience**
Previous **Chef Mark Sekita prepares a dish**

THREE MORE TOKYO CHEFS PUSHING CULINARY BOUNDARIES

✳ **Florilege** At Florilege, which recently moved to a new location in Azabudai Hills, pioneering head chef Hiroyasu Kawate has created a dining-as-theatre experience. Guests sit at a grand table d'hôte, or host's table, while the cadre of chefs meticulously prepare an environmentally sustainable menu. Kawate harnesses the techniques of French cuisine, but the pretension stops there. It's a communal experience where the wine flows as freely as the conversation between guests and staff. 🌐 **aoyama-florilege.jp**

✳ **Den** Den in Shibuya, voted Asia's best restaurant in 2022 by the World's 50 Best group, is like a Japanese homestay experienced through food. Chef Zaiyu Hasegawa has elevated the repasts of his childhood to the realm of the exquisite, whether it's 'Dentucky' chicken wings stuffed with steamed mochi rice or a vibrant medley of Japanese garden vegetables. But there's one principle to which he's stayed true: eating out should never be a chore. 🌐 **jimbochoden.com**

✳ **Spice Lab** You might not have hauled yourself all the way to Japan to eat Indian food, but hear me out. The philosophy at Spice Lab is to celebrate Japanese ingredients, Indian spices and the culinary sensibilities of both cultures. A kaleidoscopic assortment of small bites, evoking the flavours of Indian street food and presented on a ceramic pillow is the tasting menu highlight. If you need more convincing, executive chef Tejas Sovani also had a stint at Noma in Copenhagen – awarded the world's best restaurant on five separate occasions – so he has sufficient credibility in the kitchen. 🌐 **spicelabtokyo.com**

NIHONSHU: JAPAN'S NATIONAL ALCOHOLIC BEVERAGE

An interesting fact: sake in Japanese means 'alcohol.' So, if you ask for sake in a restaurant and the staff brings out a beer menu or wine list, it's perhaps because they have misunderstood you. The rice wine we often refer to as sake is called nihonshu, and though I'll use them interchangeably here, the latter is the term to avoid confusion.

Domestically, nihonshu consumption has taken a hit since it peaked in 1973, with most casual drinkers now favouring beer, whisky-soda highballs or tea-based drinks like oolong high (oolong tea with shochu and ice.) There are around 1800 licensed nihonshu breweries in Japan today, a sharp drop from the 30,000 in existence in the 19th century, but many of the traditional brewing heartlands remain in good health. Kyoto, Niigata and Hyogo Prefectures can all stake a claim to producing Japan's best rice wine, though breweries in Tohoku, like Niizawa and Otokoyama Honten in Miyagi Prefecture or Hokushika in Akita Prefecture, are no strangers to nabbing gold medals at the Fine Sake Awards.

Nihonshu culture can be complex and a little intimidating for the uninitiated. There are numerous varieties and styles, influenced by terroir, the type of rice used and how much it is polished, the freshness of the water, how much brewer's alcohol is added and the number of enzymes in the koji (see p. 88).

A degree of snobbery comes with the territory, but the following recommended breweries and shops are based on personal preference, nothing more:

Hakkaisan

This Niigata-based brewery is well known throughout the country, and if a Tokyo izakaya only stocks a couple of nihonshu varieties, Hakkaisan's dry but fragrant junmai ginjo will likely be one of them.

◉ hakkaisan.com

Kubota

Another Niigata-based brewery, Kubota was established in 1985 to meet the needs of Japan's shifting food culture. Most varieties are crisp, clean and dry, meaning they pair well with most cuisines and don't grate on the palate. I'm not usually a sparkling *sake* fan, but Kubota's version is super delicate.

◉ asahi-shuzo.co.jp

Yosamusume

At the foot of the mountains in northern Kyoto Prefecture, sixth-generation *sake* master Shiro Nishihara brews farm-to-table *sake* – Yosamusume's rice paddies are a few hundred yards from the front door of the brewery. Nishihara is innovating in line with a changing market, producing a tasty but flexible *junmai* that retains its flavour when heated up, and a sweet, floral *sake* created using white wine yeast.

yosamusume.com

Otokoyama

Not to be confused with Otokoyama Honten in Miyagi Prefecture, Otokoyama in Hokkaido has been producing *sake* in some form since the Edo period. At the company museum in Asahikawa you can sample several varieties, but the slow-aged Kanshu is a great option when you're in a pinch.

otokoyama.com

Meishu Centre

Not a brewery, but this *sake* shop in Tokyo's Ochanomizu district is built for people who don't know where to start. It has friendly staff and 100-plus bottles on the shelves, most of which you can drink by the glass before deciding if you want to buy.

nihonshu.com

Top **Nihonshu is Japan's drink of choice**
Bottom **Meishu Centre**

Barrels of nihonshu (commonly referred to as sake)

Top **Shochu can be distilled from all sorts of food products**
Bottom **Brewing shochu**

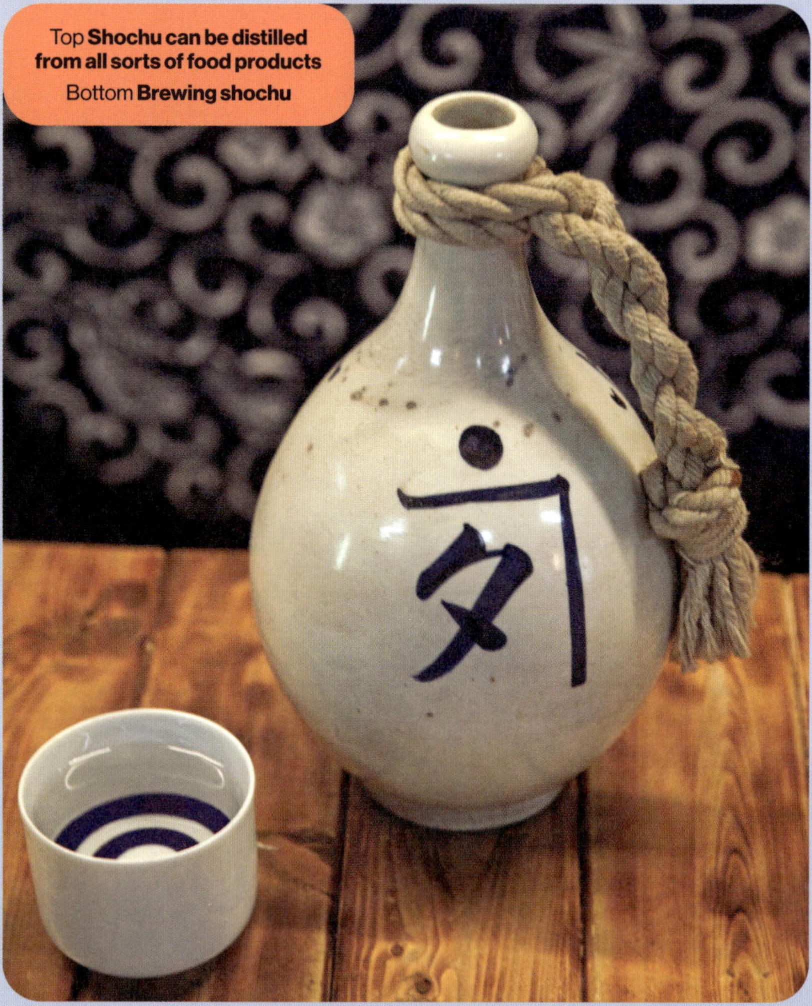

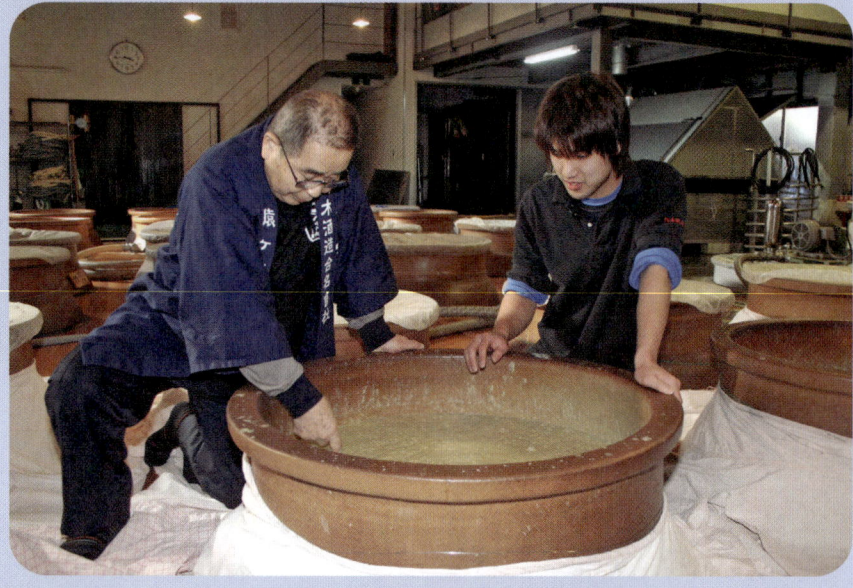

THE SPIRITUAL HOME OF SHOCHU

⊙ **KAGOSHIMA**

What is shochu? An interesting question and one to which I've never heard a convincing answer. So, I'll provide a vague one: it's a distilled spirit made from one or several of up to 53 government-approved crops to be considered honkaku (genuine), and these crops are as wide ranging as potatoes, barley, carrots, brown sugar and rice. I find the taste is somewhere between whisky and vodka, though often there's a lingering bitterness that takes time to appreciate.

One thing is certain – Kagoshima, a sunny, seaside city in the south of Kyūshū, is the spriritual home of shochu. The city has a fascinating cuisine culture – deep-fried fish paste, pickled herring and raw chicken are all meibutsu (regional specialties) – which pairs well with the locals' favourite liquor.

Shochu made from satsumaimo, or sweet potatoes with purple skin and yellow flesh, is the most abundant here because the crop flourishes in Kagoshima's volcanic soils. It was once described to me as 'fire water for the samurai', as it was used to make fulminated mercury for the firing caps of military rifles in the late 1800s. Because it was being produced in such abundance, some entrepreneurial distilleries refined their techniques to make more palatable versions for drinking.

Satsumaimo shochu, locally known as karaimo shochu, has a hint of natural sweetness, and is therefore a fine accompaniment to salt-based foods. Brands like Satsuma Shuzo (satsuma.co.jp/english) and Hamada Syuzou (hamadasyuzou.co.jp/en) are good places to start navigating the world of shochu, while Yokaban, an izakaya on the lively Flamingo-dori yokocho (alley), has a liver-busting *shochu* menu that keeps enquiring drinkers on their toes all night.

IS SAPPORO THE KING OF JAPANESE BEERS?

⊙ HOKKAIDO

Japan isn't known for being culturally diverse, but the victual arts conceal a host of foreign influences. Japan pinched tempura from Portugal, ramen from China, *yakiniku* from Korea, pastry techniques from France, cocktails from America and whisky distillation from Scotland.

Beer, which is now the nation's favourite tipple, was adopted from Europe in the late 1800s, and after decades of refinement, Japan now produces some of the crispest lagers in the world. Asahi is undoubtedly the best-known brand, partly because it revolutionised the domestic beer market in the late 1980s and partly because of marketing. In Asakusa, the former low city of old Edo, you'll find Asahi adverts on walls and billboards, Asahi taps in every *izakaya* and the iconic Asahi Beer Tower, a golden skyscraper that looks like a freshly poured draft with a frothy head, housing the company headquarters. The employees operating out of its 22 stories must be an industrious bunch because Asahi has boomed overseas, too, with 19 production facilities in eight countries across Europe alone.

When Asahi announced it was changing the recipe of its flagship beer, Super Dry, in 2023, it caused quite a stir – though the differences, for even the most discerning drinkers, proved to be subtle. Subtlety could also be ascribed to the flagship lagers of Asahi's competitors, Sapporo and Kirin, both of which are brewed with rice, meaning they're lighter bodied and less malty than the European beers on which they were modelled. Those who prefer rich beers may favour Sapporo's Yebisu, a golden brew named after the Shinto god of fishermen and fortune, or Premium Malts, a hoppy beer made by whisky giant Suntory.

Which beer tops the podium is a frequent source of disagreement among imbibers. Sapporo is my personal favourite – it's more viscous than Kirin and Asahi, with a cleaner taste – and I can trace my love of it back to a trip to Sapporo City in 2018.

Any beer drinker will tell you, when you arrive in the capital city of Hokkaido, you feel an inexorable pull towards the Sapporo Beer Museum, a taphouse and former Meiji-era brewery with all the red-brick grandeur of an Edwardian manor. In the museum's Genghis Khan Hall, the air smells like beer and charred meat, and bib-wearing diners down steins the size of their heads and tend to chunks of lamb sizzling on convex skillets (resembling the headgear worn by the eponymous Mongolian warlord). The Oktoberfest-in-Bavaria atmosphere is disarming, but only until you sit down are you tasked with drinking as much Sapporo beer and eating as much lamb as you can in 100 minutes. That's when you settle in and start ordering drafts of some of the world's crispest lager while watching lamb fat dribble to the rim of the grill, where it cooks an assortment of seasonal vegetables.

I've had plenty of Japanese beers that have tasted like gulps of ambrosia itself: a can of Yebisu after a hard day's work, a draft of Asahi to punctuate a hike or a chilled bottle of Kirin on a scorching summer's day. But to drink Sapporo lager in the place of its creation is to taste Japanese beer at its very best.

🌐 sapporobeer.jp/english

Sapporo is one of many popular Japanese beers on the market

Left Sapporo and Yebisu on display in a supermarket

Sapporo Beer Museum

THE SCIENCE OF BREWING WITH KEN MUKAI

⊙ KOCHI

Craft brewing has become big business in Japan. Microbreweries are popping up across the country, many of them using local ingredients or leftover produce to create 'sustainabeers' that promote economic development and rural revitalisation.

Ken Mukai's brewery, Mukai Craft Brewing, is about as rural as they come. The California native and his Japanese wife Masako opened the brewery in the outskirts of Niyodogawa, high in the Shikoku mountains, in 2020. It was an inauspicious time to launch a business, but Mukai, who had been travelling to Japan every year since the 1990s, said the move was never about making money. He wanted to revitalise a region he had grown to love, to attract new residents to Niyodogawa and stem the tide of population decline.

'We get a monthly residents' magazine, and on the back page they have population statistics,' Mukai tells me over a selection of ales in the brewery's Blue Brew Taproom. 'Every month we lose 10 to 20 residents to death. It's like a mini obituaries section.'

Four of his signature beers have unusual, numbered names that are dedicated to Niyodogawa – 2410, when rendered in kanji script, can be read as ni-yo-do; 439 is the name of the highway that runs into town; 89 is the percentage of forest cover in Niyodogawa; and 17 is the number of residents per square kilometre.

'We're now down to 13.5 residents per square kilometre,' says Mukai. 'My goal has always been to get that number up to 18. We might not make it, but we're going to try.'

Of course, Mukai hopes people come to Niyodogawa for the beer, but he insists there are plenty more reasons to stay in town. He encourages guests to go to farmers' markets or festivals held at local shrines. The Shimonanosato hotel, run by former students in what was once Niyodogawa's elementary school, sits on the riverbank opposite the brewery, while the pack-rafting and canyoning guides operate a few kilometres downriver at Nakatsu Gorge.

Mukai concedes that brewing high-quality beer is the only thing directly under his control, but even his journey to that was a little unorthodox. After spending 23 years as a science teacher in the California public school system, a drunken conversation with a friend in Japan about starting his own brewery in Kochi Prefecture soon turned into a brick-and-mortar reality.

It was a baptism of fire. Mukai had to learn how to assemble the industrial brewing equipment, handle substances he'd only ever taught in chemistry class and tinker with his old homebrewing techniques and ingredients he'd never heard of to produce beer at scale. One advantage he had at his disposal, however, was Niyodo Blue, the epithet for the

freshwater that courses through the adjacent river gorge.

'The levels of chemicals in the artesian springs are almost undetectable,' he says. 'Everybody adds certain salts to their beer to adjust things like the mouthfeel or the sense of hoppy-ness. But historically, the water source guided the different styles ... The water source here is so pure, I can make any style of beer. I've got a blank canvas.'

Given his chemistry background, Mukai loves the experimental aspect to this. He makes multiple versions of each beer, shaping the flavour profile with new ingredients delivered to his door by local farmers, before deciding which one ends up in the kegs. The 89 is an English-style pale ale infused with the floral notes of endemic kuro-moji leaves. The Mountain Fruits sour ale combines the cherry-like goumi with kuwa (mulberry) and yamamomo (red bayberry). The 17 is a satsumaimo stout, made with Japanese sweet potato, and the 439 is an IPA flavoured with Niyodo green tea. The 2410 is a classic Belgian white with a local spin, using ginger and sansho peppers, the latter of which Mukai harvests himself.

Mukai says he's still iterating upon his recipes, but the changes are minute; perhaps those only a perfectionist would discern.

He also has newer, experimental beers – like the Dark Forest IPA – on tap at Blue Brew before they can earn a place on the bottled roster. On my visit to the taproom, I make my way through most of the chalkboard menu. The beers are great – even the Belgian white; a style I usually find soapy – but I'm still surprised at how clearly I can taste the botanical ingredients.

'That's always the challenge,' says Mukai. 'How do you make a beer that celebrates our town but is also of high quality, where people say, "I need to get me some more of that"? That's our philosophy.'

 mukaicraftbrewing.com

Top **Mukai Craft Brewing**
Bottom **The brewery is a must-see destination for beer lovers**

MODERN MIXOLOGY

⊙ TOKYO

Japan loves a good concept. And one you'll hear time and again, in reference to various disciplines, is kaizen, the concept of continuous improvement. Perhaps that doesn't seem so novel, but when it's applied with rigorous attention to detail, with laser focus on every incremental improvement, innovators can turn their products from good to great to best in class.

Japanese mixologists know all about this. In the 1920s, when Japan was in a prolonged period of Western imitation – adopting foreign dress styles, using bricks and concrete as building materials, employing English-language teachers in schools – the first cocktail bars appeared in Tokyo's Ginza neighbourhood. The owners were mostly disciples of Louis Eppinger, a German cocktail pioneer raised in America who ran the bar at the Yokohama Grand Hotel at the turn of the 20th century. At first, the cocktails they served were nothing fancy – perhaps mizuwari (whisky and water) or whisky-soda highballs.

It wasn't until the 1970s when Japan was wealthier and imbibers were becoming increasingly discerning, that cocktail makers really began to innovate. One oft-cited example is ice balls, invented by Niigata-based bartender Masaaki Wada on the pretense that it would take the ice longer to melt.

Much like in traditional Japanese cuisine, seasonality soon became a key theme in Japan's cocktail bars. Why use overripe produce imported from abroad when fresh botanicals are available at the local farmers' market? Is there any need to plop an olive in a martini when you can harness the flavours of a fresh bamboo leaf instead?

Japanese mixology has been on an upwards trajectory for decades, and the hype hasn't gone unnoticed. By 2008, *Bon Appetit* magazine had declared Tokyo the cocktail capital of the world. And to this day, cocktail enthusiasts still flock to Ginza, an area of chic boutiques and stylish department stores that lend it an air more European than Eastern. Some estimates say there are around 350 bars here, many of which could hold a candle to the top cocktail bars in London, Singapore, New York or Barcelona.

Some of these bars, for better or worse, are still locked in the early 1900s. Step into Bar Sherlock (bar-sherlock.jp) or Bar Musashi (@bar_musashi) and you'll find staff in three-piece suits, antique furnishings, maybe some slow jazz tumbling out of the speaker system and businessmen holding court in hushed tones. Gaslight Eve (bar-gaslight.com) cuts a similarly antiquarian figure. But there is a key difference. Chief mixologist Naomi Takahashi put paid to the belief that making cocktails is a man's game when she became the first Japanese woman to win a grand prize at IBA World Cocktail Championships for her Wisteria aperitif in 2013. Her goal, aside from blowing your socks off with her mixology skills, is to bring more women into the industry – which is often reflected in the bar's staff and customer base.

Not every Ginza bar looks like a scene from a Victorian epistolary novel, though. Bar Orchard (@barorchardginza), run by affable husband-and-wife team Takuo and Sumire Miyanohara, is much quirkier. The couple have decorated their bar with paraphernalia collected at flea markets or on overseas travels, some of which are repurposed as receptacles for drinks. There is no menu, either. Instead, you'll pick a fruit from a bowl on the counter – this will be the cocktail's base flavour – and they'll do the rest. It's not uncommon to get a foamy, apple-based cocktail served in a little bathtub or a banana-coffee-rum infusion in a cappuccino cup. Under other circumstances this could come across as gimmicky, but multiple appearances in the list of Asia's 50 Best Bars prove the Miyanoharas have the skill to back it up.

The crazy thing is the standard is getting higher. Some bars, like Benfiddich in Shinjuku or the SG Club (sg-management.jp) in Shibuya, are like high-end, Prohibition-era moonshine operations, except the homemade spirits don't threaten to blind you. Gen Yamamoto (genyamamoto.jp) in Azabujuban has built its stellar reputation on a seasonal *omakase* cocktail tasting menu. At Gold Bar (goldbaratedition.com) in Toranomon, the blackened interior makes it feel like you have wandered into a land of shadows. Whether by design or chance, however, this heightens your other senses, giving every sip of your

reimagined Golden Era cocktails an extra bit of bite.

Cocktail drinking in Tokyo is by no means a cheap endeavour – you can demolish a nightly budget in a matter of minutes. But when drinking is elevated to high art, when every aperitif and digestif is there to be savoured and every botanical and ingredient sings in perfect harmony, sometimes the wallet just needs to take a hit.

Top **Innovative cocktails in Tokyo**
Bottom **A Ginza bar serves an elevated drink**

"Fire is treated with equal parts trepidation and reverence, which is evidenced at the nation's fire festivals."

FESTIVALS & EVENTS

KANAMARA MATSURI: FESTIVAL OF THE STEEL PHALLUS

⊙ KANAGAWA

My timing couldn't be worse. It's a muggy April afternoon in Kawasaki, my t-shirt is clinging to my back like cellophane, the entire population of the Tokyo Metropolitan Area – all 37 million and change – has arrived at Kawasaki Daishi Station at the same time, and they're all walking in the same direction.

Officious-looking men wearing the unmistakable uniform of the Japanese crowd controller direct people into a narrow shopping street using colourful batons and whistles. In between their piercing shrills, I hear the distant sounds of chanting, clapping and stomping – the rhythm and beat of a tribal war dance. Against my better intuition, and perhaps in the interest of journalistic integrity, I follow the people following the noise. The mob ahead is long and thick – an appropriate

Celebrations at the Kanamara Matsuri
Opposite **Phallic souvenirs on display**

description given what people are straining to see: a procession of erect model penises on top of portable mikoshi (floats).

It's not out of the ordinary for the penis to be venerated in Japan. I have been to shrines with phallic iconography everywhere and others where expertly carved penises congregated around a small altar or kamidana ('god shelf'). Penises are thought to represent strength and vitality, or in some instances, the unity of man, woman and earth. But at the Kanamara Matsuri, the penis embodies the hero of a folktale, in which an envious demon takes refuge inside a newlywed woman's vagina. A blacksmith then comes to the rescue, fashioning a magical metal penis to excise the demon from the woman's body – hence the festival's main float, the Kanamara Fune Mikoshi, houses a huge steel phallus adorned with shide streamers, indicating sacred objects in Shinto lore.

As the parade marches on and the crowd begins to disperse, I venture into the festival market at Kawasaki Daishi Temple, a sprawling Buddhist complex that draws thousands of visitors for hatsumode, the year's first prayer. Amid the sizzle of okonomiyaki and yakitori stalls, men, women and children ogle phallic souvenirs and suck on penis-shaped lollipops. Some are wearing penis hats, others have purchased bright-pink penis t-shirts and a group of middle-aged men pose for photos with prosthetic penises dangling from their noses. I find it all a little odd, truth be told, but the wider historical context puts it into perspective.

The metal phallus from the myth is enclosed within Kanayama Shrine – one of the festival venues – where couples pray for fertility and happy marriages. Since the Edo Period, when Kawasaki was a brothel-

filled post town on the old Tokaido Rd, sex workers have come here to pray to the gods of blacksmithing to prevent STDs. The shrine and accompanying festival have also become icons for Japan's gay, trans and drag communities, who use it to normalise different sexual orientations and celebrate sex positivity.

It's perhaps easy to cite the festival as a classic example of 'whacky Japan'. But such cliches miss the point. There is a sense of liberation and freedom to the Kanamara Matsuri that extends beyond the confines of its crass iconography. It is the Japanese festival scene writ large: under every eccentric facade lies a deeper meaning.

🌐 kawasakidaishi-kanko.com/english/matsuri/kanamara.html

NAKIZUMO CRYING BABY FESTIVAL

⦿ TOKYO

The Nakizumo Crying Baby Festival has been held at Tokyo's Sensoji Temple (and other venues throughout Japan) for the past 400 years. In line with the old proverb that 'a crying baby makes a healthy baby', thousands of parents attend the festival in late April to make their children weep with the aid of sumo wrestlers. The proceedings mirror the format of a sumo bout: two wrestlers, each clad in mawashi loincloths and armed with a baby, compete against one another in a dohyo (wrestling ring). Rather than fight, the sumo jiggle and coax the babies in their arms; the winner being the baby that cries first. If neither is stirred to tears, men with demon masks will enter the dohyo to seal the deal.

⦿ www.gotokyo.org/en/spot/ev017/index.htmll

AWA ODORI

⊙ TOKUSHIMA

The Awa Odori – from Awa, the old name for Tokushima, and odori, meaning 'dance' – is part of the August Obon (commemoration of the dead) festivities in Tokushima City, and is probably the best-known of all Japan's dance festivals. The festival's origins, however, are up for debate. Some think it stemmed from the celebrations following the construction of Tokushima Castle in the early 1600s; others say it was connected to the indigo and salt trades of the late 1500s. Either way, it has flourished into an arresting, free-form style of entertainment that is tightly bound to Tokushima's identity. For four days, the city centre is effectively shut down and transformed into a stage for dance troupes, called ren, who frolic and swerve to the sound of drums, gongs, samisen and woodwind instruments.

🌐 shikoku-tourism.com/en/see-and-do/10051

Top and bottom **Performers at Awa Odori**

Opposite **Tears at the Nakizumo Crying Baby Festival**

117

JINDAIJI TEMPLE DARUMA DOLL FAIR

◉ TOKYO

Daruma, good luck talismans, are among the most recognisable symbols of Japanese spirituality. They are styled after Bodhidharma, the founder of Zen Buddhism, who was said to have meditated for nine years straight, causing his legs and arms to atrophy and fall off. He then fell asleep, and disgusted at his lack of perseverance, hacked off his eyelids to prevent it from happening again, resulting in the wide-eyed, floating head representation of Bodhidharma in his namesake Daruma doll.

Though the largest Daruma production centre in Japan is 100km (62 miles) north of Tokyo, in the Takasaki region of Gunma Prefecture, the capital hosts one of the biggest Daruma showcases every spring. At the Yakuyoke Ganzan Jie Daishi Matsuri, more commonly (and pronounceably) known as the Jindaiji Daruma Doll Fair, there are around 300 stalls selling Daruma of every size and description. Typically, Daruma are

red – an auspicious colour in Buddhism and the supposed colour of Bodhidharma's robe – which symbolises safety and prosperity. But at the festival Daruma dolls also appear in white (purity and balance), blue (career success), black (protection against evil spirits), green (health and physical well-being), orange (academic success) and as *shisa* (guardian lions), dragons and various other creatures from folklore.

Once you've bought a Daruma, you can inscribe it with a wish. The queue for the wish table, presided over by the temple's monks, is guaranteed to be long and winding. But if you have the constitution, a monk will fill in the left eye of your Daruma with a kanji character to consecrate the wish. When, and if, that wish comes true, you can mark the right eye with another character to acknowledge its fulfilment.

🌀 jindaiji.or.jp/event/darumaichi.php

Top **Daruma are a symbol of good luck**

Bottom **Green daruma represent health and physical well-being**

BEHIND THE MASK: THE TRADITION OF IWAMI KAGURA

⊙ SHIMANE

On a day like this, the tree-covered dunes of Shimane's San'in coastline are a pleasure to drive through; the sea so still it looks like a lake, sun splashing off the terracotta-coloured roof tiles. This region, 'The Province of the Gods', is associated with the Shinto creation myth and has blossomed into a heartland of kagura, a theatrical style of dance whose kanji reading translates to 'entertaining the gods'.

Japanese performance arts like kabuki and Noh and, to a degree, bunraku (puppet theatre) are preceded by their reputations. But kagura is often absent from the conversation. Not so in the Iwami region of Shimane Prefecture, where as many as 130 kagura troupes are in operation.

When I pull up to Kobayashi Kobo, a small building by the rusted train tracks running around the Edo-style onsen town of Yunotsu, 44-year-old artisan Taizo Kobayashi comes out to greet me. He's wiry, with the strong arms of a man accustomed to working with his hands, and judging by the clay dust flecking his clothes, I've interrupted the artistic process. We step into his gallery and workshop, where the walls and cabinets are fixed with exceptionally detailed masks, depicting savage demons, anthropomorphic creatures and mythological heroes.

Kobayashi crafts these masks, the most symbolic of kagura props, from clay moulds and paper fibres bound by glue and persimmon extract, which protects them against ravenous insects. There are other kagura regions in Japan – Miyazaki, Saitama, Hiroshima – but only Kobayashi and the seven other mask makers in Iwami use *washi* paper as their primary crafting material.

Unbelievably, Kobayashi has been doing this for 33 years. One day, he came across a picture book about a boy born into a family of *kagura* mask makers and was deeply moved by the story. So, at age 11, he started making daily pilgrimages to the workshop of famed local mask maker Katsuro Kakida, under whose tutelage he honed his skills.

'At first, I was only interested in making masks. But when I went to high school my friends were in a kagura group, and I wanted to be like them,' Kobayashi says. He now acts and plays music in kagura performances, and is using his crafting techniques to make wall reliefs encapsulating mythological events. 'I wanted a challenge, to see how far I could go as an artist.'

Kobayashi pulls up the PowerPoint he uses to introduce students to the grand bible of kagura scripts. He slips quickly into educator mode, and it's clear he's buoyed that young people in the region are taking an interest in kagura as an artisanal craft and performance art.

'We have two main types of kagura: kagura performed in palaces for the royal family and sato (local) kagura performed at shrines,' he says. 'From the Kojiki (Records of Ancient Matters), we get the Iwami kagura scripts, and there are 30 different stories ... But we make new scripts too. The shrine here in Yunotsu is dedicated to water and mountain gods, who can appear as dragons. So I wrote a story about those dragons.'

There's a 'festival' at Yunotsu's Tatsu no Gozen Shrine every Saturday night, a 90-minute kagura performance involving three different stories. The following night, I attend the show, played to a full house of 55 people. I sit on a cushion in the front row, my knees brushing against the foot of the stage, as the taiko drums begin their primal beat.

There are sections of strangulated dialogue – of which I can scarcely grasp a word – but kagura is a mostly visual experience, with characters stomping, cavorting and pirouetting around the stage in gold, orange and red livery. When the heroes triumph, the crowd bursts into applause as though watching 'Shotime' Ohtani hit a home run at Tokyo Dome.

At the end of the show – finishing with the tale of *Orochi*, the battle between the god Susano-o and the eponymous eight-tailed serpent – the performers remove their masks and press their faces, beaded with sweat, onto the stage floor. It's as low and respectful as bow is wont to go, in appreciation of the still-clapping audience, no doubt, but mainly to pay obeisance to the gods, hoping that they were duly entertained.

Drunk on the colour, pace and energy of the performance, I sit back and think about something Kobayashi had said to me the day before: 'The movement you have in your heart when you're a child stays with you forever ... To do kagura is to know yourself.'

🔴 kobayashi-kobo.jp

Kagura is traditionally performed in recognition of Shinto gods

Top **Masks are a significant element of kagura**
Bottom **Elaborate costumes and props are used**
Opposite **Performers are often clad in colourful, intricate fabric**

A shrine is carried at Sanja Matsuri

THE CAPITAL'S THREE GREAT SHINTO FESTIVALS

⊙ TOKYO

Sanja Matsuri

The Sanja Matsuri is a three-day festival held in Tokyo's Asakusa district, attracting more than two million visitors each May. It commemorates the founders of Sensoji, Tokyo's oldest and one of its most important temples. Friday welcomes the Daigyoretsu Parade, a vibrant procession of priests, parishioners, geisha, dancers and city officials. On Saturday, 100 mikoshi (floats) from the district's 44 neighbourhoods are carried to Sensoji and the adjacent Asakusa Shrine, where the founders were deified. The Sunday celebrations start at 6am, when participants wearing the colours of their respective neighbourhoods meet at Asakusa Shrine and compete to carry the three largest and most spiritually significant mikoshi through the streets.

◉ asakusajinja.jp/en/sanjamatsuri

Sanno Matsuri

The Sanno Matsuri, a full version of which is held only in even-numbered years, features a parade that begins and ends at Hie Shrine, where the guardian deity of Tokyo is enshrined. During the approximately nine-hour procession, the parade stops at the Imperial Palace, where the chief priest offers prayers to the emperor and his family.

◉ tenkamatsuri.jp

Kanda Matsuri

The Kanda Matsuri is a mid-May festival, taking place only in odd-numbered years, to ensure the continued good health and prosperity of the citizenry. The main procession starts and ends at Kanda Myojin Shrine, which enshrines Daikokuten, the deity of harvest and matrimony; Ebisu, the deity of fishermen and wealth; and Taira Masakado, a deified samurai and lord revered for his courage and perseverance. During the Edo period, the Kanda and Sanno Matsuri were the only festivals allowed to pass through the Edo Castle grounds. A fierce rivalry developed between them, so it was decided they would be held in alternate years.

◉ kandamyoujin.or.jp/kandamatsuri

THE DEMON MESSENGERS

⊙ AKITA

In Northern Ireland when children are badly behaved, they're often threatened with, 'Stop that, or the *man* is gonna get ye'. Whoever this unnamed shadowy figure is, and what his intentions are, remain unclear. But he strikes fear into mischievous children, nonetheless.

In Oga, a coastal town in Akita Prefecture, there is an entire folk tradition built around keeping children in line. Rather than planting an image in children's minds, the threat manifests itself in a much more tangible way. In the dead of night on New Year's Eve, snow blanketing the land and icy winds whipping across the peninsula, the townsfolk listen out for the unmistakable snarls and blood-curdling cries of Namahage, terrifying creatures in Shinto folklore. Men dressed in straw coats and red or blue masks with bared teeth and furrowed brows bound into people's homes, the smell of sake thick on their breaths, demanding any lazy or disrespectful children be handed over. If the Namahage are successful, the unsuspecting children, amid pleas and floods of tears, promise they will behave forevermore.

In an era where gentler parenting techniques are encouraged, some baulk at the idea of terrorising their children in the name of pedagogy. But for Gretchen Miura, a New Jerseyan who settled in Oga more than 20 years ago, and her husband Keno, the priest at Oga's Dairyuji Temple, the Namahage tradition plays a much more fundamental role in locals' lives.

'The myth is reflecting what is needed in the community,' says Gretchen. 'The winters are so harsh here – there's a wind and an intensity to Oga that I haven't experienced elsewhere – that Namahage is important for staying in touch with each other, for checking on your neighbours, making sure they're okay.'

Growing up in Oga, Namahage have always been part of Keno's life. 'Parents protect their children from Namahage, which strengthens the bond between them,' he says. 'Also, children in Oga are considered tough, and I think Namahage are the reason.'

The Namahage myth binds the Oga Peninsula's diffused population and gives the region communal purpose as it faces the same depopulation struggles that plague much of rural Japan. That's perhaps why it has endured for so many centuries, with some versions of the folktale suggesting the Namahage were sent from China to Japan by Emperor Wu of Han, sometime before his death in 87 BCE.

The Namahage New Year ritual is still consigned to local households. But the Namahage Sedo Festival, taking place over a weekend in February each year, has capitalised on the growing interest in one of Japan's most unusual folk traditions. When the Namahage actors don their costumes, they embody the part as though Academy Awards were on the line. Beckoned by the sonorous beat of taiko drums, they hurtle down from the mountains with torches and curved knives and charge into the crowds of onlookers screaming, 'Naku-ko wa ine ga?' ('Where are all the crybabies?').

'A lot of people misrepresent Namahage as being like ogres,' says Gretchen. 'But the local community sees them as *kami-sama*, as deities, or at least messengers. It's an auspicious visit, a blessing for your family.'

🌀 oganavi.com/sedo/en

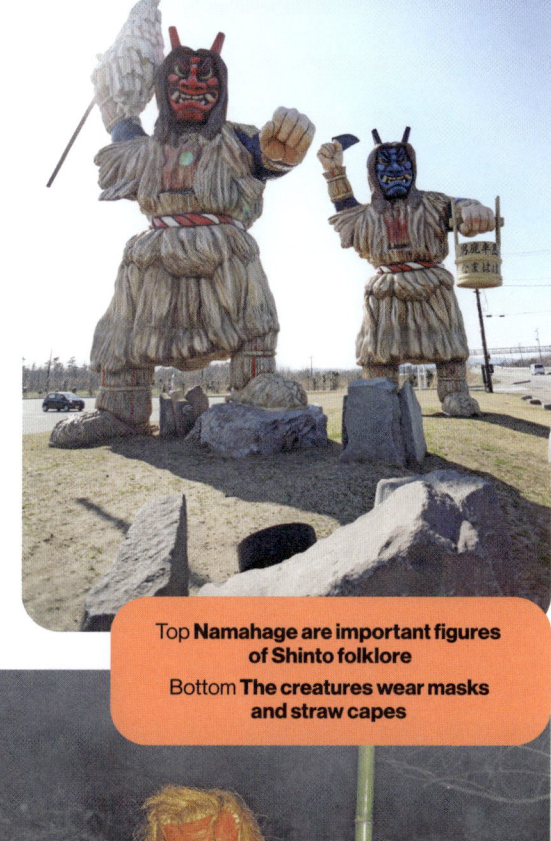

Top **Namahage are important figures of Shinto folklore**
Bottom **The creatures wear masks and straw capes**

FIRE FESTIVALS

⦿ AROUND JAPAN

In the days of antiquity, fire was a fearful phenomenon in Japan. It was dangerous to a culture that built its castles, temples and dwellings from wood and paper, and it could erupt from the archipelago's 100-plus volcanoes, causing devastation in nearby settlements. But it was also used to heat gassho-style, thatched-roof homes, cook food over the *irori* (sunken hearth), smith weapons and farming tools and fire pottery and porcelain.

As such, fire is treated with equal parts trepidation and reverence, which is evidenced at the nation's fire festivals. At the Oniyo Fire Festival, held at Fukuoka's Daizenji Tamataregu Shrine each January, men in loincloths brave the near-freezing temperatures to carry and climb atop a series of flaming torches each weighing more than a tonne. This rite has been carried out for 1600 years to exorcise demons and ward off evil spirits. The Nachi Fire Festival in mid-July sees parishioners dressed in white run down the stone steps at the Grand Shrine of Kumano Nachi Taisha carrying 12 burning bamboo torches, each representing one of the 12 deities enshrined

there. The Taimatsu Akashi, the last of Japan's three great fire festivals, takes place in November in Fukushima Prefecture. During the celebrations, pyres, effigies and flaming artworks are erected to honour warriors who died when the great samurai Masamune Date laid siege to Sukagawa Castle in 1589.

Hanabi matsuri, or fireworks festivals, are also key dates on the calendar. The most famous is the Sumidagawa Fireworks Festival in Tokyo, first held in 1733 to commemorate lives lost to famine, but the largest is the Nagaoka Fireworks Festival, where 20,000 explosives are launched into the air over Niigata's Shinano River each August.

🌐 tamataregu.or.jp

🌐 kumanonachitaisha.or.jp/ougimaturi/ougi.html

🌐 sukagawa-kankoukyoukai.jp/Event/page08.html

🌐 sumidagawa-hanabi.com

🌐 nagaokamatsuri.com

SNOW AND ICE FESTIVALS

⊙ AROUND JAPAN

Northern Japan is home to some of the snowiest places on earth, providing plenty of raw material for regional snow festivals. The most popular is the Sapporo Snow Festival, which transforms several locations in Sapporo into wintry dreamscapes for a week each February. Artists from Japan and abroad create magnificent artworks from packed snow, with all the deliberation and intricacy of history's great sculptors. Snow may be pretty when blanketing rural landscapes, but it takes on a fresh appeal when fashioned into dragons, stingrays and foxes, or towering depictions of Tsuruga Castle, Notre Dame Cathedral and the White House.

The 450-year-old Yokote Kamakura Festival in Akita Prefecture was once dedicated to a water deity. It has since expanded to become a community-wide event celebrating the enduring beauty of snow. In preparation for the festival, locals craft kamakura (igloos) throughout the town, each emitting its salubrious glow into the frigid night air. In Yokote Park, there are igloos where guests eat grilled rice cakes and drink amazake, a low-alcohol drink made from fermented rice, while along the banks of the Janosaki River Beach sit hundreds of miniature igloos illuminated by candlelight.

The Zao Juhyo Festival in Yamagata is perhaps the most unusual snow festival in Japan. The Zao region is known for its stratovolcanoes, ski resorts, *onsen* towns and an abundance of fir trees. When cold winds travelling from Siberia hit the Zao firs each winter, they coat the trees in an icy rime, creating gnarled and erratic shapes known as juhyo, or snow monsters. The juhyo are then bathed in multicoloured lights come nightfall, producing an extraterrestrial visual effect.

🔗 snowfes.com/en

🔗 yokotekamakura.com

🔗 kankou.yamagata.yamagata.jp/zao/winter/jyuhyofes_2023-2024

Top **A spectacular snow sculpture**

Bottom **Guests sit in kamakura at Yokote Kamakura Festival**

Opposite **Nachi Fire Festival**

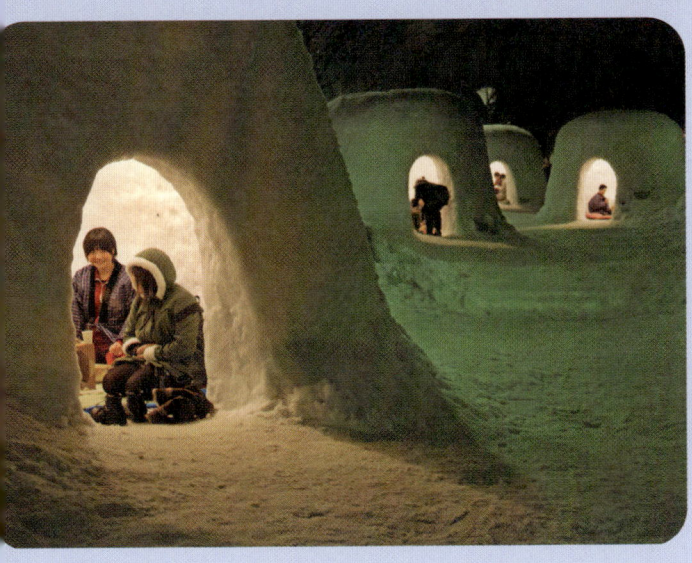

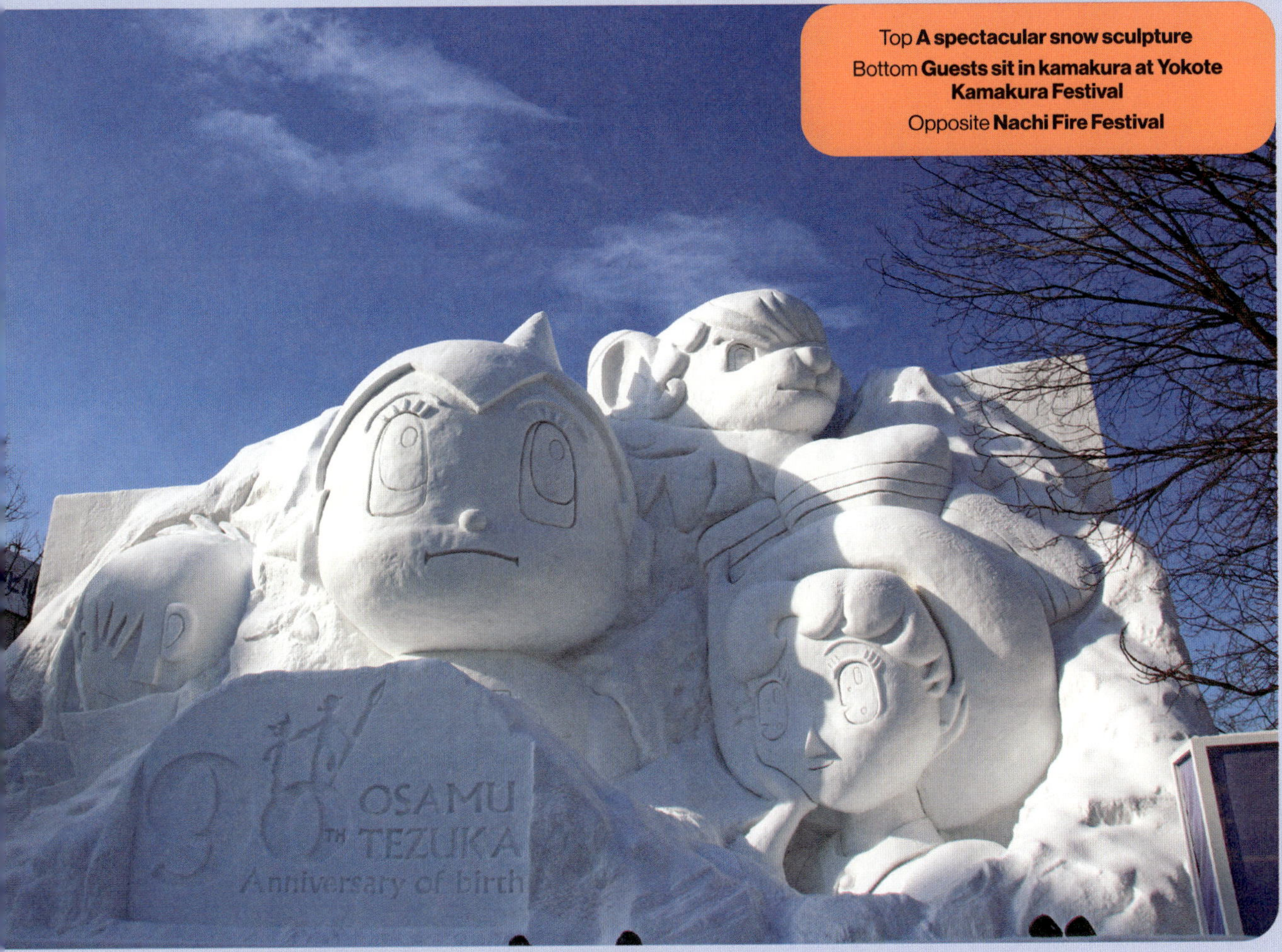
OSAMU
TEZUKA
Anniversary of birth

SNOW MACHINE FESTIVAL

◉ **NAGANO**

Hakuba, one of Japan's most popular skiing destinations and host of the 1998 Winter Olympics, is the perfect location for a five-day music festival: the resorts are concentrated in a compact area, the slopes cater to skiers and boarders of all levels (some Snow Machine tickets come packaged with lessons), the mountain villages are charming and the onsen aplenty, and it's one of the most internationalised regions in Japan. So it's no surprise the organisers of Australia's successful Wine Machine festival adapted their model for the Nagano pistes. Snow Machine – operating on the tagline of 'Apres All Day' – lands towards the end of the ski season in March and celebrates the sounds of Australian dance, electronic and house music. For those who prefer something more palatable on the eardrums, singer-songwriters and indie rock bands also appear on the lineup. (The organisers also launched Snow Machine Niseko, a sister festival in Hokkaido, in spring 2025.)

🔗 snow-machine.com/jp

FUJI ROCK FESTIVAL

◉ **NIIGATA**

Fuji Rock is Japan's largest annual music festival, attracting between 100,000 and 150,000 visitors. The name is a slight misnomer, though; the festival no longer takes place at the foot of Japan's most famous volcano, but in the snowless ski fields of Naeba in Niigata each summer. The two main stages – Green Stage and White Stage – have hosted an eclectic cast of international headliners over the festival's nearly-30-year history, including the Chemical Brothers, Foo Fighters, Gorillaz, Red Hot Chili Peppers, Green Day and Queens of the Stone Age. The smaller stages and marquees focus on local musicians, folk artists and up-and-coming J-rock bands.

🛈 en.fujirockfestival.com

YAMAGATA INTERNATIONAL DOCUMENTARY FILM FESTIVAL

◎ **YAMAGATA**

The Yamagata International Documentary Film Festival (YIDFF) is a biennial event held in the mountain valley city of Yamagata in October. The festival celebrates emerging Asian filmmakers crafting nonfiction narratives and encourages discussions on the raw and expressive power of documentary filmmaking. The New Asian Currents program casts a wide net, with subversive stories about social upheaval, political unrest, the nature of identity and the people left behind by a continent marching towards a post-industrial future. Recent entries in the international competition have included topical narratives like *Eastern Front*, which follows a Ukrainian medical battalion at war with Russian forces, and *Inside the Red Brick Wall*, covering the Hong Kong protests of 2019.

🔗 yidff.jp

KYOTOGRAPHIE INTERNATIONAL PHOTOGRAPHY FESTIVAL

⊙ **KYOTO**

Photography lines the walls at Kyotographie

Opposite **Yamagata International Documentary Film Festival celebrates filmmaking**

Kyotographie was launched in 2013 by photographer Lucille Reyboz and lighting director Yusuke Nakanishi, both of whom believed Japan needed solid platforms for communication with the outside world following the 2011 Tohoku earthquake and tsunami. Taking its name from the city where it's held, Kyoto, the festival places photography as a primary form of artistic expression and uses the city's old-world structures, flagstone streets and modern architectural spaces to enhance the emotive force of the photos exhibited there. The themes are by no means restricted to Japan: you might find ethnographic studies of Amazonian tribespeople in one space and photos of an Iranian women's uprising in another. There are also several masterclasses led by international photographic artists throughout the month-long event.

🔘 kyotographie.jp/en

WORLD COSPLAY SUMMIT

⊙ AICHI

Cosplay has spread throughout the world, but it remains an inherently Japanese phenomenon – even throwing the words 'costume' and 'play' together to form an ungainly portmanteau is a quirk of the modern Japanese language. At the World Cosplay Summit in Nagoya, thousands of otaku and cosplay influencers gather to primp and pose in the elaborate regalia of characters from their favourite Japanese manga, anime and video game franchises. The summit features a parade, photo spots, live dance performances, talk shows and a championship starring cosplayers from around the world. The over-the-top performative nature of the championship – and given the participants are representing their countries – gives it a warped-reality Eurovision feel that rarely strays into the realm of taking itself too seriously.

🔗 worldcosplaysummit.jp/en

Cosplayers in Nagoya
Opposite top **Gyoza dumplings**
Opposite bottom **A gyoza-themed manhole in the streets of Utsunomiya**

UTSUNOMIYA GYOZA FESTIVAL

◉ TOCHIGI

Most cities in Japan have at least one meibutsu, a regional specialty, that is often some kind of food. In Utsunomiya, Tochigi Prefecture, gyoza dumplings have become such a source of civic pride that the citizenry established both a gyoza committee and a gyoza festival. Over a weekend in November, the city's top gyoza chefs set up stalls in a city park, cooking up gyoza in its many varieties: yaki gyoza (fried), age gyoza (deep-fried), sui gyoza (steamed and served with broth) or hanetsuki gyoza (with crispy 'wings'). Waiting times at individual stalls can be long, but festivalgoers get great bang for their buck with each plate of dumplings costing only a couple hundred yen.

gyozakai.com/information/37

SHIMONOSEKI DAY OF FUGU FESTIVAL

⊙ YAMAGUCHI

Fugu (pufferfish), a seafood delicacy that's been immortalised in Western pop culture, from *The Simpsons* to *The Office,* is notorious for its ability to poison unless prepared with the utmost care and precision. In Shimonoseki, on the coast of Yamaguchi Prefecture, chefs have plenty of experience in removing the fish's tetrodotoxin-containing organs – and carry specific licences to prove

it – so the local fugu festival at Haedomari Market has grown into one of the most authentic culinary showcases in Japan. Pufferfish Day is 9 February, but just to confuse things, the festival takes place on 11 February, a national holiday, and features fresh pufferfish sales, fugu sashimi, fugu nabe (hotpots), an auction, a raffle and other fugu-related festivities.

TOKYO FURUSATO MATSURI

⦿ TOKYO

The goal of the Tokyo Furusato Matsuri, or 'Hometown Festival', is to gather the best of Japanese regional cuisine under one roof. Taking place over several days at Tokyo Dome, the festival involves hundreds of food vendors from all corners of the country whipping up meibutsu (regional specialities) for the thousands of visitors in attendance. You can chow down on Miyagi beef, sea urchin croques or Hokkaido seafood and follow it up with matcha mont blancs or traditional okashi (sweets) from Kansai, Chugoku or Okinawa. There are hundreds of local tipples on offer, too, from craft microbrews to sake from some of Japan's top distilleries. Choreographed dance and music performances are also on show, proving that culture in the regions isn't confined to restaurant kitchens.

🖱 event-td.com/gotochi/weekend/2024

Tokyo Furusato Matsuri is a celebration of Japanese cuisine
Opposite **Fugu statues in Shimonoseki**

Performers at Tokyo Furusato Matsuri

Hiroshima is the oyster capital of Japan

Opposite **Customers buy oysters on Miyajima**

MIYAJIMA OYSTER FESTIVAL

⊙ HIROSHIMA

You'd be hard-pushed to find better oysters in Japan than those on Miyajima, a small island off the coast of Hiroshima famed for the 'floating' Itsukushima Shrine. It's apposite, therefore, that it would host Japan's top oyster festival during the February oyster season, with stalls selling the seafood aphrodisiac in a variety of ways: raw, grilled, fried, swimming in broth, smothered in ponzu, dressed with grated wasabi or tempura battered. For a food-obsessed nation like Japan, it's little surprise that queues build up quickly during the event, so it's best to get down early and prepare yourself for a saline breakfast.

⊙ miyajima.or.jp/english/event/event_kaki.html

"With their focus on loyalty, discipline and valour, they aren't simply styles of combat, but lessons for life"

ACTIVITIES & SPORTS

JAPAN, THE HOME OF MARTIAL ARTS

⊙ AROUND JAPAN

In a country where a warrior class held control for so many centuries, it stands to reason that complex martial arts would arise in lockstep. Japanese martial philosophies, however, view violence as a last resort, showing the imprints of Buddhist, Taoist and Confucianist DNA. With their focus on loyalty, discipline and valour, they aren't simply styles of combat, but lessons for life hammered into the liturgy of battle preparation. As the great Miyamoto Musashi pithily put it: 'Never stray from the Way'.

The depth and breadth of the martial arts Japan has pioneered is staggering. Most people will be familiar with karate, judo and jiu-jitsu, perhaps even sword arts kendo and iaido, or self-defence-based aikido. But Japan also gave rise to kyudo, the way of the bow; naginatajutsu, the art of wielding a naginata polearm; ninjutsu, guerilla warfare and espionage tactics; suijutsu, combative swimming; and Okinawan kobudo, the old martial way of Okinawa.

Sumo is one of Japan's oldest and most culturally significant martial forms. While many fighting styles evolved in conversation with Buddhism, sumo was borne out of Shinto ritual. Bouts were often held at shrines to bring good fortune and bountiful harvests, and sumo was referenced in the *Kojiki*

(712 CE) and *Nihon Shoki* (720), Japan's founding historical texts. Though public interest has waxed and waned over the past few centuries, the sport has entered a boom period, partly kickstarted by its expanding global reach.

Top **Okinawan kobudo**

Bottom **Kyudo, the way of the bow**

Opposite **Martial arts have significant history in Japan**

Top **Fukuoka Grand Sumo Tournament**
Bottom **A sumo wrestler in the ring**
Opposite **Ryogoku Kokugikan National Sumo Arena in Tokyo**

A GUIDE TO WATCHING SUMO IN JAPAN

Nothing turns heads in a Japanese room like the entry of a sumo wrestler. Not only are they gargantuan men in a country of comparatively small people, but they're often viewed as exemplars of Japan's exacting moral standards.

Both their size and their ritualistic approach to the sport is laid bare at live events: the tossing of salt to protect the wrestler from injuries; the stomping of feet, called shiko, to drive away evil spirits and encourage the growth of crops; or the eventual slap of flesh on flesh when the bout begins.

Sumo tickets have become commodities as rikishi (wrestlers) have taken to the airwaves to promote the sport to a new generation, while more inbound tourists are planning their trips to coincide with one of the big national tournaments.

The six Honbasho (Grand Sumo Tournaments), each lasting 15 days, take place as follows:

* **January** Ryogoku Kokugikan National Sumo Arena, Tokyo

* **March** EDION Arena, Osaka

* **May** Ryogoku Kokugikan National Sumo Arena, Tokyo

* **July** IG Arena, Nagoya

* **September** Ryogoku Kokugikan National Sumo Arena, Tokyo

* **November** Fukuoka Kokusai Center, Fukuoka

The bouts usually start around 8.30am, but these feature lower-ranking sumo and are therefore deemed less exciting. Crowds will flood in around lunchtime, in preparation for the juryo (second-highest division) and makuuchi (highest division) fights in the afternoon. The final bout, or musubi-no-ichiban, will typically feature one or more yokozuna (grand champions) battling it out for supremacy in the ring.

Tickets for Grand Sumo Tournaments are available at Ticket Oosumo, the Japan Sumo Association's recommended ticket portal, and at the independent Buy Sumo Tickets website. They go on sale around one month before the event's opening day.

🔴 **sumo.pia.jp/en**
🔴 **buysumotickets.com**

BASEBALL CRAZY: JAPAN'S ADOPTED NATIONAL SPORT

◉ **AROUND JAPAN**

There are plenty of acclaimed sports venues in Japan: the Ryogoku Kokugikan National Sumo Arena; the Nippon Budokan, spiritual home of martial arts; Grand Prix stalwart's Suzuka Circuit and the Fuji Speedway; Yokohama Stadium, host of the 2019 Rugby World Cup final; and the Japan National Stadium, host of Tokyo 2020. But perhaps Meiji Jingu Stadium takes the biscuit.

A red-brick colonnaded baseball ground in the heart of downtown Tokyo, it opened in 1926, making it the second-oldest baseball stadium in the country. (The oldest, incidentally, is Hanshin Koshien Stadium near Kobe, home of the National High School Baseball Championship, arguably the most beloved and fever-pitched ball game of the year.)

Meiji Jingu's home team, the Tokyo Yakult Swallows, might not be the dominant force they were in the 1990s, but the stadium has a long history of welcoming luminaries of the game – it's one of only four remaining stadiums worldwide where Babe Ruth once played – and on one fateful day in 1978, the on-field action inspired Haruki Murakami to become an author. Plans to bulldoze and relocate the stadium have drawn so much ire from the public because of Japan's deep-rooted fascination with baseball. Sumo might be the official national sport, but there's no arguing that *yakyu* (baseball) is the one that's captured the nation's heart.

Nothing embodies this better than perpetually smiling Shohei Ohtani, a once-in-a-generation talent, a whip-fast pitcher and beefy slugger, who's broken more records than Guinness and has been compared, not unreasonably, to the legendary Ruth. Affectionately known as 'Shotime', his national hero status was cemented further when he nabbed a contract with the LA Dodgers in 2022 worth US$700 million, the most expensive in North American sporting history.

Ohtani may be smashing homers an ocean away, but his continued success has emboldened the love of baseball at home. Go into any residential area of a Japanese city, and the available turf is taken up not by football fields, rugby pitches or tennis courts but by baseball diamonds and

pitcher's mounds. Bars across the country are covered in baseball memorabilia and posters singing the praises of the local team. It's Japan's most-attended spectator sport, and by quite some distance.

Nippon Professional Baseball is split into two divisions, the Central League and the Pacific League, each consisting of six teams. Regular season games are played from late March through October, almost every day of the week (bar Monday), with tickets usually available on the day. Some teams are renowned for their die-hard fanbases, like the Yokohama-based BayStars, the Hanshin Tigers of Nishinomiya and Tokyo's Yomiuri Giants, meaning tickets are harder to acquire, particularly for games on weekends and public holidays.

Baseball tickets are available for purchase on team websites, but English-language support and user-friendliness vary. They're also available at third-party sites like Klook and Japan Ball Tickets or at convenience stores.

🌐 japanballtickets.com/index.html

JAPOW: WINTER SPORTS CULTURE IN JAPAN

⊙ **AROUND JAPAN**

Japan has grown into one of the world's peak winter tourism destinations because skiing or snowboarding on the fabled 'Japow', the moniker for Japan's unparalleled powdery snow, has become the winter sports equivalent of finding El Dorado.

It often surprises people that Japan receives as much snowfall as it does. Even Hokkaido in the north has a middling latitude – it's aligned with Rome, Madrid and New York – and its mountains are low-lying compared to the great, soaring ranges of Eurasia and the Americas. But, of course, meteorology is more complex than that. Japan is the world's snowiest country because freezing arctic winds from Siberia pick up moisture as they travel across the Sea of Japan, and when these winds hit the mountains in the north, they rise and cool, releasing themselves as heavy snowfall.

As any snow junkie in Japan will tell you, it's not just the consistency and volume of snow, but the quality. This is down to the complex, right-place-right-time merging of geographical and climatological processes, but suffice it to say, the amount of air trapped in the stellar dendrite snow crystals is in excess of 90 per cent, resulting in the fresh, fluffy snow dumped on Japan's ski resorts throughout the winter.

Niseko usually takes the plaudits for having the country's best powder. Its slopes, chalets and hotels bag consistent nominations at the World Ski Awards, with Niseko United winning the best ski resort in Japan in consecutive years from 2013 to 2016. But the snow in other popular resorts, like Hakuba and Nozawa Onsen, both of which hosted events at the 1998 Winter Olympics in Nagano, and on the slopes around Sapporo, home of the 1972 Winter Olympics, are also known to send skiers and boarders into fits of ecstasy on early-morning powder runs.

As the term Japow has been popularised, however, so too have the resorts most associated with it. This has caused once-quiet mountain villages to become swarmed with deep-pocketed foreigners, causing prices to skyrocket – a bowl of ramen in Niseko now costs around three or four times what you'd pay in Tokyo – and locals to go elsewhere in search of more affordable lifestyles. Not everyone sees this as a negative; these areas have internationalised faster than anywhere else in the country, meaning the levels of spoken English are much higher, in turn making them easy places for non-Japanese to travel, live and work. But from an ethical tourism perspective – and in the interest of having a more authentically Japanese experience – this trend emphasises the need for winter tourists to broaden their horizons.

While Japan's resorts are concentrated in the north and along the Sea of Japan coast, particularly in Niigata and Nagano, there are ski venues running all along the spine of the Honshū mainland, and even into Shikoku and Kyūshū.

Furano Ski Resort in Hokkaido

Opposite **Winter scenery in Nozawa Onsen**

WHERE TO SKI/ SNOWBOARD IN JAPAN

◎ **AROUND JAPAN**

Myoko Kogen, Niigata

Myoko Kogen is an up-and-coming resort area in Niigata, just over two hours from Tokyo by bullet train. It's in a similar place to where Hakuba or Niseko was 10 or 15 years ago, and as outside interest in Japan increases and more people are looking for alternatives to the most crowded and priciest resorts, Myoko Kogen is raising its hand as a viable replacement. The area receives around 14m (46ft) of snow per year, with regular snowfall on consecutive days. There are five main resorts here – Akakura Onsen, Akakura Kanko, Ikenotaira Onsen, Myoko Suginohara and Seki Onsen – and several more within driving distance.

🌐 myoko.jp

Appi Kogen, Iwate

Winner of Japan's best ski resort in 2022 and 2023, Appi Kogen has established itself as a genuine frontrunner in the domestic ski scene. Straddling two mountains, the resort has 21 runs, including long, groomed pistes, mogul terrain, a snow park and a kids' ski school.

The hotel options have expanded in recent years, too: alongside the local ski lodges, guesthouses and ryokan, international chains like Holiday Inn, InterContinental and Crowne Plaza offer ski-in, ski-out accommodation. The ski season here is beefy, lasting from December till early May.

🌐 appi-japan.com

Rusutsu Resort, Hokkaido

Rusutsu is no stranger to the podium, either – it was awarded Japan's best ski resort in 2017, 2018, 2019 and 2021 – and is a great alternative to the likes of Niseko and the other resorts near Sapporo. Meaning 'the path at the foot of the mountain' in the indigenous Ainu language, Rusutsu is a 90-minute drive from the Hokkaido prefectural capital and is one the largest resorts on the island. It has 36 runs across three mountains, fresh powder dropped consistently throughout the season and is renowned for its backcountry trails, tree skiing and heli-skiing.

🌐 rusutsu.com/en/rusutsu-in-winter

Zao Onsen, Yamagata

Zao Onsen is one of the largest and most comprehensive resorts in the Tohoku region, with around 50km (31 miles) of ski trails. One of the area's biggest draws is skiing through the juhyo (snow monsters), fir trees covered in an icy rime that turns them into gnarled stalagmites – though the same weather that creates this phenomenon can be a blight when you want to hit the slopes. Zao Onsen grew more organically than most ski towns, so it has retained much of its old-world aesthetic, and it has been a popular hot spring bathing spot for almost two millennia, with sulphuric spring water that alleviates aches, chronic pain and skin conditions and strengthens blood vessels.

🧭 zao-spa.or.jp/english

Palcall Tsumagoi Resort, Gunma

Palcall Tsumagoi was a product of the 1980s bubble era, when skiing became a viable leisure activity to the newly affluent masses. Much of the ageing infrastructure remained in place until it underwent a facelift in 2014, merging with nearby Baragi Kogen Tsumagoi, leading to several World Ski Awards nominations over the proceeding years. It's still largely the preserve of Japanese skiers and boarders, meaning you're aware that you're actually in Japan – a fact that needs reminding in the more internationalised resorts. Tsumagoi village is also a 25-minute drive from Kusatsu Onsen, one of Japan's finest hot spring areas.

🧭 tsumagoiskiresort.life/en

Top and bottom **The popular slopes of Zao Onsen**

ALTERNATIVE WAYS TO HIKE MOUNT FUJI

⦿ YAMANASHI, SHIZUOKA

'A wise man climbs Fuji once. Only a fool climbs it twice.' – Ancient Japanese proverb

It's been a long time coming, but Mount Fuji has finally begun to reject the annual hordes of hikers swarming across its slopes like termites on a mound. In 2024, local authorities introduced a cap of 4000 climbers per day and a hiking fee of ¥2000 to the Yoshida Trail, the most popular and well-provisioned route. They also sought to prevent 'bullet climbing' – hiking the volcano overnight to watch the sunrise at the top – by only permitting visitors at night if they have a reservation at one of the mountain lodges.

The Yoshida Trail, even before hikers became personae non gratae, was never the most attractive of courses. Hour upon hour of wending over volcanic rubble and scree, braving switchbacks in the face of erratic weather and standing in single file behind hundreds of fellow hikers is not my idea of a good time. You'll often hear that Mount Fuji is an easy climb. Such statements belong to the ill-informed and internet bravado. It's well maintained and equipped for a 3776m (12,388ft) peak, but this is the highest point in the country: typhoons, snow storms, rockslides and sub-zero temperatures can arrive without much notice.

The general rule is to go during the 'official' hiking season, July and August, or with a licensed tour operator, like Fuji Mountain Guides, which also conducts tours in the early summer and autumn. With the Yoshida Trail operating at peak capacity, the alternative routes – the Subashiri, Gotemba and Fujinomiya trails – are worth consideration.

Note: Bring coins for restrooms, a bag to carry your rubbish and a stick for walking. Yoshida and Subashiri Trail accommodation can be rented through Japan Mountain Huts (japanmountainhuts.com). Gotemba Trail accommodation is available at fujisan223. com/rule/stay/gotemba, and Fujinomiya Trail accommodation is available at fuji-tozan. com/04_lodge.html (both in Japanese only).

Subashiri Trail

– The Subashiri Trail begins at the Subashiri Fifth Station (accessible by car or bus) at 1970m (6463ft) above sea level
– The ascent will take five to seven hours, the descent two to four
– It's Fuji's greenest route, with the tree line running as high as 2700m (8858ft), though it merges with the busy Yoshida Trail after the eighth station

Gotemba Trail

– A long and gently sloping trail that starts at the Gotemba Fifth Station (accessible by car or bus) at 1440m (4724ft) above sea level

– The ascent will take eight or nine hours, the descent around four hours. On the way down, volcanic sandy tracks, called osunabashiri, allow hikers to slide down at pace (spats or gaiters recommended)

– There are few amenities until around the seventh and eighth stations, so provisions are necessary for the first half of the ascent

– While this is the quietest and most leisurely of Fuji's trails, its scenery is the least interesting

Fujinomiya Trail

– This trail has the least elevation gain of the four main routes up Fuji, beginning at the Fujinomiya Fifth Station (accessible by car and bus), approximately 2400m (7874ft) above sea level

– The ascent takes between five to seven hours, the descent two to five, depending on congestion

– Fujinomiya is the second-busiest trail, partly because it's the easiest to access for hikers coming from Shizuoka and west Japan

– It also offers a route to Mount Hoei, a secondary peak formed by a volcanic eruption in 1707

PURIFICATION AND REBIRTH: HIKING JAPAN

◉ AROUND JAPAN

In Japan, the notion of retreating, hermit-like, into the mountains has held cultural sway for centuries. Mountains provide refuge to the kami, divine Shinto spirits, and the wandering souls of the dead. They're spaces where one can attain special powers through ascetic shugendo practice or satori (enlightenment) through endless hours of meditation and repose. They're admired for their aesthetic virtues, yes, but primarily mountains represent a literal and symbolic struggle; hiking is less an act of conquering a foe and more a purification rite giving way to rebirth.

Around 73 per cent of the Japanese landmass is mountainous, with more than 12,500 named mountains therein, many of which have hiking trails etched into their slopes. Shrines, temples, cairns, *jizo* bodhisattva statues or magnificent stones inscribed with epitaphs tell tales of the mountain's past, while torii gates or towering cedars demarcate the material and spiritual worlds.

Mount Fuji, a stratovolcano straddling Yamanashi and Shizuoka Prefectures, is Japan's most famous mountain. It's been an object of worship since at least the seventh century, but even before that, the sight of its perfect conical structure dominating the skyline would surely have turned the most faithless of people pious.

It isn't just pilgrims that flock to its trails now. Estimates suggest around 200,000 people climb the 3776m (12,388ft)

peak every summer – and long queues on the slopes provide solid anecdotal evidence – with some marching up in crystal-clear conditions, while others have to battle the elements. I know this all too well: in two attempts at climbing Fuji, I've been halted before the summit by roaring typhoons. It may be Japan's Chomolungma, the Goddess Mother of the Earth, but I've decided to lace up my hiking boots elsewhere.

Even within the Tokyo prefectural limits, the options are plentiful. Mount Takao in Hachioji is a popular (and easy) hike for denizens of the capital, though it gets dreadfully busy during the cherry blossom and autumn seasons, and the views from the top are nothing special. Mitake and Kawanori, isolated and thickly forested mountains in Tokyo's Okutama region, have more challenging, yet much more rewarding, trails.

Tokyo's neighbouring prefecture, Kanagawa, has some great hikes during the spring thaw season, with mountain summits like Kintoki, Tonodake and Ogusuyama looking across clear skies towards Fuji. Mount Oyama is a popular pilgrimage spot here, especially during summer, when the Choyukai – a group of tattoo artists and people covered in horimono, contiguous works of body art drawn using a manual *tebori* technique – march to the Shinto shrine at the top.

More advanced alpinists may look to Japan's tallest mountains, concentrated in the Japan Alps around Yamanashi, Shizuoka, Nagano and Gifu Prefectures. There are 23 mountains over 3000m (9843ft), including peaks like Yarigatake and Hotaka. Connected by a vertigo-inducing ridgeline, with an infamous section called the *daikiretto*, or 'big cut', which requires rock climbing over steep drops with the aid of chains and bolts, these mountains draw keen hikers to Japan each year.

Another, Mount Tate (better known as Tateyama), is considered one of the 'Three Holy Mountains', alongside Fuji and Hakusan. This epithet – which is somewhat misleading, given it's hard to find an unholy mountain in Japan – can't be attributed to any definitive source. But it speaks to the point: Japan's mountains are sacred realms, rooted in the nation's collective consciousness.

Top **A map of Mount Fuji's hiking trails**

Bottom **The scenic Mitake**

CLIMBING TO NAGEIREDO, JAPAN'S MOST DANGEROUS NATIONAL TREASURE

⊙ TOTTORI

Nageiredo is one of those ancient monuments that stops you in your tracks and makes you think, *how?* Built on stilts in an inaccessible recess near the summit of Mount Mitoku, and dating to the early eighth century, its existence makes almost no sense. They say the holy man and founder of Shugendo, En no Gyoja, used powers gained from years of asceticism to launch the temple into its current resting place (Nageiredo means 'Thrown-in Hall'). Its true origin story, lost to the annals of history, is doubtless just as mystifying.

Nageiredo is often described as Japan's 'most dangerous national treasure'. And sure, if you tried to scale the near-vertical rock wall from the top of Mitoku to the temple's wooden veranda, you'd probably end up as carrion on the forest floor below. But this characterisation is really just a catchy marketing ploy.

Mitoku's summit is 900m (2953ft) above sea level, and in fairness, the route is coarse and unpredictable, as though charted by a priest who'd had too much to drink. Rather than a series of steps carved into the granite, there are boulders connected by chain links, protruding tree roots that serve as ladders, and barely identifiable paths along narrow ridges.

When I arrive at Sanbutsu-ji, the temple at the foot of Mitoku, the priest Ryojin-san looks at my hiking shoes as if to say, 'No, no, no, these won't do at all.'

He hands me a pair of roughspun waraji (straw sandals), like someone had hacked two chunks out of a basket and glued straps to them.

'Seriously? I have to wear these?' Usually, I'd be more accommodating, but it's early March, and the snow has yet to fully thaw.

He says something about tradition and practicality, the relationship between the soles of my feet and the mountain. It's clear I'm fighting a losing battle.

I slip on the waraji and we set off on the trail. Mitoku is isolated, rising from the eastern end of Daisen-Oki National Park in Tottori, Japan's least-populated prefecture. There isn't another soul in sight.

'Now repeat after me,' says Ryojin-san, as if to break the silence. '*Zan-ge zan-ge ... Rokkon shojo.*'

I repeat the recitation – 'Repent, repent; purify our six senses of perception' – chorusing the words, over and over, synching it to the tempo of my feet. To cleanse the rokkon, your five senses and consciousness, one must undertake a hardship that shows

deference to nature. Out here, on this hallowed trail, it's easy to decouple oneself from the worldly desires the Buddhists believe to be the source of all our suffering.

I see votive offerings at the base of an ancient tree, a poignant reminder of those who have walked the trail before me, who undertook a sacrifice in response to something greater than themselves. I stop at two wooden temples, Monjudo and Jizodo, with their *ukiyo-e*–like views of the Chugoku mountains, and ring the two-tonne, 800-year-old Shorodo bell, perhaps to inform the gods I'm coming. The trail end then looms, a rock tunnel ('the womb') signifying the pilgrim's rebirth.

I slide through and look at Nageiredo, hanging there, like it could collapse at the slightest puff of wind. I don't believe it is held up by any force other than those governed by the laws of physics. But still it makes no sense. 'How?' I say to no one in particular. *How?*

Nageiredo is built on stilts near the summit of Mount Mitoku

BRUCE DILLON TALKS SURFING IN KUROSHIO

⦿ **KOCHI**

I've long had a theory that Japan is so clean because it deposits every metric tonne of rubbish on its beaches. Granted, a lot of the seaside detritus – nets, buoys, buckets, PET bottles, toothbrushes and all manner of footwear – has either washed ashore or can be attributed to commercial fishing activity, while local municipalities likely don't have the funding, personnel or wherewithal to maintain beach upkeep. But it's disheartening all the same.

On occasion – and this is the salient point – I find an exception that proves the rule. Such is the case at Ubuki Beach, a 4km (2.5-mile) expanse of sun-baked sands running along the Kuroshio seafront in Kochi Prefecture.

I'm here to meet Bruce Dillon, owner of Hata Surf Dojo and a Kuroshio resident (on and off) for the past 30 years. Having spent most of his youth living and surfing on Australia's Gold Coast, Dillon began to feel like he was on shifting sands. The area was becoming more populated and the beaches overcrowded with inbound surfers, so in 1995 he came straight to Kochi Prefecture on a working holiday visa, an unusual route for a first-time visitor, and immediately jibed with Japan's rural surf lifestyle.

Kuroshio is far from the trodden trail, just the way Dillon likes it. A one-and-a-half-hour flight from Tokyo, followed by another couple hours behind the wheel (or a wing and a prayer with public transport), with little in the way of infrastructure, accommodation or restaurants and nightlife. That said, a figure-eight highway around Shikoku is on the drawing board, and though it will bring more tourists, businesses and money, Dillon has mixed feelings.

'If it's locals making the coin and it's not disappearing into other people's pockets then that's good,' he says. 'It's a natural progression, I guess, so no one's really fighting it.'

Japan's surfing industry has trended upwards over the past decade, helped by the inclusion of surfing at the Tokyo 2020 Olympics and the popularity of *Chasing Waves*, an eight-part docuseries on Japan's surf culture.

'It's lost that bad-boy image,' Dillon says. 'It attracted a different market, women started surfing, and it really just grew from there.'

Kuroshio might not cut it for big-wave chasers, unless a strong typhoon swell hits in the late summer, but the quality of the surf here is undeniable. While chunks of Japan's tsunami-prone coastline have been bastioned with tetrapods, huge concrete jacks designed to quell wave energy and coastal erosion, Kuroshio is largely concrete-free.

'We're pretty lucky,' says Dillon. 'We've got these open beaches, which are wide and spread out, so if you're not a high-level person, then it's heaven because you can find your own peak.'

Kuroshio's surf season runs from April through October, but like any activity dictated by the whims of nature, what you get on any given day is a toss-up. So Dillon is always keeping his eye on the forecast.

'If I know the waves are gonna be good, I'm up at 3am, chasing it,' he says. 'And it's so fickle and hard to read, that often we get great waves with no one else around.'

🌐 hatasurfdojo.com

WHERE ELSE TO SURF IN JAPAN

✳ **Tsurigasaki Surfing Beach, Chiba** Tsurigasaki was selected as the surfing venue for Tokyo 2020 and welcomes as many as 600,000 surfers each year. Mixing trade winds and typhoon swells, Tsurigasaki's waves typically break around 1.5m (5ft), but they can pose a stiff challenge during the peak summer season. Several world-class athletes have cut their teeth on this beach, including Hiroto Ohara, the first Japanese surfer to win the US Open, as well as international competitors Reo Inaba and Tenshi Iwami.

✳ **Shonan Coast, Kanagawa** Local surfers claim the Shonan Coast to be the home of surfing in Japan. Their claim is a good one: running from Atami to Miura, and straddling Kamakura, Fujisawa and Zushi, the coast includes beach breaks, reef breaks and river mouths, and is dotted with surf dojos and equipment rental shops. When the waves swell, so does the surfing population, given the Shonan Coast's proximity to Tokyo.

✳ **Okinawa** The advantage of surfing in Okinawa is that the subtropical climate keeps the waters temperate. Plus, the island chain has nearly 300 degrees of swell channel, so your surf options are plentiful. The Sunabe Seawall near the capital, Naha, is renowned for its sections of reef break; while Hedo Point on the main island's northern tip gets hefty swells during typhoon season.

✳ **Miyazaki** One of Japan's most southern prefectures, Miyazaki is at the centre of Kyūshū's surf culture. Kisakihama, sprawling across 3km (1.9 miles) of Pacific coastline and home to pretty consistent waves year-round, is probably the most popular beach here – it held the ISA World Surfing Games in 2019. But the Kaeda River Mouth, ideal for intermediate surfers, and Okuragahama, which has hosted numerous regional and international surf competitions, offer great alternatives.

Top **Cycling is hugely popular in Japan**
Bottom **Biking through Japan's greenery**

JAPAN ON TWO WHEELS

⊙ AROUND JAPAN

Recently I came across some statistics – of varying veracity, it must be said – on the popularity of cycling in Japan. There are one hundred million cyclists across the country, stated one source. Tokyo is the world's most bicycle-dense megacity, claimed another. One website averred that Japan was now the world's third-greatest cycling nation after the Netherlands and Denmark.

We can quibble about the data-gathering methodology, but one thing is for sure: Japan is a great place to ride a bike. Seeing mothers and homebound commuters on mamachari, push bikes built for carrying groceries and children, is part of the rhythm of everyday life in the cities. Most major urban areas sit on flat coastal plains and river basins, providing navigable (and not particularly strenuous) turf for travellers on two wheels. To that end, Tokyo, Yokohama, Kyoto, Osaka, Hiroshima, Fukuoka and Sapporo all have e-bike share schemes – like Docomo, Hello Cycling and Luup – and various bicycle tour providers.

The Shimanami Kaido, which receives up to 300,000 cyclists per year, has become the poster child of bicycle tourism in Japan. This 70km (43.5-mile) cycling route, tracing lazy S-shapes from Honshū to Shikoku by way of suspension bridges and roads bisecting a small, mountain-riddled archipelago, is long enough to be an achievable challenge for novices and short enough to be bundled into a longer journey for experts.

Frankly, it surprises me that the Kaido constantly finds itself on lists of the world's best cycling routes. The coast has been smothered in more concrete than a Tadao Ando building and lots of the townships have morphed into hopelessly depressed sites of industry. But to each their own. Elsewhere in Japan, though, there are rural roads paved to perfection and rewarding mountain slogs reaffirming its reputation as a cyclist's nation.

MORE CYCLING ROUTES IN JAPAN

* **Biwaichi, Shiga** Cycling around Lake Biwa, the largest lake in Japan, has become a popular enough pastime to spawn the sobriquet 'Biwaichi', short for *Biwako isshu*, meaning 'a loop around Lake Biwa'. The route covers around 200km (124 miles) of mostly flat terrain and is divided into the 150km (93-mile) northern section (Hokko) and the 50km (31-mile) southern section (Nanko) by the Biwako Bridge. The road along the lake's eastern front is particularly prepossessing: it hugs the water's edge for most of the way, skirts past historic town Omihachiman and the castle cities of Hikone and Nagahama and finally ascends into the mountains at Kinomoto.

* **Ring Ring Road, Ibaraki** The Ring Ring Road in Ibaraki Prefecture is so called because it forms a circular shape around Lake Kasumigaura (repetition of the word 'Ring' apparently emphasises just how circular – which is odd, given it's not circular at all). Around 180km (112 miles) long, the Ring Ring Road has been divided into shorter sections. The most popular is a long, flat path hugging the lake and guiding cyclists past castles, flower parks, shrines, temples and ancient *kofun* (burial mounds). There's also a course heading towards Mount Tsukuba, following an abandoned railway line, with an optional 25km (15.5-mile) hill climb.

* **The Noto Peninsula, Ishikawa** The Noto Peninsula, a windswept hook of land reaching 100km (62 miles) into the Sea of Japan, has gone from a place of quaint anonymity to one of the most popular cycling destinations in the country. It's famed for its terraced rice paddies, rocky promontories, spring and summer wildflowers and port towns with exceptional seafood, like Wajima, where the morning market is more than 1000 years old.

Given the lack of hilly terrain, advanced cyclists can power through the peninsula in three or four days, whereas novice and intermediate Noto cycling tours may last more than a week. Weather plays a factor, too: winters are notoriously harsh here, and in even spring, summer and autumn, it can rain one out of every three days.

* **Fuji Five Lakes, Yamanashi** If there's one thing I've learnt about Mount Fuji over the years, it's that she looks much better from a distance than she does up close. And to see her at her most besotting, there are few better vantage points than from Fuji Five Lakes. The lakes – Yamanaka, Kawaguchi, Saiko, Shoji and Motosu – gather around the base of the stratovolcano, each with a well-paved path around its perimeter. Depending on the route, the cycle could be anywhere from 40km (25 miles) to 100km (62 miles), with elevation gain between 100m (328ft) and 450m (1476ft). Fuji is revealed in its highest definition in winter and early spring when the sky is clearest, particularly from the shores of Lake Motosu – a view immortalised on the old ¥1000 note.

* **Tsushima Island, Nagasaki** I think it's fair to say that few travellers had heard of Tsushima before Sony-owned game studio Sucker Punch revealed it was making a samurai epic called *Ghost of Tsushima* (2020). Set during the first Mongol invasion of Japan in 1274 on an island between Korea and Kyūshū, it sold more than five million copies in its first four months. Since then, interest in Tsushima has spiked, and some intrepid explorers have taken to the island on two wheels. The islets of Aso Bay, the Kaneda fortress ruins, the Korean-style Kankoku Observatory on the island's northern tip – there's plenty to keep you pedalling along Tsushima's 900km (560-mile) coastline.

Riding through Imabari

"Hiroshima should always stand as a cautionary tale, and that peace – the most utopian of human ideals – is still worth striving for."

HISTORY

THE REMNANTS OF FEUDALISM: CASTLES IN JAPAN

⊙ AROUND JAPAN

Traditional architecture in Japan can be broadly split into two categories: the architecture of religion and the architecture of war. The latter takes the form of shiro (castles), multi-storey keeps surrounded by moats, baileys, gates, watchtowers, battlements and jokamachi (castle towns). Though cityscapes have changed drastically in the past couple of hundred years, many modern cities, from Himeji to Kanazawa to Nagoya, still unfurl from a central castle.

Warlords erected such fortifications with haste and vigour during the Sengoku Jidai, or Warring States era (1467 to 1615), during which Japan was ravaged by internecine conflicts. But if castles weren't destroyed during a siege, they were just as likely to perish in a fire or be damaged by an earthquake. They fared little better following the Meiji Restoration of 1868, when the Tokugawa Shogunate was abolished and power restored to the emperor. Japan strove to emulate the West, envisioning a future of civilisation and modernity. Castles were reminders of its feudal past, a symbol of a nation left in the wake of the industrial revolution, and as such, they had to be torn down.

Centuries of constructing and deconstructing castles have left just over 100 standing, only 12 of which are considered 'original' – meaning the tenshu, or main keep, isn't a replica built after 1868.

Bitchu Matsuyama Castle
Opposite **Matsumoto Castle**

Bitchu Matsuyama Castle

A 13th-century mountaintop castle in Okayama, also known as the Castle in the Sky.

Hikone Castle

This 400-year-old castle, overlooking the waters of Lake Biwa, is one of the best-preserved in the country, having never seen battle.

Himeji Castle

Towering over Himeji City, the 'Castle of the White Heron' is often deemed Japan's most beautiful and was the first site in the country to be awarded World Heritage status (alongside Hōryūji Temple in Nara) in 1993.

Hirosaki Castle

This 17th-century castle in Aomori is renowned for its winter snow lantern festival and the 2600 cherry trees blooming on its grounds each spring.

Inuyama Castle

Inuyama Castle's keep has been designated a National Treasure, but its most notable feature is the view it commands over the surrounding Kiso River valley.

Kochi Castle

Lords tended to retreat to castles only when their domain was under attack, but Kochi Castle doubled as the permanent residence of the daimyo, and even today it's full of manicured gardens and plum and cherry trees.

Marugame Castle

Erected on huge cyclopean foundations – the tallest stone walls in Japan – Marugame Castle looks more like a neolithic site than a 16th-century fortification.

Maruoka Castle

A bit of a miscategorisation here; Maruoka Castle was levelled during an earthquake in 1948 and reassembled with 80 per cent of the original materials.

Matsue Castle

The last original keep in the San'in region, Matsue Castle stands in a charming part of the city, surrounded by an old samurai quarter and the heron-filled Jozan Park.

Matsumoto Castle

Matsumoto's Crow Castle embodies the eras of war and peace; it has strong fortifications and a hidden inner floor for ambushing attackers, as well as a moon-viewing room in its south-eastern wing for relaxing on autumn evenings.

Matsuyama Castle

Built on a hill rising 132m (433ft) above a lowland plain and arranged in a series of terraces, Matsuyama Castle has one of the most distinctive appearances of all Japanese castles.

Uwajima Castle

This keep on the west coast of Ehime Prefecture is one of the smallest and most unassuming of Japan's feudal structures.

ALEX KERR ON RESTORING JAPAN'S OLD BUILDINGS

◉ **AROUND JAPAN**

When you see all the Instagram posts and YouTube videos of atmospheric shrines and temples, it's logical to assume Japan excels in preserving its old buildings. But this is only half true. The country is awash in *akiya* (abandoned homes) – statistics put the number at 8.5 million, though some estimates suggest it's closer to 11 million – often bedecked with coped-tile roofs, elegant *fusuma* doors and traditional gardens. Yet they are deemed outdated and valueless.

Alex Kerr, a longtime Japan resident and the author of books like *Lost Japan* and *Dogs and Demons*, has been renovating such homes for more than half a century. His first project was a thatched-roof farmhouse in Tsurui, a hamlet set amid the steep gorges of Iya Valley, in which he envisioned life as a hermetic sage, drinking tea on the veranda by day and painting calligraphy deep into the night. Working on the principle of 'old world aesthetic, present-day comfort', he understood that living in a traditional Japanese home didn't have to mean draughty corridors, leaky ceilings and scarcely a piece of furniture in sight.

'Old world aesthetic, present-day comfort is pretty much a standard idea worldwide,' says Kerr. 'It's only in Japan where that's considered revolutionary.'

He says this stems from an 'ingrained philosophy of modernism', whereby Japan still feels it's playing catch up with the pace of progress in the West and that old buildings are unwelcome relics of a bygone era.

'With residential buildings, Japan went one of two ways,' he adds. 'The government would declare it a cultural treasure, and it would be fabulously [preserved] down to the square millimetre – exquisite – but you couldn't put in an electric plug, you couldn't change the shape of a window. It was unlivable but perfect: a museum piece. Or, it was torn down and you built something out of concrete and plastic. It was one or the other.'

Over the last 30 years, Kerr has given close to 600 talks on the importance of preserving Japan's traditional architecture. The main challenge has been proving to bureaucrats that it's possible to marry wood, tatami flooring and traditional plaster with plumbing, electricity, central heating and modern furnishings, and that it's worth doing because it can help revitalise the ageing rural regions that need it most.

'Now we're seeing a seismic shift and the restoration of old houses is really taking off,' he says. 'Tourism was the turning point because they realised these houses could make money.'

Kerr, along with teams of carpenters, builders and contractors, has restored old buildings throughout Japan – including an apothecary in Mikuni Town and a collection of *kominka*, literally meaning 'old houses', on Ojika Island – opening them as accommodation for travellers. Even Chiirori (chiiori-stay.jp), the House of the Flute, his first renovation project and former home in Iya Valley, is open for reservations.

Kerr admits the houses of his heart are built of thatch and timber, with sunken hearths and smoky wooden beams, buildings that evoke an ancient age, when aesthetic sensibilities were wilder and freer. But he doesn't believe houses need to be old to have value. Provided they use traditional materials and a traditional sense of space, he says, they're embodying an ethos that's worth preserving.

Top **Alex Kerr**
Bottom **Akiya are more prevalent in rural areas**

REFRAMING HISTORY THROUGH THE LENS OF PEACE

⊙ HIROSHIMA

If you were anywhere near the hypocentre of the atomic explosion that decimated central Hiroshima on 6 August 1945, there were two things that might have saved you. First, sheer why-the-hell-me luck. Second, maybe, if you were underground.

Some of the most chilling survivor testimonies come from people who happened to be under the city when Little Boy sent supersonic shockwaves across the sky. Akiko Takaura, a 20-year-old Bank of Hiroshima employee, was dusting her desk in the vault when a bright white flash knocked her unconscious. Seven teenage girls, 'mobilised students' surreptitiously tasked with sending military communications, were stationed in a subterranean bunker. Nomura Eizo, an office worker, happened to go looking for his paperwork in the basement at around 8.15.

'That's when it happened. I heard this massive explosion,' Nomura later wrote; his words now printed on the wall of the basement. 'There was a sharp pain, and when I went to touch my head, there was something sticky dripping from it ... from deep in the darkness, I could hear a man shouting for help. The shouts continued, and then, they turned into sobs: terrible, wailing sobs.'

Most travellers go to Hiroshima to see its haunting Peace Memorial Museum. It's a strange experience as a tourist, walking around in glum, graveyard silence, looking at burnt children's clothing, faces wrought with anguish and honeycombed with blisters, a human shadow scorched into stone, vivid and violent artworks depicting Death, destroyer of worlds. No wonder visitors gather in the lobby afterwards, staring listlessly into the void.

Elsewhere in the 3km (1.9-mile) blast radius, the facts and data points become more tangible. The hypocentre marker, standing anonymously on a side street. The trees that somehow withstood the explosion. The basement where Nomura survived and a 140,000-stone monument that honours the original death toll. Fukuromachi Elementary School, reconstructed after the bomb, where a new generation of children play in the schoolyard, joined by the ghosts of their predecessors.

Hiroshima may be shorthand for atrocity. But since the 1950s, the city has tried to reframe its narrative through peace. You walk along Peace Blvd towards Peace Park and enter the Peace Memorial Museum. Eriko Abiko, a peace activist and owner of Hachidorisha Cafe – where she holds events in which customers can talk to hibakusha, A-bomb survivors – says the authorities do a really good job of presenting an image of peace, but it's mostly lip service. *Barefoot Gen*, for example, a powerful and moving manga series about a child who survived the bombing of Hiroshima, has been nixed from the local peace curriculum because it casts the Japanese government in a critical light. Much was also made of the G7 being held in Hiroshima recently, though Abiko says it was more about the politics of peace than its practical application. But she believes Hiroshima should always stand as a cautionary tale, and that peace – the most utopian of human ideals – is still worth striving for.

So did Tamiki Hara. A Hiroshima-born poet and advocate for peace, he committed suicide in 1951 because President Truman was considering the use of nuclear weapons in the Korean War. One of his poems, like a pithy last will and testament, is inscribed on a footpath near the Atomic Bomb Dome:

Engraved in stone long ago
Lost in the shifting sand
In the midst of a crumbling world,
The vision of one flower

Hiroshima, 1945

WHERE WORLDS COLLIDED

◉ **NAGASAKI**

When you look at Nagasaki on a map, its surprisingly cosmopolitan history begins to make sense. It hangs off the coast of western Kyūshū, almost like it's trying to escape into the East China Sea, and is closer to the likes of Busan, Jeju and Shanghai than to the longstanding centre of power in Tokyo.

During the Age of Exploration, when the empires of western Europe were racing to colonise the East, Nagasaki was one of the first ports in 'the Japans' at which their ships would drop anchor. Jesuit priests did just that in the 16th century, turning Nagasaki into a secret Christian stronghold, evidenced by an unusually large collection of churches and cathedrals littered throughout the greater prefecture. Oura Church, the Basilica of the Twenty-Six Holy Martyrs of Japan – named in honour of those crucified at the behest of Toyotomi Hideyoshi in 1597 – is arguably the prettiest Christian building in the country.

But nothing quite encapsulates Nagasaki's unorthodox past like Dejima, a fan-shaped, artificial islet constructed off the coast in the 1630s, initially to intern Catholic missionaries from Portugal. Japan then introduced *sakoku*, a policy designed to eliminate foreign influence, banning colonial ships from entering Japanese harbours and banishing the remaining Portuguese interlopers.

Dejima was then designated as a trading port for the Dutch East India Company and would remain so for the next 200 years, a fascinating slice of history beautifully realised in David Mitchell's novel *The Thousand Autumns of Jacob de Zoet*. Japan was still fiercely isolationist and treated the Dutch with much trepidation, but the Tokugawa Shogunate spotted an opportunity. It enlisted the Protestant Dutch in its crusade against the Portuguese Catholics and permitted the trade of Japanese camphor, porcelain, lacquerware, silver and rice in exchange for sugar, silk, cotton, *materia medica*, animal skins and Western science. The last of these was perhaps the most important: the word *rangaku*, from *orandagaku* ('Dutch studies'), referred to the entire body of Western technical knowledge theretofore unknown in Japan.

Dejima still exists, bound on three sides by reclaimed land. On crossing over the wooden footbridge, one steps into a world not dissimilar to that which housed the clerks, merchants, doctors, scholars, shipwrights and servants of the Dutch East India Company. The wood-framed buildings on the 15,000 sq m (161,459 sq ft) patch of land have been reconstructed from old maps and drawings, each one filled

with illuminating exhibits, artworks and period artefacts.

The Christmas banquet exhibit in the Chief Factor's Residence is perhaps the most illuminating of all. Though the Dutch were on Dejima for a long time, most of them never enjoyed it, nor were they really that welcome. With Christianity outlawed, Christmas had to be celebrated under the guise of Dutch Winter Solstice, a time during which company employees got festively drunk and deeply homesick and dreamed of the god they'd left behind.

Where Dejima would stand out in most Japanese cities, it fits quite comfortably in Nagasaki, a city with Japan's oldest Chinatown, church spires jutting above a modern skyline, a terraced garden built by a Scottish merchant and shippoku cuisine, a shared meal sometimes mixing Japanese, Chinese and Dutch elements. It's the city of warakan, of 'mixed cultures', as locals like to say. And once, in the not-so-distant past, it was Japan's lone window to the world.

Top **The incredible Oura Church**
Bottom **Nagasaki, overhead**

"Spirituality has also played a key role in Japan's artistic development, seeping into the core of almost every discipline."

ART & CULTURE

WHO ARE THE AINU? JAPAN'S LOST PEOPLE

⊙ HOKKAIDO

It's telling that in the seven years since I moved to Japan, I've heard the word 'Ainu' mentioned in public discourse only a handful of times.

'Simply put, it's because Japan succeeded with assimilation,' says Kanako Uzawa, an Ainu scholar, artist and rights advocate. 'The government is willing to support anything related to Ainu culture and language, but they don't pay much attention to indigenous rights.'

The Ainu are a minority ethnic group who once thrived in the northernmost reaches of Japan. Archaeological evidence suggests their descendants were nomadic peoples who came to Hokkaido via a land bridge from Siberia more than 20,000 years ago. A common Ainu culture then emerged around the 12th or 13th century, but it wasn't until the Edo period, when Japan wanted to monopolise trade in the north and exploit Ainu resources, that tensions began to arise.

The Ainu were formally acknowledged as an indigenous people of Japan in 2008, which was seen as a watershed moment for a country that prides itself on homogeneity. But advocates argue the next step is more important: being granted rights to land, fishing, hunting, resources, socioeconomic development and political representation.

Recent research has suggested there are up to 10,000 Ainu living in and around Tokyo and more than 13,000 in Hokkaido. But this is mostly guesswork. 'How to define Ainu is difficult because we're all mixed,' says Uzawa. 'Self-identification is very important.'

Uzawa was raised in Tokyo (where she was reluctant to speak about her Ainu heritage) and often travelled back to her family in Nibutani, Hokkaido, where 80 per cent of the population are considered Ainu. So, identity has been central to her work in academia – she has researched Ainu culture and indigeneity – and as a multimedia artist. Uzawa creates performance pieces: playing Ainu instruments, like a mukkuri (a stringed flute), or choreographing dances that explore humanity's innate relationship to the natural world.

'I do it to develop who I am and to strengthen my Ainu identity. But I also want to challenge what Ainu art is,' she says. 'I want my art to highlight the discussion of indigenous rights, and to bridge academic and artistic discourse.'

Ainu history has its cultural hallmarks: bear woodcarvings, thatching techniques and a tradition of face tattooing. But Uzawa says it's much broader than that.

'The culture consists of language, food, traditional knowledge of vegetation – people still go to the mountains to gather plants – and performing arts,' she continues. 'There is an

"Ainu boom" right now; many people are going to Hokkaido to learn about Ainu culture. Maybe this can be a positive thing.'

In 2021, Uzawa established *Ainu Today,* a knowledge-sharing platform to disseminate Ainu culture through scholarship, advocacy and art. It raises such questions as, 'What does it mean to be Ainu in the 21st century?' So I pose this to Uzawa.

'A sustainable way of living was part of Ainu culture ... Contact with that may teach us valuable lessons that are different from the ones we grew up with,' she says. 'But one should also be free to express oneself. And as a public speaker, I have to convey the right information, that culture is not a static thing. It should be innovative and creative and expressed in different forms.'

🜂 ainutoday.com

WHERE TO LEARN MORE ABOUT AINU CULTURE

✳ Akanko Ainu Kotan In Ainu culture, the number six is important: it has its own numerical value but can also be interpreted as meaning 'many' or 'lots'. At the Akanko Ainu Kotan, an Ainu settlement on the shores of Lake Akan in eastern Hokkaido, Ainu culture is disseminated through six traditional ways of life: interacting, making, eating, inheriting, unleashing and living with nature. Inside the settlement's timber and thatched-roof buildings are craft shops whose artisanal wares reflect the animistic beliefs of the people, theatres and galleries exploring Ainu life and indigeneity and restaurants serving Ainu cuisine. ⊙ **akanainu.jp**

✳ Upopoy – National Ainu Museum and Park With the numbers of Ainu-language speakers and craftspeople dwindling, Upopoy (from the word meaning 'singing together in a large group') aims to promote, revitalise and expand the reach of Ainu culture. The museum has a permanent exhibition featuring six key themes from an Ainu perspective – language, universe, lives, history, work and exchange – as well as a special exhibition room and a 96-seat theatre for short films. The open-air park adjacent to the museum reflects the connection between Ainu culture and the natural world through crafts, architecture, the Path to the Ainu Spirit walkway, an outdoor performance area and several species of flora prized by the Ainu for their ceremonial or practical usages. ⊙ **ainu-upopoy.jp/en**

✳ Nibutani This district of Biratori Town overlooking the Saru River was once called Pipaushi, meaning 'a place rich in shells' in the Ainu language. Today, Nibutani is the settlement with the largest percentage of Ainu residents in Japan, and as such, it has preserved many hallmarks of Ainu culture. At the Nibutani Kotan, artisans demonstrate carving and embroidery techniques in the renovated cise (thatched-roof dwellings). The Nibutani Ainu Culture Museum is also here, charting the history of Ainu settlers in the Saru River basin through four distinct zones: Ainu Zone (Ainu Way of Life), Kamuy Zone (Dramas of the Gods), Mosir Zone (Blessings of the Earth) and the Morew Zone (A Tradition of Figurative Art). ⊙ **biratori-ainu-culture.com/en/ trip/nibutani-kotan**

✳ Sapporo Pirka Kotan As the capital city of Hokkaido, and the gateway to the island for most visitors, Sapporo provides the most accessible introduction to Ainu culture. The Ainu Culture Promotion Centre, also known as the Sapporo Pirka Kotan, is a tactile version of the Ainu museum experience, with 300 exhibition items, including handicrafts, weaving and cooking tools and clothing made from bark fibres, which visitors can hold and inspect. ⊙ **www.city.sapporo.jp/shimin/pirka-kotan**

✳ Hokkaido Museum The Hokkaido Museum, fringing the Nopporo Forest Park in the Sapporo outskirts, takes a bird's-eye-view approach to exploring the nature, history and culture of Japan's northernmost island. One of the permanent exhibitions looks at the development of Ainu culture in Hokkaido, as well as on Sakhalin and the Kuril Islands in the Sea of Okhotsk, and the eventual clashing of social and cultural mores when Japan appropriated the Ainu and their land into its growing empire in the late 19th century. ⊙ **www.hm.pref.hokkaido.lg.jp/en**

THE BLOSSOMING OF JAPANESE ARTS AND CULTURE

◉ **AROUND JAPAN**

The Edo period (1603–1868) was a time of profound change in Japan. The Sengoku, or Warring States, era had come to an end after 150 years of near-constant bloodshed. Tokugawa Ieyasu had slain his final challenger at the Battle of Sekigahara and united Japan under the rule of the Tokugawa Shogunate. With no enemies to thwart and no real reason to embark on resource-depleting conquests, he laid down his sword and Japan entered a sustained era of peace. As a result, arts and culture flourished.

Merchants and prosperous city dwellers bought elaborate byobu (multipanelled screens) and festooned their walls with kakejiku (hanging scroll paintings). Fuelled by a growing thirst for tourism, ukiyo-e artists flooded the market with woodblock prints depicting scenes of natural beauty. Teahouses proliferated throughout the country, where geisha versed in the arts of conversation and music entertained sake-soaked elites. As their swords grew blunt, the samurai engaged in cultural pursuits and decorated their manors with high-class ceramics, purchasing wares from Arita in the south and Kyoto in the west. It was a great time for storytellers, too: Noh, kabuki (both forms of stylised theatre) and bunraku (puppet theatre) performers regaled audiences with Japanese folktales and epic accounts of battles past.

It was also the era of Sakoku. A national policy established to quell the spread of Christianity and monopolise trade, it enforced limited contact with the outside world. While the seafaring empires of Europe were hellbent on colonising the east, Sakoku equated to a door firmly shut. With little outside interference – save for Dutch and Chinese traders in Nagasaki – the arts evolved in isolation. This is partly why the arts of this period are considered so singular today: look at a painting of a makeup-clad kabuki actor, a neatly stitched kimono embroidered with cranes and wagasa umbrellas or an origami frog and immediately you know from where these items hail.

But nothing remains permanent. Traditional Japanese arts make up a much smaller share of the market today, and are often confined to museums, exhibitions or rural craft heartlands, such as Kyoto by the Sea (*see* p. 208), that provide pottery, lacquerware and ornamentation to hotels and restaurants. When we think of Japanese art in the 21st century, it's probably the polka-dotted sculptures of Yayoi Kusama, the video games of Nintendo and Square Enix, the animated masterpieces of Studio Ghibli or the novels of Haruki Murakami.

That's not to say that tradition holds no sway or influence. After all, would there be such a thing as anime and manga without kabuki? Could the Gutai Group, teamLab or other experimental collectives have existed without dyed-in-the-wool conventions to push back against? Would Hiromi Kawakami or Banana Yoshimoto have even become novelists without an appreciation of traditional Japanese aesthetics and literary ideals?

Spirituality has also played a key role in Japan's artistic development, seeping into the core of almost every discipline. Whether it's the polytheistic animist beliefs of Shinto or the more formalised doctrines of Buddhism, we see spirituality's signature everywhere – in the concept of the soul in Japanese literature, in the ever-present odes to nature in kakejiku paintings and in the minimalist designs that have defined the work of artisans for centuries.

THE ART ISLANDS: AN ORIGIN STORY

◉ OKAYAMA, KAGAWA

The Seto Inland Sea makes a good first impression. Perhaps you'll first see it from the port of Takamatsu, or maybe you'll be waiting for a ferry in Onomichi. If you're lucky it'll be at sunrise or sunset, when pastel colours merge and settle on the horizon and the mountainous islands appear as silhouettes rising from the water.

Donald Richie must have experienced a similar hit of adrenaline when he visited in the 1960s because only an enraptured author could have penned a book like *The Inland Sea*, a love letter to the region that remains a seminal travelogue more than half a century later.

Richie travelled throughout this archipelago strewn across a lake-like body of water between Honshū, Shikoku and Kyūshū, believing the Japanese were the last people who stood in reverence of the natural world.

But the book was also a eulogy: he was convinced the Seto Inland Sea marked an endpoint for old Japan. He wanted to observe what people were like when they had time and space, believing it was one of the final opportunities.

His words proved prophetic. Technological upheavals and improved transport networks encouraged a brain drain to Japan's major cities. Now, you're as likely to find ghost villages, abandoned schools and municipal buildings reclaimed by nature as you are fishing and farming communities living off the fruits of the land.

There is an element of paradise lost. All it took was a philanthropic billionaire with a lofty ambition to find it again.

When publishing magnate Soichiro Fukutake first travelled to the Seto Inland Sea in the 1980s, he was shocked by what he found. The islands were rapidly ageing and had become sites of industry, with refineries built on Naoshima and Inujima and illegal waste dumped on Teshima. He wanted to rejuvenate the region and knew there was only one way to do it: through contemporary art.

But Fukutake needed a collaborator. So he joined forces with Tadao Ando, an architect whose style is likened to haiku poetry, where nothingness and empty spaces are the essence of meaning.

Ando's inaugural project was the Benesse House Museum, named after Fukutake's firm. Overlooking a bay on Naoshima, the museum-cum-hotel combines its solid concrete foundations with large apertures gazing towards the Inland Sea and outdoor artworks by the likes of Yayoi Kusama, Shinro Ohtake and Hiroshi Sugimoto. Icons of the global art world, from Andy Warhol and Walter de Maria to David Hockney and Jean-Michel Basquiat, feature elsewhere in the compound.

With the museum's opening in 1992, Naoshima became the first of Japan's art islands. But Fukutake's vision grew; he wanted to create an artistic utopia as an antidote to the 'monstrous cities' found throughout Japan. There are now 12 designated art islands and two ports that feature in the Setouchi Triennale, a once-every-three-years festival that invites artists from across the world to pay homage to the history of the Seto Inland Sea. It's not a fly-by-night process, either. Many of the most immersive and thought-provoking exhibitions are given a permanent place on their host island.

It all harkens back to one of the late-Richie's original sentiments: that there are still people who don't want to eradicate the natural world. Fukutake and his collaborators have successfully adapted themselves to it. They have offered themselves to it and have even come to terms with it.

🧭 setouchi-artfest.jp/en

Top and bottom **Unique and interactive sculptures are found throughout the islands**

FIVE ART ISLANDS TO VISIT

* **Naoshima** Home to the art islands' origin story and most of the region's museums, Naoshima has become a towering force in Japan's contemporary art scene. Even for well-established artists, getting a piece in the Benesse House Museum, the Chichu Art Museum or the Art House Project – which takes place across several akiya (abandoned homes) – is considered a massive coup. Naoshima is also one of the few islands with a range of high-quality accommodation options.

* **Teshima** Teshima is Naoshima's larger, if less-heralded, neighbour. Artworks are dotted across the gently rolling landscape near the coastline, but it's the Teshima Art Museum that attracts most of the footfall. Combining the creative visions of artist Rei Naito and architect Ryue Nishizawa, the museum sits at the corner of a rice terrace and was designed to look like a water droplet at the moment it strikes the ground. Oval openings in the structure's concrete shell allow the sights, sounds and smells of the natural world to infiltrate the viewing space, emphasising the seamless connection between architecture and environment.

* **Megijima** Of all the popular stories in Japanese folklore – and there is no shortage – the journey of Momotaro, the 'Peach Boy', is perhaps the most retold. It's a classic underdog tale with a dash of Eastern mysticism, following Momotaro, who joins forces with a dog, a monkey and a pheasant, to defeat a band of malevolent ogres living on a nearby island. People now believe that island to be Megijima, thanks to a cave with interconnected chambers – the Ogres' Lair – on its highest peak. Visitors often make a trek through the mountaintop caverns their first port of call. But there are some great artworks in the coastal village, too, like Shinro Ohtake's MECON, an abandoned school revitalised with vibrant pops of colour and tropical flora, or Island Theatre Megi, a disused warehouse converted into an old Manhattan-style picture house.

* **Ogijima** The confluence of art and reinvention feels particularly strong on Ogijima. A small island with a village clinging to the hillsides, artists use old and disused homes as blank canvases for their work. Often these works focus on distortion or shifting perspectives, like Akinorium, a house full of self-propelling 'sound objects' that throw moving shadows across the room, or the Room Inside of the Room, in which every wall, object and ornament has been turned 90 degrees.

* **Oshima** At a glance, nothing on Oshima looks amiss. The squat, grey buildings may be a little ugly, but the densely wooded hills or the hazy outline of distant islands are much more likely to grab your attention. This is, however, the paradox of Oshima: the prepossessing natural beauty belies its troubled past. It was once an island leprosarium, where people suffering from leprosy were interned under Japan's since-disbanded leprosy prevention laws. The Setouchi Triennale introduces contemporary artworks that tell the story of the leprosarium's inhabitants. Under less empathetic stewardship, it could have become an exercise in dark tourist voyeurism, but of all the feelings the art on Oshima evokes, the most enduring is hope.

Top **Memory bottles on Ogijima**
Bottom **Ogijima art installation**
Opposite **Even the stairs offer interesting optics, Naoshima Island**

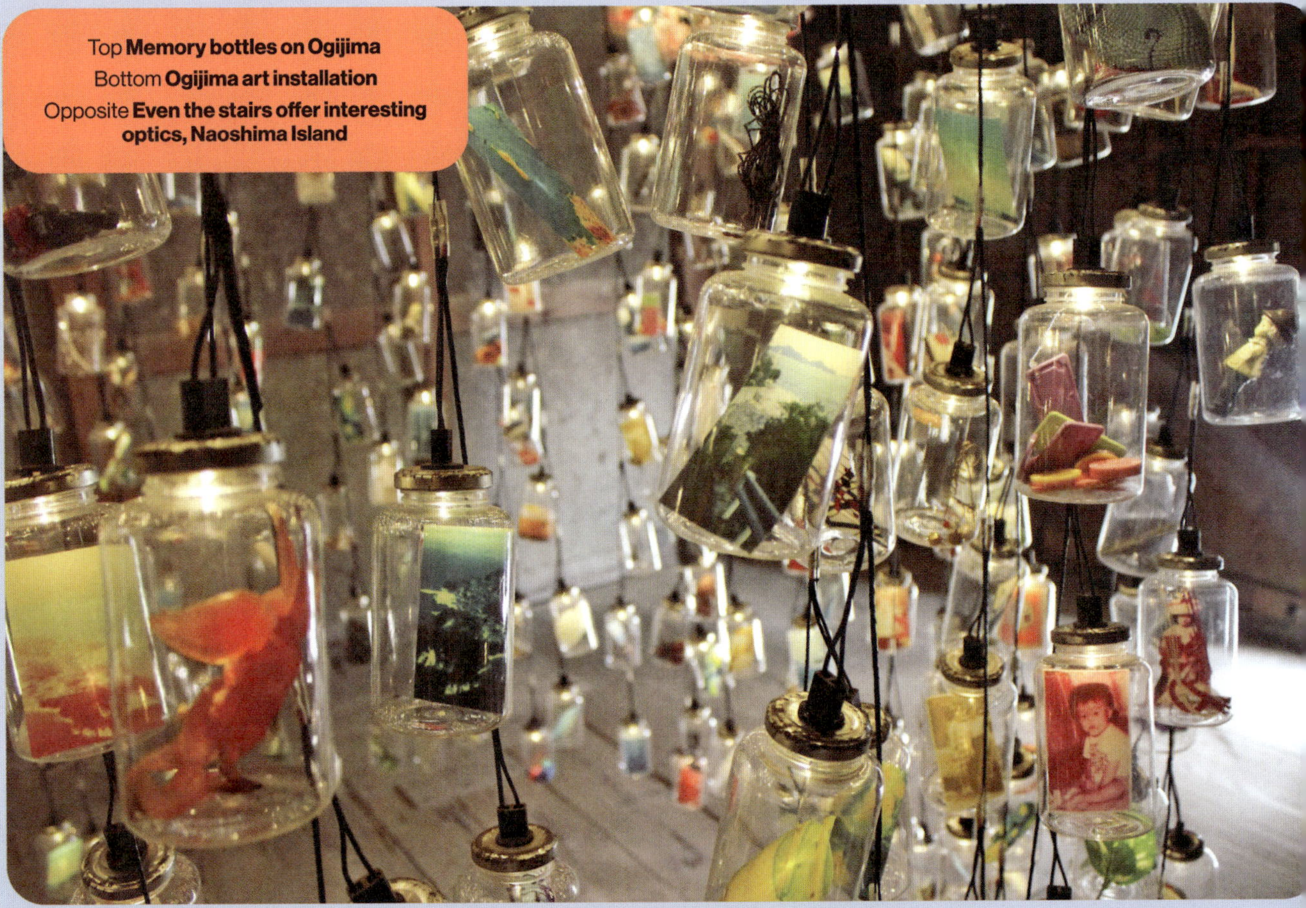

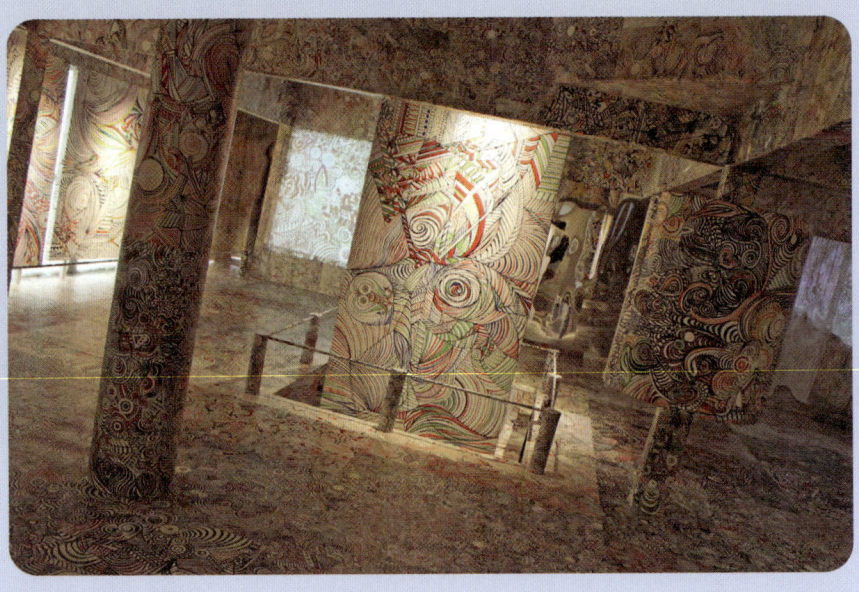

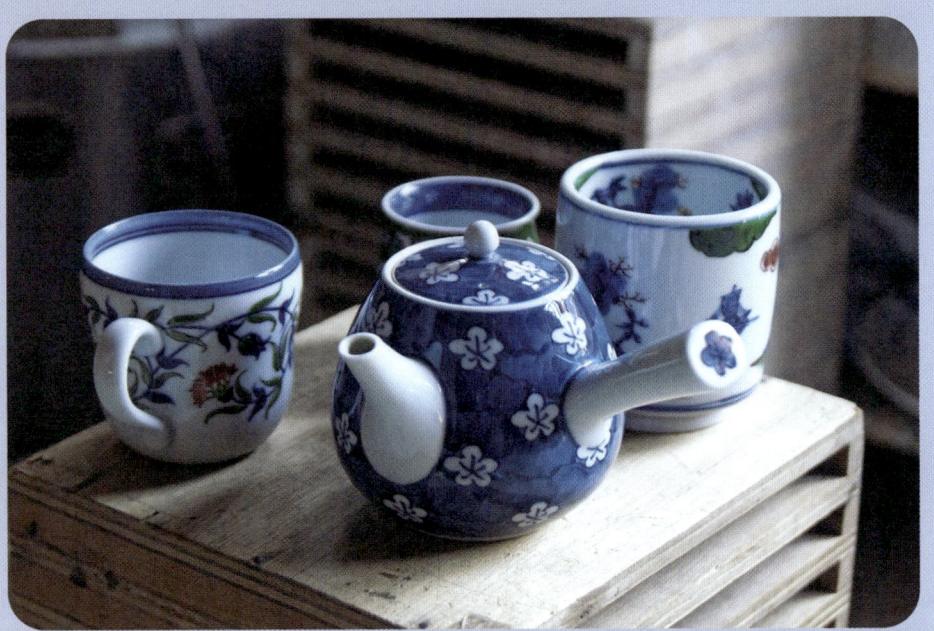

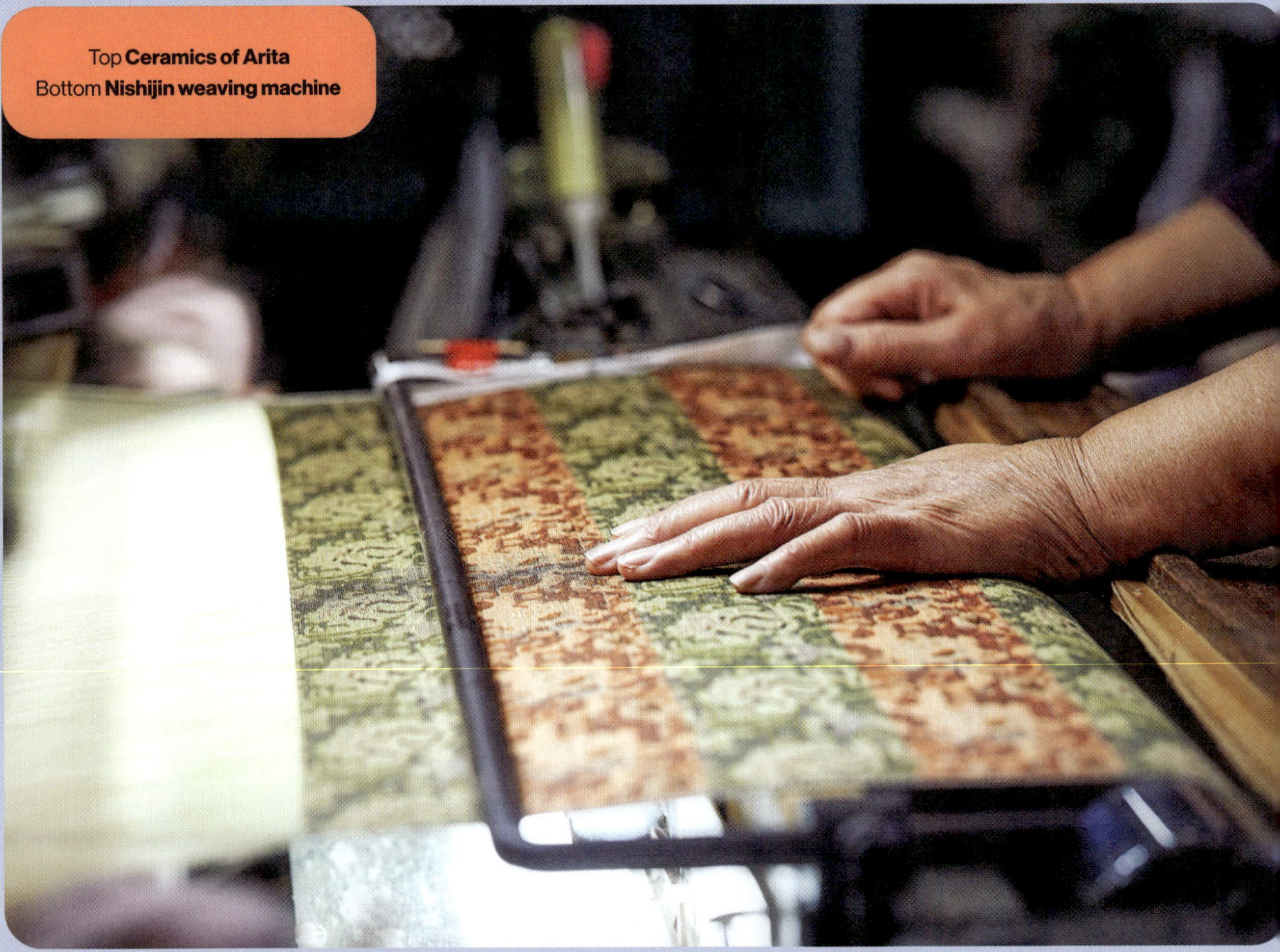

Top **Ceramics of Arita**
Bottom **Nishijin weaving machine**

KOGEI: TRADITIONAL CRAFTS OF JAPAN

◎ AROUND JAPAN

Crafting is inseparable from Japanese culture; for centuries it was the lifeblood of the body politic. Some forms, like ceramics and lacquering, have been around since the Jomon era (14,000 to 300 BCE) when the Japanese archipelago was home to disparate tribes of hunter-gatherers. Artistic influences then filtered in from Eurasia, more crafts were introduced by Chinese imperial delegates in the Middle Ages and others were developed during the Edo period.

Today, nearly every town, city and prefecture in the country has a strong tradition in at least one craft form. There are also more than 240 kogei – officially designated traditional crafts – which are assigned based on five key criteria:
1. The object produced must be made for everyday use
2. It must be handmade
3. The artisan must use traditional techniques that are more than 100 years old
4. They must use raw materials
5. The production process must take place in a designated region of Japan

Kogei comprise a vast range of artistic disciplines today: the Nishijin brocading techniques of Kyoto; the woodcarving tradition in Inami, Toyama Prefecture; the Kawanabe Butsudan altars of Kagoshima; and the prized ceramics of Arita in Saga.

In Japan, it is not just the quality of the crafts, but the sheer dedication of the artisans. Many approach it not as a vocation, but as a calling; to be an artisan is to find one's ikigai, one's reason for being.

THE ARTISANS OF KYOTO BY THE SEA

◉ KYOTO

It's the tail end of winter and a curtain of rain hangs over the mountains of northern Kyoto Prefecture. At Miyazu Bay, the sea and sky are watery shades of blue-grey and the wood-framed buildings hunched by the coast are dripping like a wrung-out cloth. I slide open the door of one nestled by the shoreline. A faint warmth comes from a kettle on the stovetop. The room has all the ordered chaos of a workshop: a haphazard stock of mallets, looms and baskets of fibres; and scarves, obi belts, coasters and tote bags hanging from every surface and fixture.

Hiroko Sakane greets me, one of the wisteria weavers of the Kyoto by the Sea region, and the last living in Kamiseya village, the only place where fuji-ori (wisteria weaving) has been passed down to the current generation. Though Sakane worked in the textile industry in her youth, she only took up fuji-ori when her husband died suddenly 17 years ago. She was warned it would be a long and labour-intensive journey, but she felt a deep, ancestral pull towards the craft.

'Back in the Jomon period, any place you had wisteria, people were likely doing wisteria weaving,' Sakane says. 'But with the industrialisation of cotton and silk innovation, most textile producers shifted to those materials.'

In Kamiseya, and the nearby mountain villages, the weather was too cold and the people too impoverished to raise silkworms, so the craftspeople continued using wisteria – and were it not for their persistence, the ancient techniques may have died out. But since the Wisteria Weaving Preservation Society was established in 1989, fuji-ori has witnessed a revival.

'The artisans are still mostly women,' says Sakane of the society's 130-plus members. 'But people from other weaving industries are also transitioning into wisteria because they have the right knowledge base.'

Still, she's nervous about the future of fuji-ori, unsure if it's viable as a way of life in the modern world. It's strange to think as I admire the handiwork in one of her intricately woven,

Top **Tamiya Raden**
Bottom **Fuji-ori (wisteria weaving)**

barley-coloured scarves, trying to fathom how it began its life as a bundle of rough and unappealing fibres.

'Wisteria weaving is so personal. We go into the mountains ourselves and select the wisteria,' Sakane says. 'I don't want to betray the mountain. So, when I'm making the thread and weaving the wisteria, it's always with respect to where it came from ... The final product should be like holding a mirror to yourself.'

Fuji-ori is one of several heritage crafts in the north of Kyoto staring into an uncertain future. The ethereal beauty of Gunze silk, washi papermakers preserving 800-year-old techniques and urushi (lacquerware) artisans using some of the finest tree sap in the country – all have seen precipitous declines in the post-industrial era.

It's a trend swordsmiths understand all too well. Tomoki Kuromoto, Kosuke Yamazoe and Tomoyuki Miyagi, all in their thirties, started Nippon Genshosha because they realised the sword-making industry needed a fresh outlook. Each had grown up watching samurai films and jidaigeki (period dramas) – where swords fly from scabbards at the slightest indiscretion – so it was a lifelong ambition fulfilled when they built a smithing forge in a vacant house in rural Kyoto.

When I visit Nippon Genshosha's soot-stained workshop, Kuromoto and Miyagi are fashioning a blade. It is an act of nonverbal communication: Kuromoto sets the rhythm by tapping on the anvil; Miyagi does the heavy lifting, shaping the steel with wallops of his sledgehammer. Miyagi entreats me to have a go, and I do my best to beat the living bejesus out of the red-hot metal, amazed that an act of brute force can – with better technique – create an object of such uncompromising beauty.

'Sword-making techniques have remained pretty much unchanged over time,' Miyagi tells me. But modern blacksmiths need a licence to craft swords in Japan, so the number of practitioners is dropping each year. 'Maybe 200 people have the licence, but there are only around 100 that are still making swords.'

Admittedly, the market for swords has dwindled. The samurai class was abolished in 1871, the Japanese Self Defense Force has little use for melee weapons and collectors are mostly interested in period swords and ancient hamon (blade patterns).

The Nippon Genshosha blacksmiths are bridging the gap between craft and art by presenting swords in eye-catching and experimental ways, like casting high-quality katana in blocks of resin. They've also started a YouTube channel with high-production-value videos in a bid to reach new audiences.

'For a thousand years, swords were made as weapons,' says Miyagi. 'We're still making traditional swords that could function as weapons. But always present in our consciousness is that what we are making are works of art.'

It's art for art's sake, perhaps. But that's an approach their neighbours, the silk-weaving experts at Tamiya Raden might sympathise with. Their journey started in 1977, when textile artisan Katsuichiro Tamiya wondered if the polychromatic mother-of-pearl shells found along the Kyoto coastline could be woven into chirimen silk. An audacious hypothesis, but one that he verified after two years of trial and error. Kyoji Tamiya, Katsuichiro's son and the current owner of the business, is continuing his father's pioneering techniques, inspired by the hikibaku method, whereby gold or silver leaf is pasted onto thin strips of washi paper then woven into fabric.

When I walk through the door of Tamiya Raden's studio, Kyoji's wife, who is introduced as Tamiya-san, shows me into a display room. It's faintly illuminated, allowing the shimmering, iridescent kimono centrepiece to engulf the space. Embroidered with phoenixes and mandala-like flower patterns, the whole fabric of the robe appears in motion, as though reflecting its origins in the sea.

Like a philistine, my first thought is, what would this cost? Millions of dollars, I'm assured. But how does someone look at hard, brittle shells and envision this kimono?

'Kyoji's antenna is always tuned,' Tamiya-san says. 'He's always getting ideas and inspirations from different places. That's actually what takes the most time, thinking about how all these things come together.'

Tamiya Raden, unsurprisingly, has made a splash in international artistic circles, including an appearance at Paris Fashion Week and collaborations with watchmaker Harry Winston and sound company Bang & Olufsen. But when I ask Tamiya-san what the future of mother-of-pearl weaving looks like, she leaves me wondering.

'There are not many people who know this technique,' she says. 'In fact, only Kyoji knows the entire process.'

It feels unjust that such a bewitching artform – that any of these artforms – might have an expiry date. But then again, this is a culture that so often finds beauty in impermanence.

'Even cherry blossoms fall,' wrote the poet Yosa Buson, 'and the branches soon forget their bloom.'

🌐 kyotobythesea.com

🌐 gensho.jpn.com/index_en.html

🌐 fujiori.jp/fuji_en.html

🌐 tamiyaraden.com

Nippon Genshosha

Top and bottom **Blacksmiths at work at Takefu Knife Village**

THE KNIFE MAKERS OF TAKEFU VILLAGE

⊙ FUKUI

If you were to wander into Takefu Knife Village at midnight on New Year's Eve, you'd be greeted by the clink of hammer on red-hot steel, the puff and wheeze of a pair of bellows and sparks dancing in the inky night air. Three designated men, kitted out in white robes and lacquered headdresses, would be performing the year's first forging, a sacred rite in a region whose history of smithing goes back to the year 1337.

Japan is famous for its steel. For centuries, the katana, wakizashi and tanto swords used by samurai were the pinnacle of blade craftsmanship. These techniques have since migrated into the culinary realm, where Japanese artisans forge kitchen knives, meat cleavers and filleting tools prized by chefs across the world.

In Takefu Knife Village, set within a valley of rice paddies in central Fukui Prefecture, some of the country's most venerated blacksmiths ply their trade. The open-to-the-public workshop brings together 13 different knife companies and more than 40 artisans, one of the greatest concentrations of knife makers in the country. Some producers, like double-bevel specialist Anryu Knives or single-edge blade maker Kitaoka Knives, have been in the business for several generations.

Knives produced in the village are used in Michelin-star kitchens and line the shelves on culinary shopping streets, like Tokyo's Kappabashi Dori. There's also a direct shop in the village, stocking a range of knives with arresting hamon (blade patterns) and decorative handles.

🕸 takefu-knifevillage.jp

THE MARSH OF GOLD: TRADITIONAL CRAFTS IN KANAZAWA

◉ ISHIKAWA

Kanazawa is a city of great distinction. A former Buddhist fiefdom, colloquially known as the Peasant Kingdom, it underwent a significant transition in the late 16th century when it fell under the control of the Maeda clan, one of the Edo period's most powerful feudal lineages.

They transformed it into a city of grand samurai manors and scholastic achievement, with neighbourhood divisions, gardens and plazas and an intricate water system. Kanazawa became a repository of fine art and craftsmanship, partly due to the clan's glamorous warrior culture. No longer embroiled in conflict, the samurai embellished their homes and armour with kinpaku (gold leaf), increasing the demand for gold leaf products and attracting kinpaku artisans from across the country.

Kanazawa retains many of these pre-industrial cultural hallmarks: its well-preserved samurai district, refurbished wooden teahouses and pillared Noh stages and a *kinpaku* industry that produces 99 per cent of Japan's gold leaf.

While gold leaf might be a source of civic pride – it's even referenced in the city's name, which means 'Marsh of Gold' – there are 22 designated kogei (traditional crafts; *see* p. 207) in Kanazawa, more than in any other city in Japan. For hundreds of years Kanazawa's artisans have produced lacquerware for jewellery boxes, kitchen utensils and tea caddies. Some found success in dying silk kimono with the kaga-yuzen technique – characterised by its use of five basic colours: indigo, crimson, ochre, dark green and purple – or creating fishing flies, folk toys or butsudan altars. Others became masters in porcelain, embroidery, decorative metal inlaying or futamata paper crafting.

Kanazawa crafts are admired for their advanced techniques and their ability to thrive despite the changing needs of modern society. But they are also bound by something more abstract: a 'Kaga' style, which takes its name from the former domain comprising Kanazawa. This quality, which somehow connects artforms as different as pottery and paper making, combines the opulence of Maeda clan tastes with the subdued spiritual flavour of Buddhism.

When strolling around Kanazawa – recommended when a lateral rain isn't sweeping in from the Sea of Japan coast – you see signs of the city's craftsmanship everywhere: in the old castle grounds, in the grand 17th-century garden of Kenrokuen and

Kanazawa, Higashi Chaya

in the Higashi Chaya geisha district. Even chic modern restaurants, like Coil, which combines temakizushi (hand-rolled sushi) with a self-serve tea ceremony, or the Plat Home bistro, display utensils, ornaments and crockery that speak to the region's artisanal heritage.

Museums have proliferated throughout Kanazawa, too, like the Japan National Crafts Museum – the only national museum dedicated to Japan's kogei tradition – the Ishikawa Prefectural History Museum, the Kaga-Yuzen Kimono Centre and the Yasue Gold Leaf Museum. But there is one that far surpasses them in terms of cultural significance and clout.

The D.T. Suzuki Museum, named after an influential Buddhist philosopher and one of

Kanazawa's favourite sons, was created to summarise his voluminous writings and provide a contemplative space that would invite self-reflection. It also hints at how Zen influenced – and was perhaps inextricable from – the crafting culture of the region.

Suzuki believed technical knowledge was not enough. 'One must transcend techniques,' he wrote, 'so that the art becomes an artless art, growing out of the unconscious.'

- www.momat.go.jp/craft-museum/en
- coil-japan.jp
- plathome2530.wixsite.com/plat-home
- kanazawa-museum.jp/daisetz

LAFCADIO HEARN'S GHOSTLY MATSUE

◉ SHIMANE

I'm never quite sure if Lafcadio Hearn's life was more remarkable or unlikely. Born in 1850 to a Greek mother and Irish father on an island in the Ionian Sea, he was abandoned by both parents by age seven. He was then foisted upon a pious great-aunt in Ireland until age 13, sent to a boarding school in England where he lost sight in one eye during a playground accident and after the family estate dried up, found himself alone and penniless on the other side of the Atlantic. Yet somehow he managed to have one of the most inspired – and criminally underappreciated – literary careers of the late 20th century.

As a muckraking journalist and obsessive crime reporter, an intrepid traveller and cultural ethnographer, he chronicled life in the margins, whether it was drinking with emancipated slaves in Cincinnati, learning the harbour-front songs of sailors and stevedores in New Orleans, recording Creole proverbs and recipes or living with the islanders of Martinique. He arrived in Japan aged 40 and moved to Matsue, a small castle town in the interior. In many ways, it was the paradise he'd always longed for, and though Hearn would only live there for 13 months, neither his heart nor his legacy would ever leave.

His time in Matsue was one of keen observation, informing works like the acclaimed *Glimpses of Unfamiliar Japan* (1894). But it was his fascination with the gruesome that really buttressed his Matsue legend. Scarred by the abandonments of his youth, and the ghosts, creatures and mysterious entities that haunted his dreams, he found a Stockholm-syndrome-like solace in the kaidan (stories of strange or supernatural origin) and folktales rooted in the region. 'The ghostly,' he believed, 'represents always some shadow of the truth.'

'Hearn did not simply collect local folktales and present them as they were, but rather infused them with a literary soul and retold them, weaving them into short works of literature,' says Bon Koizumi, Lafcadio Hearn's great-grandson. As a child, Koizumi, who is also an honorary professor and folklorist at the University of Shimane and director of the Lafcadio Hearn Memorial Museum, had little interest in his ancestor's work. But he later found himself drawn to these stories, acknowledging their power to transcend literary and cultural boundaries.

'Hearn was not Western-centric, Christocentric or anthropocentric, but rather open-minded and unprejudiced in his approach to his subjects,' says Koizumi. 'Hearn's thought connects people with people; people with different cultures, people with nature, the dead with the living, and tells us the importance of symbiosis.'

Matsue's northern quarter, where Hearn lived with his wife Setsu Koizumi, is one of the most charming stretches of urban Japan, with its bottle-green moat and yakatabune (pleasure boat) cruises, its flocks of herons swooping from treetop to treetop and its crescent-shaped bridges and former samurai residences fronted by coped-tile walls and overhanging pines. The Lafcadio Hearn Memorial Museum and Lafcadio Hearn Former Residence sit on the traditional Shiomi Nawate St – fitting for tributes to a man who detested Japan's Western assimilation. A Matsue Ghost Tour, a two-hour walk to locations that inspired his tales, narrated by a local storyteller, has also been developed in Hearn's honour.

'Hearn's masterpiece, *Kwaidan*, was written 120 years ago in his study in Tokyo,' says Koizumi. 'But it was in Matsue that Hearn learned of the existence of yokai (ghosts), such as Yuki Onna and Rokurokubi, that appear in the book. The abundance of ghost stories is a sign of the strong awe that the people of [Matsue] have for nature and the other world.'

Top **A statue memorialises Lafcadio Hearn in Matsue**

Bottom **The gardens of Lafcadio Hearn's former home**

THE LAST GAIJIN BOOKSHOP

◉ TOKYO

There's a good chance you'll have heard of Asakusa. People flock to this historic district in northern Tokyo to see Sensoji Temple, strut around the streets in period attire or travel in the back of a hand-drawn rickshaw. But seldom do they cross the river and pass through the looking glass, into a rough-hewn, antiquarian, wood-furnished world that is a hub of literary culture yet fiercely unpretentious.

There's a familiarity to Infinity Books. The mingled scent of air freshener and musty paper. The names and titles on fraying spines that remind us of stories we'll never forget. The collection of instruments that are played every weekend but look like they've not been touched in years. The gruff Yorkshireman, Nick Ward, cocooned by his novels and PC monitors in the corner.

I round the counter and take a seat beside him. He pours me a pint, reminds me this isn't a bar and starts me on a tab, as usual. We've told each other our stories many times, often accompanied by ice-cold shots of Jagermeister, each rendition inflected and coloured in a new way.

'When I was young, I was surrounded by books,' he says. Nick's mother used to edit uncorrected proofs for a publisher, which attracted an eclectic cast of characters to his council house in Harrogate. 'And that's when I realised that books might be important.'

Nick spent his youth frequenting the pub and the library in equal measure. While both proved formative, it was in the latter he found windows into worlds beyond North Yorkshire and a repository of knowledge he thought inaccessible.

'Even after that, I always used to collect books and have books all over the shelves in my house,' Nick says. 'It was like a security blanket; I always felt safe surrounded by books, even if I hadn't read them.'

When, decades later, Nick opened Infinity Books, the digital era was already underway, brick-and-mortar bookshops were on unfirm ground and the market for secondhand English bookshops in Japan – never the most futureproof to begin with – was more precarious still.

But he survived by diversifying: teaching English, running live music events (where his old pub licence comes in handy), selling new books by Japanese authors in translation or old books online through third-party retail sites. Other independent English-language bookshops in Tokyo have pulled down

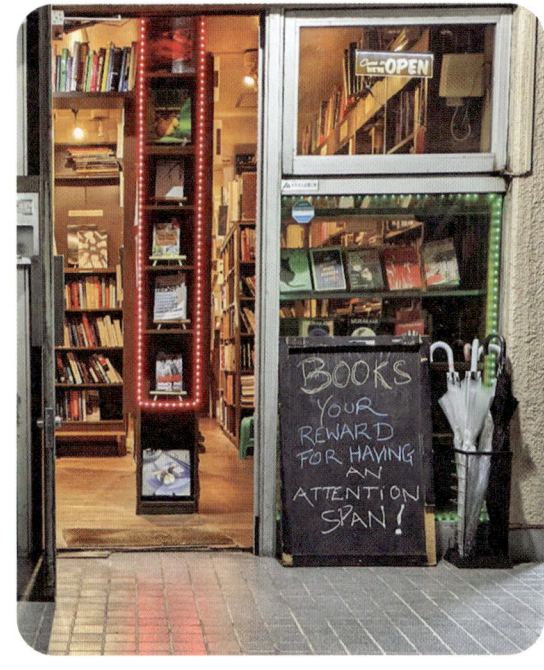

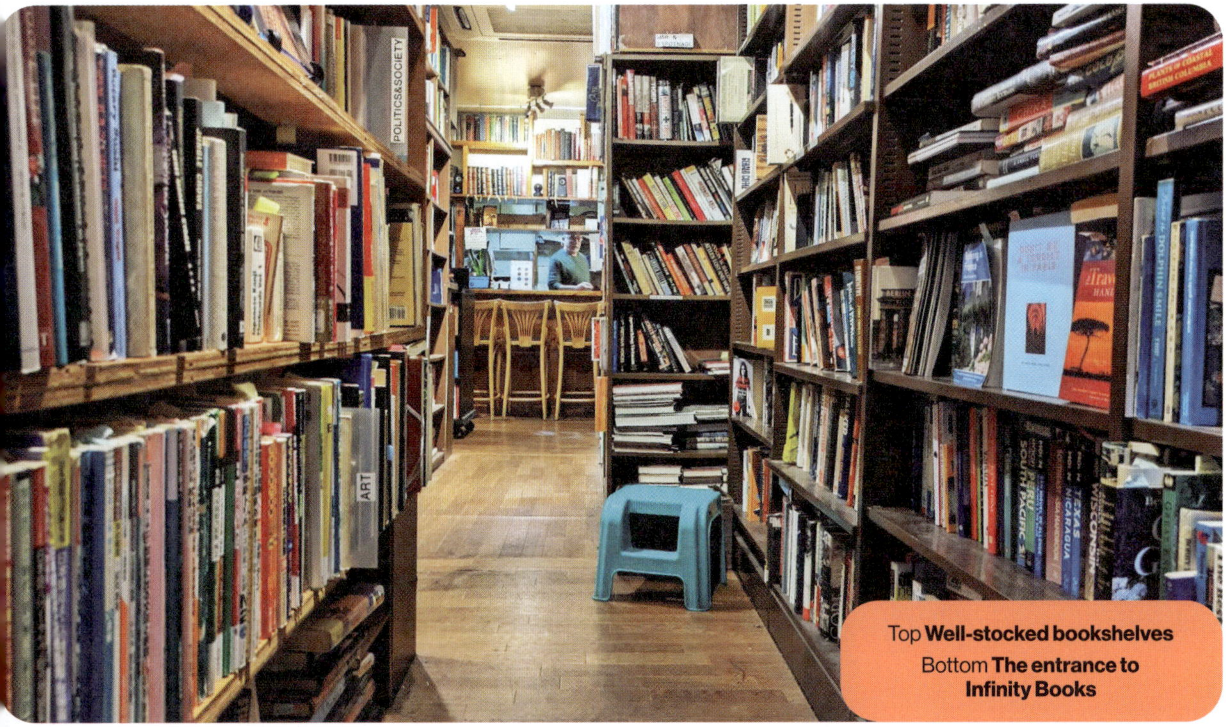

Top **Well-stocked bookshelves**
Bottom **The entrance to Infinity Books**

their shutters, while Infinity Books has just celebrated its 10th year.

'I get imposter syndrome; it's like I don't really own the place. The books own the place; they're the ones that bring the atmosphere,' he says. 'And just think of the *time*, and the number of people that have touched and read these books. There's a resonance from that; you can feel it.'

Nick always says you have to be crazy to run an independent bookshop these days. But there is method to the madness.

'Without wanting to sound cliche, I think bookshops are the soul of every town, of every city,' he says. 'It's the soul of a past tradition and it will never die. You can't kill it off completely.'

infinitybooksjapan.com

EXPLORING THE VANISHING WORLD OF JAPANESE JAZZ KISSA

◉ TOKYO

When I arrive at Eigakan, a jazz kissa in northern Tokyo, it's as though I'm surveying the room through grainy 35mm film. A sepia-coloured speaker system engulfs one end of the room, like a musical shrine projecting its instrumental sermon to the few in attendance. The walls, yellowed by decades of tobacco smoke, are covered in movie posters and vintage record covers. The shelves are stacked with old camera equipment and thousands of vinyl LPs. The clutter is accumulative; not the sort of mess one could make overnight.

I spot James Catchpole, a writer and podcaster also known as Mr Ok Jazz, sitting at a table nursing a bottle of Guinness. I take a seat, order one too. Catchpole has been documenting Japanese jazz kissa for the past two decades, and recently contributed an essay to a photobook by Northern Irish photographer Philip Arneill, called 'Tokyo Jazz Joints', named after their audiovisual archive project begun in 2015, for which they visited hundreds of kissa throughout the country.

'In Japan, a city the size of Milwaukee or Cleveland could have six jazz kissa,' he says, his voice competing with the clamour of a saxophone solo. 'Being in these places reminds me that this country loves jazz more than any other country in the world. It's not even close.'

That doesn't mean kissa culture is in rude health. Jazz kissa, coming from the word kissaten (cafe), are cafe-bar-listening spaces, which rose to prominence in the 1950s and 1960s when Japan was in a period of social upheaval. Liberal students, who opposed the ruling elite, found kinship in jazz, a musical genre bound to the spirit of revolution, and frequented cafes where they could listen to imported records by Thelonious Monk or Art Blakey, Miles Davis and John Coltrane. They'd sit and smoke cigarettes, drink cups of coffee or maybe a few beers and plan the next protest or riot, never considering that these halcyon days were numbered.

Tokyo, the epicentre of jazz in Japan, has lost about 100 kissa since the 1970s as neighbourhoods have gentrified and ageing proprietors have struggled to find successors. Catchpole hopes that documenting them can stem the tide of decline.

'There was no concept of opening these places with a profit motive. The Masters (owners) did it because they loved the music and they just wanted to hang out and drink,' he says. 'It was their declaration that they were leaving Japanese society; they weren't going to be salarymen; they were entering the night world. There are consequences to that, but there's also a lot of freedom.'

Catchpole found a spiritual home in jazz *kissa*, too 'because these guys love music the way I love music. And they're doing it the way I've always wanted to.'

Yoshida-san, the owner of Eigakan, has set his sights on retirement, meaning this kissa once voted the best in the country might soon be playing its final track. But Catchpole is intent on giving it a second life, and is using funds raised through a Kickstarter campaign to preserve the record collection and speaker system. There's even talk of reopening Eigakan in a new location, with Catchpole

and his business partner, DJ Hiroko Otsuka, as the custodians.

'When I bring people to jazz *kissa*, they're like, "What is this world?"' says Catchpole. 'They're blown away by the passion, the love, the knowledge ... The music is a big part of that. But really, it's about the culture. And that's what I want Eigakan to continue to be: part of the community.'

🔗 tokyojazzjoints.com

🔗 tokyojazzsite.com

Eigakan, Tokyo

CATCHPOLE'S JAZZ KISSA RECOMMENDATIONS

Catchpole has been to hundreds of jazz kissa and has found that each has its own distinct charm and aura, dictated by its location, the personality of the Master, the style of jazz favoured and even the luminaries who have drunk or left signed memorabilia there. But generally, port towns, because they were closer to outside influence, have greater concentrations of these establishments.

* **Yokohama** Catchpole says Yokohama, the city he calls home (though it's effectively an extension of the Tokyo urban sprawl), has 'a lengthy history of jazz cafes and live clubs.' He's a big fan of Downbeat, a dark and smoky jazz bar that's been in operation since the 1950s, and Minton House, a popular haunt for jazz musicians near the city's Chinatown district. The riverside Noge area is home to more great jazz spots, including Jazz Spot Dolphy and Noge Junk.

* **Kobe** Catchpole likes the international vibe of Kobe and notes that it's home to some of the oldest remaining kissa in the Kansai area. 'Java, Mokuba's Tavern and Jam Jam are three wonderful jazz kissa,' he says, 'all with very distinct and unique atmospheres that really capture the magic of kissa culture.'

* **Kochi** It's frequently noted that people in Kochi enjoy a night out. They obviously enjoy their jazz, too, with quirky spots like Cafe Creole in the heart of the city. But for Catchpole, Mokuba, hiding down a gloomy alleyway, is 'awesome – a classic – and it's the oldest one in Shikoku.'

Top **Karaoke is hugely popular in Japan**

Bottom **The signature neon sign of a Karaoke Kan location**

KARAOKE CULTURE JAPAN

◉ **AROUND JAPAN**

There's something symbolic about deciding to miss your last train home. It's usually done while working your way through a stiff drink, glancing furtively at your watch. You know you'll be entering No Man's Land, stranded in an alcohol-fuelled purgatory till the birds remember how to sing. Most of the bars and izakaya will be closing, all morality and decorum begins to disappear, even the shelves in the convenience stores look somehow forlorn. But this is when the karaoke parlours come alive.

In the 1960s, Japan gave the world karaoke, literally meaning 'empty orchestra', and it has grown into an indefatigable industry. No matter the chain of karaoke parlours – Karaoke Kan, Big Echo, Manekineko, JOYSOUND – the scenes are always familiar. The distant wails of off-key revellers filtering into the lobby and an officious receptionist waiting to direct you to your room. Perhaps there's a selection of costumes hanging from

a rack like a non-corporeal *danse macabre* or a weary staff member cleaning up vomit in room 401.

Karaoke in Japan is usually a private affair. Visitors are designated rooms with tablets for jukeboxes, two microphones (for nailing duets) and flatscreen TVs showing the lyrics. Nomihoudai (all you can drink) and tabehoudai (all you can eat) options are common – you can make orders from a corded telephone fixed to the wall – while closing times are almost unheard of.

Like a creature from some ancient myth, karaoke rooms feast on time. And when you tumble out and dawn has broken across the land, you're often given pause to wonder where all those hours went.

JAPAN'S MOST CINEMATIC KARAOKE EXPERIENCE

If you've seen *Lost in Translation*, Sofia Coppola's 2003 Oscar-winning film about two lost souls finding connection in the alien megalopolis of Tokyo, you'll likely remember the city standing alongside college grad Charlotte (Scarlett Johansson) and fading actor Bob Harris (Bill Murray) as the third principal character. From Shibuya's famous pedestrian crossing to the swanky New York Bar in Shinjuku's Park Hyatt hotel, the film is just as remembered for its excellent lead performances as for the distinct language and storytelling of its urban setting. One of the most beloved scenes sees Harris sing a raspy and plaintive rendition of 'More Than This' by Roxy Music in a gloomy Tokyo karaoke parlour. The actual karaoke rooms in which the scene was filmed, rooms 601 and 602 in the Shibuya Udagawacho Karaoke Kan, are still available for visitors to book. You can do this online or with the reception staff in the lobby.

🌐 karaokekan.jp/shop/detail/30

THE TRAJECTORY OF JAPANESE FASHION

⊙ AROUND JAPAN

There was much ado about Japan's changing fashion tastes in the post-Edo era. With the doors to the West finally open, the Japanese were shedding their jinbei, yukata and kimono for yofuku (Western clothing) – tailored suits, close-fitting bodices and variable hemlines – while the men lopped off their chomage topknots and grew moustaches.

Many commentators and influential writers, like Yukio Mishima and Junichiro Tanizaki, abhorred the trend toward Westernism; the latter's short story *Aguri* – the Japanese pronunciation of 'ugly' – about a man who becomes besotted with a pale woman in Western dress, was a not-so-subtle expression of his dissenting views.

By the time Japan's economy boomed in the latter half of the 20th century, and the postwar constitution had enshrined freedom and secularism in Japanese law, people were free to wear what they pleased – and now had the disposable incomes to attain the apparel they desired. Japanese fashion at this time was influenced by hippie culture, rock n' roll and the swinging sixties, which eventually segued into bodikon (body-conscious dress), hip-hop clothing, casual sportswear and shell suits.

But now we're seeing the reverse effect, with modern Japanese styles influencing global fashion culture. We see this through designers like Issey Miyake and Yohji Yamamoto, who combined artistic ideals like wabi-sabi with androgynous designs, or through the return of Japonisme – the use of Japanese motifs and artistic sensibilities in Western art and fashion – inspired by the works of Kenzo Takada and Hanae Mori.

Japan's fashion boom was born out of the fact that apparel is one of the true forms of personal expression in a society that values conformity and collectivism. The same people who wear identical suits Monday to Friday might look like they've strutted off the cover of *Vogue* or *GQ* come Saturday. This means the major fashion districts are doing a good trade.

Harajuku's Cat St, the Ura-Hara backstreets and the Omotesando boulevard, all rubbing shoulders in downtown Tokyo, are a showreel for the Japanese fashion world. There are shops selling vintage clothes, branches of major fashion houses like Louis Vuitton and Balenciaga, saccharine-looking stores specialising in kawaii fashion and streetwear haunts like Worm Tokyo, which stocks some of the rarest sneakers in the city. Tokyo is also a great place for thrifting – in Japan, where people tend to take care of old goods, slow fashion accounts for 20 per cent of the market – which attracts young hipsters to the warren of alleyways in Shimokitazawa, Kichijoji and Koenji.

Osakaites would argue their city has a fashion scene to match that of the capital's. Shinsaibashi is a magnet for subcultures and fans of streetwear – it's rare to walk through Triangle Park and not be greeted by skaters and young men in beanie hats, baggie jeans and pencil moustaches puffing on cigarettes. Amemura, the 'American Village', and Orange St are full of fashion boutiques, secondhand apparel shops and independent galleries. And the old lattice-fronted stores in Nakazakicho in the north of the city can be deceiving; they house some of the most in-vogue brands in global and domestic fashion.

'Fashion is not about following trends,' Issey Miyake once said. 'It is about creating your own style.' And that's what history has shown us: Japanese fashion, though varied and influenced, has developed into something distinct.

The famous Cat Street in Harajuku

Hiroko Takahashi's modern kimono

MODERNISING KIMONO WITH HIROKO TAKAHASHI

⊙ TOKYO

Hiroko Takahashi is a perfectionist. It's the first thing she tells me when we meet in her Tokyo art studio and concept store, an airy, glass-walled structure filled with greenery and the sound of birdsong. It's an auspicious trait, given her art is defined by the two most fundamental forms: finite circles and straight lines.

'If I don't have a perfect circle or a perfect line, I can't make it work,' she says. 'Even on my grade sheet in primary school, all my teachers said I wanted everything to be perfect ... I envied the kids who didn't care about the score.'

Takahashi sits in front of a row of mannequins, each one crafted in her likeness and wearing one of her two-tone, geometric robes. Under other circumstances, I might find this self-aggrandising. But I soon discover Takahashi is down to earth and a free and easy-going conversationalist.

She knew from a young age that she wanted to be a fashion designer. Her father was an artisanal plasterer, and her mother and grandmother were knitters and dressmakers, so the concept of monozukuri (making things) was part of family life.

The kimono, a garment now reserved for ceremonial occasions, eventually emerged

as an obvious candidate for her art. Takahashi often saw the women in her family wearing kimono, and by the time she was studying at the Tokyo University of Arts, she had discovered it was the root of all Japanese textile techniques. Kimono are stitched and folded from single, 12m (40ft) bolts of fabric, called tanmono, which also appealed to her waste-free sensibilities.

Takahashi's art has been exhibited in global fashion capitals, like London and Paris, but she believes kimono shouldn't only be consigned to museums. So, it was good news when her designs caught the eye of Adidas, leading to an unlikely collaboration. Called 'adidas x HIROCOLEDGE', it includes sneakers, sportswear, yukata (robes), happi (festival jackets) and jinbei (pyjamas) bearing Takahashi's trademark patterns and stamped with the Adidas logo.

'There are traditional things that are okay to change, and things that you shouldn't change,' Takahashi says. 'As long as you don't change the thing too much so that it becomes something else.'

She has managed to strike this fine balance. Her contrasting black-and-white colour schemes and hypnotic lines are decidedly modern – perhaps the geometry even has an art-deco lineage – but there's no mistaking the traditional crafting techniques she employs.

'I respect traditional kimono patterns, but they're not really my style. So, I created new ones,' she says. 'I also wanted to focus on the shape of the kimono, which is perfect, and I didn't want to use unnecessary patterns or colours. So I developed my own style using simple things, like lines and circles, grids, that don't really have meaning.'

That hasn't stopped people from ascribing meaning to her designs, and Takahashi, to a degree, has applied meaning to them, too, using the word *shinrabansho,* which loosely translates to 'the nature of all things.'

She laughs when I ask her about this. 'Precisely because the circles and lines mean nothing, then they can become *anything.*'

There's a half-finished canvas behind me. I assess it for a moment, trying to give it meaning. I think it looks like a mandala.

'It just looks like I need to finish it,' says Takahashi. 'I'm a perfectionist.'

🔊 takahashihiroko.jp

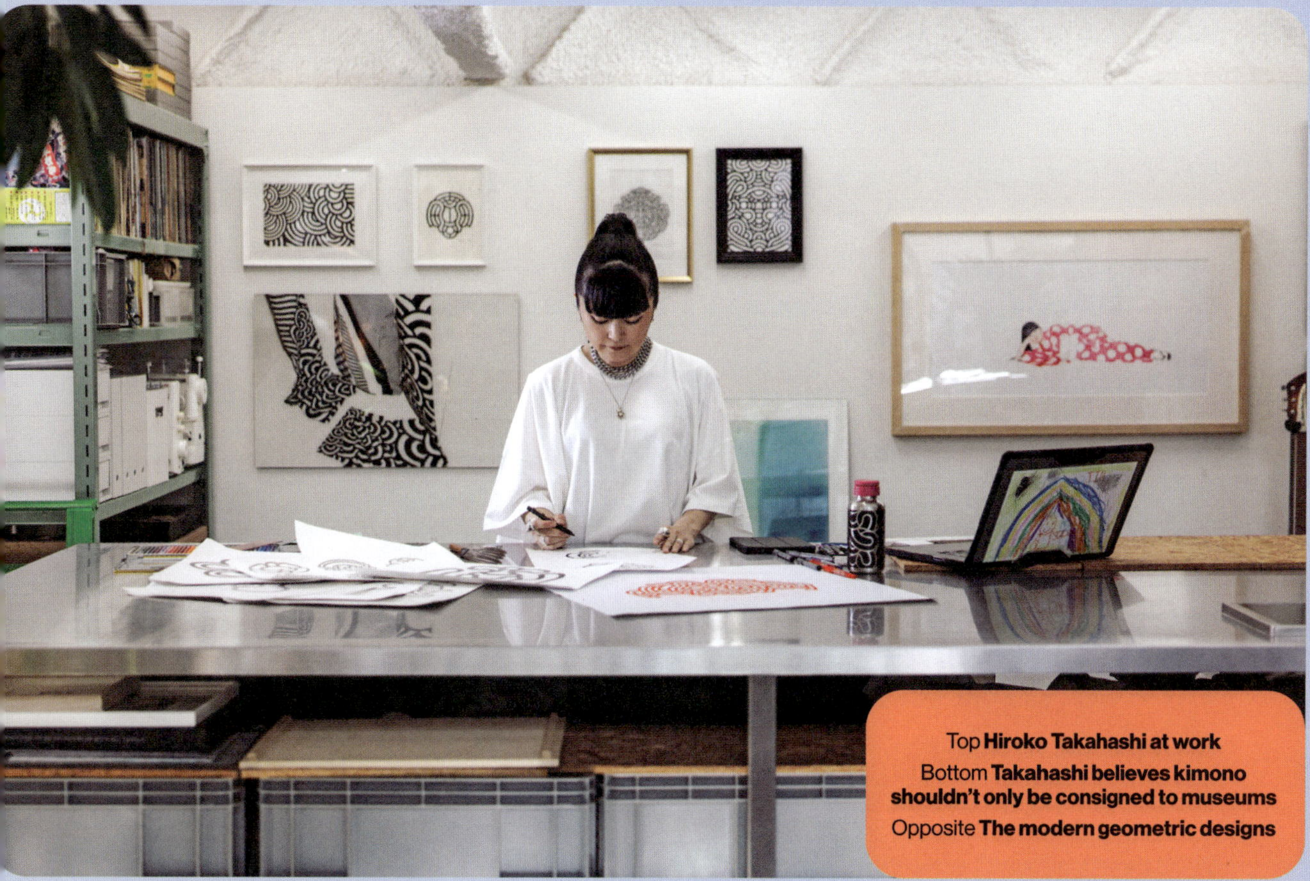

Top **Hiroko Takahashi at work**
Bottom **Takahashi believes kimono shouldn't only be consigned to museums**
Opposite **The modern geometric designs**

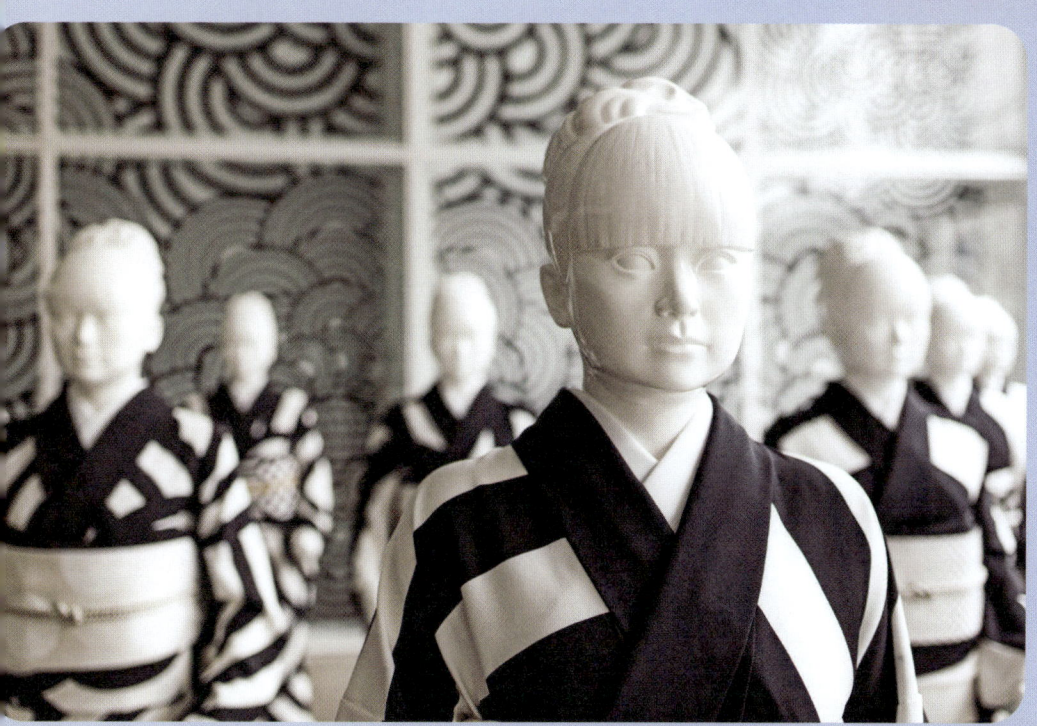

INSIDE TEAMLAB'S BORDERLESS WORLD WITH TOSHIYUKI INOKO

⊙ TOKYO

teamLab Borderless
in Tokyo

What makes a table a table? What constitutes a floor? What are the drawbacks of fixed-point perspectives? How can we harness the power of ultrasubjective spaces? If we dissolve the boundaries between an artwork and the viewer, can this alter our perceptions of reality?

I should have known from my recent visit to teamLab Borderless, arguably Japan's most in-vogue museum, that a conversation with the art collective's founder, Toshiyuki Inoko, would have been rife with phenomenological analysis. Still, my brain is bent in directions I hadn't foreseen.

Inoko thinks aloud, posing deep and probing questions and conjecting a series of answers during our lengthy conversation at teamLab's Tokyo HQ. But he's never evasive nor deliberately abstract. His background

in physics and mathematical engineering is combined with the vision and meandering mind of an artist, and it's clear he believes in the power of teamLab's art to change our relationship with the world.

'I'm genuinely interested in how humans perceive the world,' he says. 'What are humans in the first place? And can their perceptions be expanded?'

His art collective has certainly tried. TeamLab's Borderless museum, which recently moved to Tokyo's Azabudai district, was the most-visited museum by a single artist or group in 2019, the year after it opened. It's a museum without a map, a series of interconnected spaces populated by digital artworks that interact with both each other and the viewers. It might be flower creatures that scatter when you touch them, water patterns that change from ripples to swirling vortexes to crashing waves depending on where you find them or hordes of colourful butterflies that crumble like origami at the slightest contact. Walking around Borderless is a subconscious and circuitous experience; you are guided by instinct rather than any direction or purpose.

Though Borderless is often described as an 'immersive digital art museum', Inoko avoids such descriptors.

'It's not even that high-tech,' he laughs, emphasising that *experience* is at the core of his vision. 'If you're looking at a photo or video that's been captured with a lens, it fixes your perspective, narrows your focus. We've created a logical structure where your viewpoint isn't fixed, so it creates a state where your body exists within the moving image that you're looking at ... It's like when you're walking around in the forest and you're aware that you and the nature you're looking at are continuous.'

Inoko mentions 'the forest' on several occasions, which is perhaps unsurprising for a man who grew up in Tokushima, one of Japan's most rural prefectures. Venturing into the countryside in his youth clearly influenced the themes in teamLab's art.

'There was a primaeval forest behind my school,' he says. 'It was deep and dark; there were so many things growing in it to the point that sunlight didn't filter through. There were no flat surfaces, and all the roots were tangled and different types of grass grew on the trees. Each thing existed on its own, but they were also so tangled together that you couldn't perceive that they existed separately. The boundaries between them were ambiguous. This continuity is just how I saw the world.'

Even though teamLab styles itself as an 'international' collective, I tell Inoko that there's something inherently Japanese about all of this. The celebration of nature feels rooted in Shinto beliefs. The interconnectivity rings like the tenets of Buddhism. Walking through Borderless is akin to shinrin-yoku, the Japanese practice of 'forest bathing'.

I realise I'm monologuing, but Inoko just smiles. 'There probably was a strong subconscious influence,' he admits. 'But we don't think of it like that.'

Though teamLab was founded in Japan in 2001, it has exhibited its work in cities across the globe, from Beijing, Singapore and Taipei to Melbourne, New York and London. The collective also has a second permanent Tokyo space called teamLab Planets, which witnessed an equally meteoric rise to success (and recently set the Guinness World Record for the world's most visited museum dedicated to a single group in a 12-month period). Inoko pulls up a list of the 10 most-searched Google museums in 2023. Amid legendary European art museums like the Louvre in Paris, the British Museum, Amsterdam's Rijksmuseum and the Museo Nacional del Prado in Madrid sits teamLab Planets at number five.

Inoko laughs and suggests theories as to why teamLab has cemented itself in the cultural zeitgeist. I get lost in the threads as he talks about the Renaissance, the ideas of David Hockney, physical law, entropy and the invention of the lens. But one thing stands out.

'I'm interested in creating a cognitive revolution ... This transcends cultural background; it's universal to humans,' he says. 'Maybe that can lead to people seeing the world differently.'

🌐 teamlab.art

MORE ART MUSEUMS IN JAPAN

✱ **Mori Art Museum, Tokyo** Japan's most exciting, and certainly one of its most international, contemporary art museums. The focus here is on temporary exhibitions, from explorations of art's role in climate discourse to retrospectives on the Turner Prize or the works of Takashi Murakami. ⊘ **mori.art.museum/en**

✱ **Tokyo Teien Art Museum, Tokyo** It's a sign of Japan's fascination with Westernism in the post-Edo period that even members of the imperial household looked towards Europe for architectural inspiration. The Tokyo Metropolitan Teien Art Museum, a masterpiece in art-deco design, was built at the behest of Prince Asaka in the 1930s and was opened as a museum 40 years later. Bearing the artistic signatures of Rene Lalique and Henri Rapin, it combines French tapestries, Greek marble fireplaces, sliding doors with elaborate glass reliefs and exquisite geometrical design. The *teien*, or garden, fronting the museum feels more Japanese, with cherry blossoms, a wooden teahouse overlooking the pond and a collection of perception-distorting sculptures. ⊘ **www.teien-art-museum.ne.jp/en**

✱ **Enoura Observatory, Kanagawa** Photographer and artist Hiroshi Sugimoto created the Enoura Observatory to explore humanity's historic connection to art and the confluence where Japan's artistic disciplines meet. Set within the foothills of the Hakone mountains and looking towards the sprawling Sagami Bay seascape, the observatory's arches, tunnels and stages are designed to catch pools of light on the winter solstice. ⊘ **odawara-af.com/en**

✱ **Towada Art Centre, Aomori** When Kanchogai Ave, the main thoroughfare in Towada City, became desolate due to population decline, the local government looked to reinvigorate it through art. The Towada Art Centre opened on the avenue in 2008, combining an open-air museum of 16 pavilions, hosting eye-catching sculptures by Yayoi Kusama and Erwin Wurm, with a collection of gallery spaces featuring the works of Yoko Ono, Ron Mueck and Hans Op de Beeck. ⊘ **towadaartcenter.com/en**

✱ **Matsumoto City Museum of Art, Nagano** Yayoi Kusama, a pop art trailblazer and Japan's queen of polka dots, grew up in Matsumoto, and the city's namesake museum is an ode to her seven-decade career. From pointillist canvases to hypnotic pumpkins, the artworks are windows into the turmoiled mind of their visionary creator. ⊘ **matsumoto-artmuse.jp/en**

✱ **Sapporo Art Park, Hokkaido** The Sapporo Art Park, in a verdant forest south of the city, is a worthwhile diversion, but the sculpture garden, only open from April to November, is the real showstopper. The garden hosts 74 sculptures by 64 artists, highlighting the synchronicity between art and nature, and challenging the viewer's perception of where one ends and the other begins. ⊘ **artpark.or.jp/en/about**

✱ **Adachi Museum of Art, Shimane** The garden at the Adachi Museum of Art has been voted the most beautiful garden in Japan for more than 20 years in a row by *Sukiya Living* magazine, also known as the *Journal of Japanese Gardening*. Viewed from contemplative spaces within the museum, the garden employs *shakkei*, the use of natural scenery to enhance a composition, and was designed to appear, in the words of the museum's founder, like a 'living painting'. ⊘ **adachi-museum.or.jp/en**

AN OTAKU GUIDE TO THE CAPITAL

⊙ TOKYO

The word otaku, now part of the English lexicon, used to come with negative connotations. It was ascribed to anyone with a (supposedly unhealthy) passion for Japanese video games, manga, anime or 'geeky' pop culture. But modern otaku are often self-described, wearing the moniker as a badge of honour.

Gianni Simone ought to know a thing or two about geek culture in Tokyo. The author of *Tokyo Geek's Guide* and *Otaku Japan*, and a tour guide in the Japanese capital, Simone has dedicated untold hours to exploring otaku subcultures, which has often brought him to the city's big-hitting pop culture neighbourhoods: Akihabara, Ikebukuro and Nakano.

Akihabara is Tokyo's Electric Town, a district-sized Neverland for the otaku community, with towering arcade halls, multi-storey manga and anime memorabilia emporiums and shops chronologising the history of Japanese console gaming.

'Akihabara is stunning from a visual perspective, especially if you go at night with all the neon lights [along Chuo-dori Ave],' says Simone. 'Nakano has interesting shops, but almost everything is located inside a building, Nakano Broadway, which is a kind of otaku shopping mall. The main spot in Ikebukuro is called Otome (Maiden) Rd, and if you go there maybe 80 or 90 per cent of the customers are young girls.'

Many shops in Ikebukuro specialise in Boys Love manga (popular among young heterosexual women) and female cosplay outfits. If Akihabara is the otaku capital of the world, Simone reckons, then Ikebukuro is the female otaku capital of Japan.

This dispels one of the great otaku myths.

'There's always been this misconception that an otaku is a young, male nerd with poor social skills, who doesn't shower very often,' Simone says. 'But actually, the female fan contingent is huge. A lot of women – even older women – are into manga, anime, cosplay and games.'

Tokyo's manga scene provides fertile ground for the most obsessive foreign otaku because of the industry's traditional apathy towards translation.

'Until recently, the Japanese themselves didn't believe that Japanese pop culture would sell abroad,' Simone says. 'So it's still rare to find manga in English or translated into other foreign languages.'

Though popular titles – *Attack on Titan*, *Dragon Ball*, *Demon Slayer*, *Pokémon* – now have English-language editions, they are consigned to specialist foreign bookstores, like Kinokuniya Shinjuku South. But in recent years, there's been an uptick in young people

Bright lights in Akihabara

learning Japanese because they want to experience their favourite titles in the original language.

This is especially apparent for doujinshi (fanzines), a strange meta-genre that breaks every intellectual property law in the legislature. Die-hard fans will scour the shelves of K-Books in Ikebukuro or Comic ZIN Akihabara for graphic novels featuring a passionate romance between characters from two different franchises or a *Rosencrantz and Guildenstern Are Dead*–style story where bit-part characters from an epic saga become the protagonists in their own journey.

'Technically, it's illegal, of course, because of copyright infringement,' Simone says. 'But for the mainstream publishers, the doujinshi authors offer a sort of free publicity. And sometimes those indie authors are co-opted into the mainstream and offered contracts to work.'

The doujinshi scene is representative of Tokyo's otaku world: within each subculture, there are further subcultures, each with its own hunting grounds and a dedicated fandom that is far vaster than one can begin to imagine.

'If there's a city better than Tokyo for geeks, then I don't know it,' Simone says. 'In terms of both quality and quantity, you can't find another city like it.'

OTAKU NEIGHBOURHOOD WALKTHROUGH

◉ TOKYO

Many otaku stores are chains, and you'll find various branches in some neighbourhoods.

Akihabara

Yes, it's crowded, but Akihabara (affectionately known as Akiba) is the world's otaku heart.

Radio Kaikan is a good starting point, a nine-floor emporium near the station that serves as an introduction to Japanese pop culture, with a manga library, dolls, trading cards, toy sets and figurines. Animate is also worth a nosy, especially if you're up to date with the latest and trending graphic novels, while Comic ZIN and Mandarake are prime spots for dedicated doujinshi hunters.

Old-school Nintendo and SEGA fans will find immediate succour in Retro Game Camp, where the walls are lined with colourful gaming cartridges and the air is pervaded by 8-bit soundscapes. For console historians, Super Potato is a must, with heaving crowds of shoppers and immaculate and rare gaming machines crammed into the noodle-thin aisles. Retro Game Friends, a cheap mishmash of gaming nostalgia towards the northern end of the main strip, is a thrifty collector's dream.

The GiGO and Taito gaming companies host several arcades in the area, with claw machines, purikura photo booths and classic arcade franchises like *House of the Dead*,

Gundam and *Street Fighter*. But in terms of a sheer throwback to the halcyon days of coin-op gaming, nothing beats the Hirose Entertainment Yard (HEY), where you're just as likely to find salarymen playing space shooters on their lunch breaks as frantic teens breaking rhythm-game records in front of a captive audience.

Ikebukuro

Doujinshi and Boys Love (BL) fans often congregate in the manga megastores of Ikebukuro, and if you want to level up your own collection, this is where you should start – as an extra incentive, many graphic novels sold here also come with added merch, like postcards and illustration books. Women also tend to find that the female-heavy clientele in the Animate and K-Books stores on Otome Rd provides a more comfortable space when browsing for racier BL titles.

Ikebukuro has become a cosplay hub, too. If that's your thing, you might find the rare item you've been searching for in shops like K-Books Cosplay Pavilion, Lashinbang Character Palace, Assist Wig, Suruga-ya or Swallowtail. These establishments sell apparel, wigs, accessories and contact lenses to transform shoppers into their favourite anime heroines, which is perfect for Ikebukuro's annual Halloween Cosplay Festival.

Nakano

Conveniently, the otaku hotspots in Nakano are concentrated in the low-ceilinged, labyrinthine halls of Nakano Broadway. Stores scream at you with flashing lights, eccentric signage and gaudy window displays filled with manga titles, figurines, character plushies and vintage movie posters.

Apart from hosting a gaming arcade, the ground floor of Nakano Broadway acts like a ruse, concealing the legendary haul of otaku merch within the complex. Start your quest on the second floor; head to Mandarake UFO for cosplay items or the Galaxy store for secondhand video games. The third floor is all about manga and manga-related merchandise, while the fourth floor attracts collectors looking for retro action figures and geeky goods from the Showa period (1926 to 1989), when Ultraman was gracing fuzzy TV screens and robots like Golion and Dougram were all the rage.

Radio Kaikan

"When one stands on a viewpoint surveying Ogimachi village in Shirakawa-go in winter, the worlds of Hans Christian Anderson and the Brothers Grimm do come to mind"

ARCHITECTURE

DIFFERENCE BETWEEN TEMPLES AND SHRINES

⦿ AROUND JAPAN

A priest at Saikoji Temple on the Izu Peninsula once asked me if I knew the meaning of the word *baka*. 'Stupid,' I replied, hoping there was no further implication. 'Yes. But it can also mean smart. It depends on the context,' he said, as if that put an end to it. Abstractions like this illustrate an enduring truth: the divisions in Japanese religion – where one thing ends and another begins – are tricky to decipher.

Shinto, a form of polytheistic animism, has been around since at least the Jomon period (14,000-300 BCE). Adherents believe that divine *kami*, or spirits, reside in every object, creature and force in the world. It only became an established religion when it syncretised with Buddhism in the sixth century, a relationship known as shinbutsu-shugo, allowing Japan's ruling elite to appease indigenous beliefs while imbuing them with more formalised doctrine.

Japan may not be a religious country anymore, but the spiritual world is rarely beyond reach. People pay homage to nature's bounty by saying 'itadakimasu' at the beginning of a meal. They throw a few coins into the local shrine for prosperity and good luck on public holidays or in times of need. The national appreciation of cherry blossoms and autumn leaves feels like Shinto in its purest sense, while landscape gardening, shodo (calligraphy) and shinshin-toitsu-do (Japanese yoga) have their roots in Zen Buddhism. In fact, almost every cultural touchstone, from hiking and sumo to zazen meditation and ritual tea drinking, lives in harmony with Shinto and Buddhist tenets.

Because these religions share many of the same values, shrines and temples are often built within the same compound. It's a crude generalisation, but Shinto shrines are associated with life; people pray at them for good exam results, job promotions, fortune in a new business venture or rekindling the flame with the one that got away. Buddhist temples are more associated with death; their rituals deal with the nature of mortality and their clergymen perform the rites at funerals and memorial services.

At a glance, the architecture is similar, too. Shrines and temples are usually constructed with interlocking wooden beams, instead of nails and brackets, to protect them from rot or crumbling during an earthquake. They'll likely have sloping roofs with filigree and statuary and main halls enshrining a deity or Bodhisattva. But there are some telling differences.

Shrines are marked by torii gates and chozuya (water basins where visitors cleanse their hands and mouths before entering), and have thick shimenawa ropes and zig-zag *shide* streamers hanging from the main hall. Mossy rocks and fantastic trees also serve as objects of veneration in shrine grounds and are deemed as important as any of the constructions.

Temples, on the other hand, have large entrance gates and Zen gardens, perhaps a multi-storey pagoda in one corner and a belltower for calling monks to prayer in the other. Other symbols like lotus leaves, dharma wheels, mandalas and Nio statues guarding the entrance are common.

But really the differences count for little. As the saying goes, in Japan one is 'born Shinto, lives nonreligious, weds Christian and dies Buddhist'.

The peaceful Kongobuji

Shrines

Izumo Taisha, Shimane

When a shrine claims to be Japan's oldest – as several do – you'd be forgiven for thinking this was literal. Due to fires, redesigns and restoration efforts, most shrines and temples are reconstructions in a long line of faithful reconstructions. But it's believed that Izumo Taisha in Shimane Prefecture has been a site of worship for around 2000 years, and it was already deemed one of the most significant religious monuments in the country when the *Chronicles of Japan* were written in the eighth century. Izumo Taisha's Kagura Hall holds the largest shimenawa rope in Japan. Measuring 13.5m (44.3ft) and weighing almost five tonnes, it indicates the importance of the deity enshrined here, Okuninushi-no-Okami, who played a role in Japan's early development. All the Shinto deities are said to gather here during the 10th lunar month (usually around November). This time is known as Kamiarizuki, 'Month with the Gods', in Izumo, and Kannazuki, 'Month without the Gods', elsewhere in Japan.

Ise Jingu, Mie

Ise Jingu, also thought to be around 2000 years old, has earned the august nickname the 'Soul of Japan'. A complex of 125 shrines in Mie Prefecture, it honours the sun goddess and fabled ancestral deity of the imperial family, Amaterasu. Author Alex Kerr rightly observed in his book *Lost Japan* that this is a nation fascinated by secrets. The Naiku, or main inner shrine, which visitors are forbidden from entering, holds one of the three pieces of imperial regalia (the sacred mirror, yata

Rengejoin Temple

no kagami), which has been hidden there for so long no one can be sure if it exists. Still, people flock here in their millions every year.

Nikko Toshogu, Tochigi
Amid Nikko's sweep of lakes, waterfalls and forests sits Toshogu Shrine, a UNESCO World Heritage site and one of the final resting places of the great samurai Tokugawa Ieyasu – his remains were divided across multiple Toshogu shrines in Japan. The design here, featuring gold leaf and urushi tree lacquer, is unabashedly ornate. There's a five-storey pagoda indicating the five elements of existence – chi (earth), sui (water), ka (fire), fu (wind), ku (void) – in ascending order. The shogunate also summoned great carpenters from across the land to build the Yomeimon Gate and shrine halls, and they really threw paint all over the proverbial canvas. One of the subtler carvings, three monkeys hewn into the shinkyu (sacred stable), embodies the Japanese pictorial maxim, 'See no evil, speak no evil, hear no evil'.

Kumano Sanzan, Wakayama
Kumano Sanzan is the collective moniker for the three Grand Shrines of Kumano: Kumano Hongu Taisha, Kumano Nachi Taisha and Kumano Hayatama Taisha. Lying towards the southern end of Wakayama's Kii Peninsula, each shrine honours its own deities. But the shrines are often referred to as a trio, given their ancient links to the Shinto-Buddhism Unity Theory, purporting the Shinto kami to be manifestations of Buddha, and their association with one of Japan's most famous walking trails. You can reach all three by hiking the Nakahechi route on the Kumano Kodo, a pilgrimage site since the Heian period (794 to 1185) that achieved World Heritage status in 2004.

Temples
Zenkoji, Nagano
Strolling along the flagstone shopping street towards Zenkoji, a grand Buddhist edifice overlooking Nagano City, you can't help but notice the earthy-sweet smell of senko (incense) drifting from a brazier in the temple courtyard as the Sanmon Gate casts long shadows over you. Despite its size and reputation, Zenkoji is subdued, the colour of earth and wood, with little to suggest the oldest Buddhist statue in the country resides inside the main hall – though, of course, nobody is allowed to see it. Zenkoji has always been a bit of an enigma: it's run by two different sects of Buddhism, was one of the first major temples to permit women to worship and has a pitch-black tunnel that visitors traverse in search of the 'key to paradise', granting those who find it passage to the Pure Land.

Inamibetsuin Zuisenji
This temple in Inami, Toyama Prefecture, is particularly notable for its woodwork. Then again, it ought to be, given the area has been a woodworking stronghold for centuries – even today, there are around 200 artisans living in the town. The main temple hall, the fourth largest in Japan and marked by a steep, swooping roof that prevents snow from gathering in the winter, looks like a giant raptorial bird in flight. But the ranma, decorative panels carved into mythological scenes and intricate floral motifs, are what people come to see. One famous piece, known as the 'Wave and Dragon', depicts a seaborne dragon that supposedly came alive and saved the temple's main gate during a great fire in 1879.

Kongobuji, Wakayama

Koyasan is the home of Shingon Buddhism, one of the most esoteric religious sects in Japan, and it wears the weight of its history in every inch of raked gravel and pruned pine tree. With more than 100 temples and monasteries in the small mountain town, and Okunoin Cemetery, a sprawling complex of ancient tombs and cedar trees, there's no question this is a deeply spiritual place. The main temple in Koyasan, the North Star of Shingon Buddhism, is Kongobuji. It might not appear particularly special from the exterior. But inside is a series of rooms with sliding door paintings by some of the greatest Japanese artists of the past few centuries and a vast and dreamy karesansui, called the Garden of the Guardian Dragons, that far surpasses some of the more popular gardens in Kyoto.

Kosanji, Hiroshima

After spending some time in Japan – the exact amount needn't be long – you'll realise a lot of shrines and temples look pretty alike. Kosanji on Setoda Island is, in its own perverse way, a breath of fresh air. When Donald Richie first laid eyes on the bizarre fusion of European neoclassicism and Asian historical pastiche, he mused that it transcended its own triviality through size and intentions. Kosanji looks like an imaginative child was given carte blanche in *The Sims*: there are replicas of Japan's most impressive religious monuments, like Toshogu Shrine and Byodoin Temple, built using modern materials and techniques; a cave depicting the tortures of Buddhist hell; and the hilltop artwork, *Miraishin no Oka*, crafted from Italian marble and scattered with abstract sculptures.

AN ANCIENT CITY IN THE AGE OF OVERTOURISM

◉ **KYOTO**

I'd wager you're familiar with the depiction of Kyoto in popular media, a city whose atmosphere and beauty know no bounds. It's the nation's cultural capital, the home of geisha and kimono and tea ceremony, and was deemed such a treasure of the world that the Allies forwent razing it during World War II. As firebombs turned Tokyo to ash and atomic bombs obliterated Hiroshima and Nagasaki, Kyoto was left untouched. To attack Kyoto, believed US Secretary of War Henry L Stimson, would have been an assault on the culture of humanity itself.

Whether or not Kyoto remains beautiful is a matter of perception. It may have been spared during the war, but Japan's construction magnates have not necessarily extended the same courtesy. Take a look at Kyoto Station, a ghastly assemblage of steel and plate glass, and explain to me how this coheres with one of the world's great ancient cities. Or Kyoto Tower, another affront to the city's architectural tradition, rising phallus-like over its low-lying environs.

What you find amongst the ugly faux-futurism, though, is undeniably impressive. There are 17 UNESCO World Heritage Sites scattered throughout the city, standing in defiance to the state-sponsored vandalism, to pinch a phrase from writer Alan Booth,

going on all around them. And millions of tourists come to see them every month. Some temples, like Kiyomizu-dera and Ryoanji, whilst prepossessing in their own right, bear a weight of expectation that is often unmet due to the sheer volume of visitors. Is it possible to be contemplative in a Zen garden when surrounded by mobs chasing likes on Instagram? I'm not so sure.

But there are alternatives that, for reasons I've never been able to establish, attract considerably less footfall, like Byodoin, the Temple of the Phoenix, a 16-minute train ride from Kyoto Station. The main hall is a work of abstract impressionism, with two wings extending outwards and a tail in the aft, all constructed with vermillion-painted cypress wood.

Like magpies in a children's fable, people flock to Kinkakuji, a Buddhist temple covered in gold leaf that was reconstructed following an arson attack in 1950. Its sister temple, Ginkakuji, the Silver Pavilion, often plays second fiddle, even though it has one of the most tranquil Zen gardens in the city, a masterful exercise in composition, framing and perspective.

It's not just the World Heritage Sites bearing the brunt of overtourism. When you pass Inari Station, the closest stop to

Fushimi Inari, a shrine complex famous for its procession of thousands of torii gates, the entire train seems to decamp, a mass of flesh all funnelled into the same narrow walking route. Nanzenji, a sprawling acreage of temples and Zen gardens, is comparatively empty, and Heian Jingu, a palatial shrine and garden showcasing the pomp and opulence of the Heian period, is all but forgotten.

The problems that have beset Kyoto are part of becoming a popular tourist destination in the 21st century. But amid all the overtourism headlines, we'd do well to remember that this city can indeed still be beautiful. You just have to look in the right places.

Top **Heian Jingu**
Bottom **The busy streets of Kyoto**

Top **Inside Eiheiji**
Bottom **Eiheiji is a highlight of Fukui Prefecture**

EXPLORING SPIRITUAL EIHEIJI AND HEISANJI HAKUSAN

⦿ FUKUI

When I first saw Eiheiji, the Temple of Eternal Peace, in Fukui Prefecture, I was struck by two conflicting notions. First of all, I couldn't get over the scale of the place. It's huge – more than 70 buildings joined by shaded walkways – and I was unsurprised to hear it had been the headquarters of the Soto Zen sect since the monk Dogen founded it in 1244. But it is also reserved, deferring to its surroundings, even, hugging the contours of the mountains as though it had arisen naturally from the woods. Buddhist temples can, on occasion, be colourful and ostentatious, but they are at their best, most mystifying, when constructed like Eiheiji, where the size and scope exaggerates the minimalism.

If Eiheiji is the spiritual soul of Fukui, the eighth-century Heisanji Hakusan Shrine, a 40-minute drive to the east, is its quietly beating heart. Set deep within a forest of moss, where shards of sunlight are scattered by towering cedar trees, is a trifecta of small shrine buildings. The number three is important, representing the three peaks of Mount Hakusan and the Buddha triad, three key figures in Buddhist lore – a nod to the shrine's former life as a temple. Hakusan is no longer a popular site of pilgrimage, but some still make the journey here on the elusive promise that their wishes will be granted.

JAPAN'S WORLD HERITAGE THATCHED-ROOF VILLAGE

⊙ **GIFU**

As an adjective, the word 'fairytale' has rightly been demoted to cliche. Yet still, when one stands on a viewpoint surveying Ogimachi village in Shirakawa-go in winter, the worlds of Hans Christian Anderson and the Brothers Grimm do come to mind. Resting in the palm of conifer-swept mountains, all snowy thatched-roof houses huddled together, Shirakawa-go is undoubtedly one of the prettiest corners of Japan.

Thatching is used in various parts of the country – in Shikoku's Iya Valley, Kyoto's Miyama, Fukushima's Ouchijuku – but nowhere is it used on the same scale as in Shirakawa-go. The houses here, known as *gassho* (meaning 'praying hands,' in reference to their steepled shape), have been constructed in this way for more than 300 years, with pitched roofs that prevent snow from accumulating and cavernous interiors in which heat can rise and warm the entire structure.

The miscanthus grass fibres used for the *gassho* roofs are durable, but they do need rethatching every few decades. Rethatching is a community-wide effort, known locally as *yui*, and sometimes involves hundreds of villagers working in tandem. In May 2023, for example, 155 locals rethatched the 606 sq m (6523 sq ft) roof of Shirakawa-go's Myozenji Temple Folk Museum, an event that to the untrained eye would've looked more like a festival than a run-of-the-mill construction project.

The beauty of Shirakawa-go hasn't gone unnoticed. It was designated a UNESCO World Heritage Site in 1995 and in the subsequent years has grown into a popular tourist destination. The trick is now to find a balance between inbound visitors and the rhythm of local life. Because as the old Shirakawa-go saying goes, 'To live in the steep mountains is to live in Paradise on Earth.'

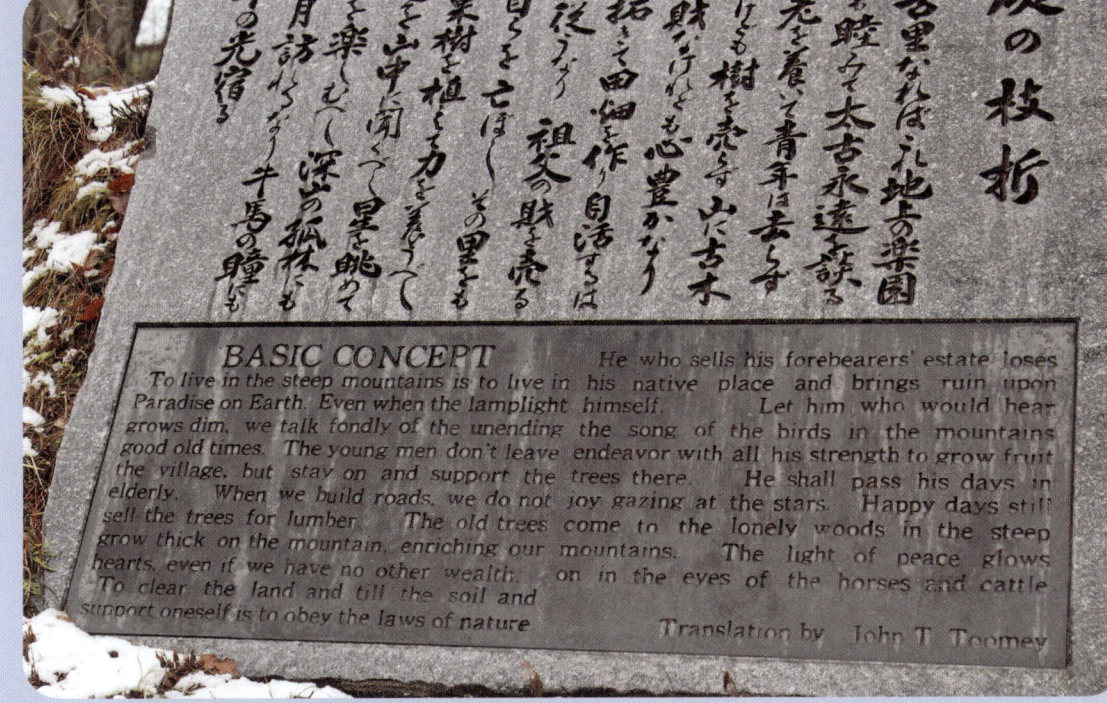

硯の枝拓

古里なれば、この地上の楽園

も睦みて太古永遠と詠ふ

光を養って青年は去らず

けても樹を売らず山ハ古木

賊けなども心豊かなり

拓きて田畑を作り自活するは

従ふなり　祖父の賊を売る

自らを亡ぼ～その里をも売る

果樹を植えて力を養って

巴と山中に開て星を眺めて

く楽むく深山の孤林にも

月訪ふるなず千馬の瞳にも

子の光宿る

BASIC CONCEPT

To live in the steep mountains is to live in Paradise on Earth. Even when the lamplight grows dim, we talk fondly of the unending good old times. The young men don't leave the village, but stay on and support the elderly. When we build roads, we do not sell the trees for lumber. The old trees grow thick on the mountain, enriching our hearts, even if we have no other wealth. To clear the land and till the soil and support oneself is to obey the laws of nature

He who sells his forebearers' estate loses his native place and brings ruin upon himself. Let him who would hear the song of the birds in the mountains endeavor with all his strength to grow fruit trees there. He shall pass his days in joy gazing at the stars. Happy days still come to the lonely woods in the steep mountains. The light of peace glows on in the eyes of the horses and cattle

Translation by John T Toomey

ALBERGO DIFFUSO: JAPAN'S PUSH FOR DIFFUSED HOTELS

⊙ **AROUND JAPAN**

The concept of *albergo diffuso*, or diffused hotels, found traction in Italy in the 1980s. The premise was quite simple: rather than build a new hotel, why not make the town itself the hotel? Does a hotel need to be concentrated within one structure, or can it be spread, *diffused,* across several old-world buildings to reinvigorate local economies?

The use case for Japan, a country where a third of the population lives in the Tokyo metropolitan area and rural populations have been declining precipitously since the 1950s, seems obvious. But it was a long-held fallacy that nobody – least of all the modern Japanese – wanted to stay in creaking old townhouses with sliding doors and tatami flooring. All it took was the government and hoteliers cottoning on to inbound visitors' fascination with traditional Japanese architecture, and soon they were turning abandoned homes and businesses into chic accommodations.

Asia's first 'official' diffused hotel was Yakage-ya Inn in Yakage, Okayama Prefecture. Yakage was once a post town on the Saigoku Kaido, a travel route between Kyoto and Shimonoseki during the Edo period. When Yakage-ya Inn opened in 2015,

breathing new life into the townscape, it provided a model for others to emulate.

Bed and Craft, a collection of six 'villas' scattered throughout Inami in Toyama Prefecture, is one of Japan's most creative examples of *albergo diffuso*. There are around 200 woodcarvers in town, and many more artisans of distinction, whose works are displayed in the renovated buildings. Tategu-ya and Kin-Naka are filled with dramatic woodwork and joinery. Tae is airy, a conduit for natural light, with commissioned lacquerware artworks on display throughout the villa. Mitu is warm and ornate, with huge cypress beams and bespoke ceramics. Tenne and Roku use the elements of nature, tree and stone, to celebrate Japanese garden aesthetics and blur the boundaries between interior and exterior.

Auberge Honmachi Mikuniminato is another interesting case. Mikuniminato straddles the mouth of the Kuzuryu River and was once a prosperous trading port welcoming kitamaebune ships carrying commodities and resources between Osaka and Hokkaido. Its Edo-period heyday is long behind it, but the introduction of a diffused hotel has given the town a much-needed

Yakage, Okayama

facelift. The hotel is spread throughout nine restored buildings and includes a French restaurant headed by Tateru Yoshino, a former disciple of Joel Robuchon. The rooms have modern comforts, like dining tables, beds and central heating, while keeping true to their roots, with traditional exteriors, cedar-wood bathtubs, Japanese landscape gardens and byobu (folding screens).

Author and Japanologist Alex Kerr has carried out a similar project on the island of Ojika. In the Kyoto by the Sea region, several residents are planning their own *albergo diffuso* in one of the sleepy seaside villages. Even in Tokyo and Kyoto, hoteliers have used similar methods to rejuvenate historic districts.

These are early days, but there is a bigger picture. Japan is one of the world's most aged nations; deaths have outnumbered births for more than a decade and some rural populations have literally vanished. If it's to reverse this decline, diffused hotels, and the locals embracing them, could play a quietly vital role.

Louis Vuitton building in Omotesando

THE GODS OF MODERN ARCHITECTURE IN OMOTESANDO

◎ **TOKYO**

It's two months out from the rainy season, but you wouldn't know it. The entire city is dripping and grey when I meet architecture guide Yuka Yoshida in Tokyo's Omotesando district. As raindrops ricochet off our transparent umbrellas, she reminds me that this area, now home to one of Tokyo's most glamorous shopping boulevards, was a train track running through arable farmland until 1915.

The government then ordered the construction of Meiji Shrine and its surrounding forest to deify the recently deceased emperor and empress. Omotesando, meaning 'front approach', became the main road to the shrine and over the subsequent decades, the architecture took on a stately air.

'There is a subtlety to the architecture,' says Yoshida. 'The facades are imposing, but they show some restraint.'

I consider this for a moment. Omotesando is Tokyo's Champs-Elysees, a 1km (0.6-mile) paean to materialism, where faux-neoclassical structures and perception-distorting buildings house the biggest brands in global fashion. Cinema-sized shop windows scream Dior, Boss, Chanel and Burberry. Subtlety is not, to put it mildly, the first word that comes to mind.

'There are implied rules that architects usually follow,' she continues. 'None of the buildings should be taller than 30m [100ft], and a lot of them are even smaller than that. They are often made with glass or concrete, so they stand out, but they're not too ostentatious. And maybe they have gardens on top, which represent the Meiji Shrine forest.'

She brings me to the new Fendi building to emphasise how easy it is to miss the brief. It certainly makes an impression, constructed from irregular blocks of stainless steel, with an art-deco-y entrance of straight lines and illuminated arches, all set above a staircase of veiny white marble.

'I was very surprised when I first saw this here,' Yoshida says. 'It's a little different from the other buildings on this street.' I concede she may have a point.

Omotesando may be home to some of Tokyo's priciest real estate, but it's also multifaceted. We slip into the sodden backstreets, a winding warren of independent apparel shops, coffee houses, hole-in-the-wall food joints and pop-up stores. This takes us down Cat St, a serpentine pedestrian lane built on top of what was once the (reportedly foul-smelling) Shibuya River. I remark to Yoshida that the architecture and businesses here are much more charming than those on the always-crammed Takeshita St, just a few hundred metres away.

She nods in agreement. 'And it's so seamless, right?'

Perhaps the reason it works so seamlessly is that Omotesando is a chronology of Japanese architecture. Meiji Shrine employs the wooden building techniques Japan used to construct monuments for centuries, before the word 'kenchikuka' (architect) had entered the lexicon. The Yoyogi National Gymnasium is the next great leap. A dramatic, sweeping design by Kenzo Tange, whom Yoshida describes as 'a god of Japanese architecture', it was built during Japan's national reinvention in the lead-up to the 1964 Tokyo Olympics. Tange combined traditional Japanese aesthetic sensibilities with modernism and concrete, inspiring the next generation of architects, like Kengo Kuma and Tadao Ando.

It's a serious feather in the cap of any architect to design a building in Omotesando, and both Kuma and Ando have joined this exclusive club. Kuma, known for his love of biomimicry and wood, designed Sunny Hills Cafe, a giant bird's nest of a structure with light flooding through gaps in the intricate latticework. Ando, Japan's undisputed king of concrete, designed the eponymous Omotesando Hills, and his artistic signature is scribbled all over it. The building's foundation is concrete, but large apertures have been carved into the facade making the interior feel spacious, less entombing – a sensation accentuated by the triangular, spiralling floor plan surrounding the central atrium.

'Ando designed it to reflect Omotesando,' says Yoshida. 'Even the angle of the floors mirrors the slope of the road.'

Younger architects, like Sou Fujimoto and Teppei Fujiwara, have also made their mark on the Omotesando cityscape, and it's only a matter of time before the architects of tomorrow are given the chance to flex their muscles here, too. While its connection to Meiji Shrine has become more tenuous, this generational approach has helped Omotesando stay relevant. Perhaps that's why Ando once said, 'Working in Tokyo has convinced me that, contrary to what people think, it is actually one of the world's most beautiful cities.'

Five More Designs to Check Out in Omotesando

Louis Vuitton Building Omotesando
Jun Aoki designed the LV building to look like a stack of Louis Vuitton suitcases, using plate-glass and rose and gold panelling. There are no floors nor walls inside; it's a series of layered spaces peppered with chic furniture and bathed in natural light. There's a gallery space on the top floor, too, holding exhibitions by international multimedia artists.

Prada Tokyo Aoyama
The Herzog & de Meuron–designed Prada building was constructed with diamond-shaped glass panels in the backstreets near Aoyama. There's a fluid connection between the floors here, allowing the interior to feel like a seamless, barrier-free extension of the city.

Omotesando Keyaki Building
The eight-storey Omotesando Keyaki Building, designed by Norihiko Dan, currently houses a Hugo Boss boutique. The outer shell is made from steel-reinforced concrete columns with coarse textures, inspired by the keiyaki (zelkova) trees lining the

Omotesando boulevard. It's an act of biomimicry showing that concrete and nature needn't always be foes.

Bottega Veneta Building

When he was commissioned to work on the TOD's Omotesando (now Bottega Veneta) Building, architect Toyo Ito started with a question: 'How can we escape the conventional notion of a wall structure?' His eventual L-shaped design drew inspiration from nature, implementing a veiny, concrete-and-glass exterior based on overlapping tree silhouettes.

The Iceberg

The Iceberg is one of the most unusual and open-to-interpretation structures in the area. Formerly the Audi Forum but now home to WeWork offices, architect Benjamin Warner's design has a polyhedral glass facade that has drawn comparisons to crystal shards, a crushed PET bottle and an iceberg, the last of which is its de-facto name.

Prada Tokyo Aoyama

"In a modern world, where the stream of endless smartphone notifications and infinite-scroll apps has caused societies to become increasingly plugged in, of course people are searching for new sources of calm."

SLOW TRAVEL

WHAT IS A RYOKAN?

⊙ AROUND JAPAN

Japan is an easy country to zip around. The Shinkansen is arguably the most efficient rail network in the world, with hundreds of high-speed trains hurtling across the country like clockwork each day. But just because you can move at pace doesn't mean you should. One of the best ways to slow down and distance yourself from the freneticism of urban life is by staying at a ryokan.

Ryokan are traditional inns – usually found in the countryside and in onsen resort towns – and often their history dates to the Edo Period, when travelling for toji (hot-spring therapy) was permitted by the Shogun. Not much has changed. Travellers still use ryokan as escapes from the city, to soak in onsen, eat locally produced food and experience a bit of R&R.

Whether they're located high in the mountains or fringing the coast, ryokan have several commonalities: hot outdoor baths with water that beautifies the skin; tatami rooms with Japanese-style futon beds; guests lounging around in traditional garments, like yukata (robes) or samue (pyjamas); a kaiseki meal for dinner and a Japanese-style breakfast; and supremely high levels of *omotenashi*, the spirit of hospitality.

There are more than 60,000 ryokan throughout Japan, but some offer considerably more bespoke accommodation than others. The Japan Ryokan & Hotel Association has certified around 1800 of these establishments based on a rigorous set of criteria, while the Ryokan Collection is a consortium of 47 of the most impressive luxury inns in Japan.

In recent years, there has also been a reinvention of the ryokan, where modern properties, like the award-winning Hoshino Resorts, fuse traditional design aesthetics with present-day comforts. You might find modular rooms with sliding shoji windows and rotenburo (outdoor baths), as well as plush furnishings, Western-style beds and air-conditioning. The idea is to recreate the atmosphere of old Edo, without making guests feel like it's 1792.

⊘ ryokan.or.jp/english
⊘ ryokancollection.com

Top **Serenity at a ryokan**
Bottom **Kurokawa Onsen is lined with ryokan**

LIVING ZEN: KISHI-KE MODERN *RYOKAN*

⊙ **KANAGAWA**

Nobuyuki Kishi is in a contemplative mood. Wearing a light linen samue, the pyjama-like clothes of the Buddhist monk, he turns his shaved head and looks out of the window.

'The view looks like a Hiroshige Utagawa painting,' he says. 'He used to paint soothing landscapes like this. The sea, the mountains.'

I take a sip of earthy sencha tea, its slightly sweet aroma fills my nostrils. I agree with Nobuyuki: looking at this scenery, the hook-shaped Sagami Bay and the great Pacific Ocean beyond, is good for the soul.

The idea for opening a *ryokan* in Kamakura, a thriving seaside town 50km (31 miles) south of Tokyo, came to Nobuyuki like a vision. 'Several years ago, I was working in the semiconductor industry and living with my grandfather,' he says. 'I was on a business trip, when suddenly I saw the image of having *gyokuro* tea with him.'

There is a ritualistic aspect to tea drinking in Japan, and for Nobuyuki, it always had therapeutic effects. Like many Japanese males who go the way of the salaryman, Nobuyuki felt burnt out by the stresses of the corporate world. Opening a ryokan, where he and his wife Hitomi could help guests seek reprieve from the rat race, felt like the perfect antidote.

Initially, Nobuyuki and Hitomi wanted Kishi-ke to be a traditional ryokan, an inn that wouldn't look out of place on the streets of old Edo. But something didn't quite feel right. 'When we came up with the idea, I was 33 and Hitomi was 28, which is quite young for this job,' Nobuyuki says. 'So we wanted to make Kishi-ke different, to reflect the reality of who we are.'

Kishi-ke is a fine balancing act, an exercise in minimalism that stays true to traditional Japanese aesthetic sensibilities without sacrificing modern comforts. It is much more youthful than the old ryokan found in Kyoto or Japan's onsen resorts, but one is under no illusions as to the historical spirit of the place. The centrepiece is a karesansui, or dry Zen garden, with a stone koi (carp), raked white gravel, a maple tree on one side and a plum blossom on the other. The guest house, which accommodates no more than four people at a time, has a washitsu, or Japanese-style tatami room, which serves as a dining and living space and as a stage for *cha-no-yu,* the tea ceremony. There are sliding doors, too, a classic feature of modular Japanese design, used to increase the sense of space and access a shaded porch overlooking the garden.

Nobuyuki is the 16th generation of the Kishi samurai family of Okayama, which has ancient links to Kamakura and Zen Buddhism. So he wanted Kishi-ke to harness the Zen *chisoku* concept, which roughly translates as 'the feeling of being fulfilled'. The implication being, if you change your environment, you're able to focus on the now, notice new things about yourself and have greater awareness of that which gives your life value. He felt the *ryokan* should be a physical manifestation of this idea and represent his ancestors' way of life. Only then could he fulfil his grandfather's wish to create something that could not be replicated.

'I'm not sure if I'm always Zen, or even if I'm religious. But maybe I do believe in something,' Nobuyuki says. 'I just want guests to feel like they are fulfilled here. I want them to appreciate being in the moment. And then maybe they can adapt that to their lives after they leave.'

While Kishi-ke was Nobuyuki's brainchild, he insists Hitomi, a former product designer at Panasonic, is the creative one. She's responsible for the artistic input, curating and designing the crockery selection and ornaments reflecting the philosophy of *wabi-sabi*, the beauty of imperfection. She also worked with Ryohei Tanaka, an apprentice of legendary architect Kengo Kuma, to bring the vision of Kishi-ke to life.

'It doesn't feel like work; it's my lifestyle,' she told me during a previous meeting. 'I want to drink tea in nice vessels, which I have created. I design them for the guests, but I also do it out of my own curiosity.'

Nobuyuki hands me a Sekisanjin stone cup, carved out of andesite and fired at well over 1000 degrees, and invites me to sit by a crackling charcoal brazier. He assumes the *seiza* position and starts preparing matcha in the old way, with arcane utensils and a bamboo whisk. It is more dance than cooking; his hands move in rhythmic, preordained lines as if there is no room for error.

The cast-iron kettle whistles, and outside, light rain falls. There's a single piece of shodo (hanging scroll calligraphy) on the wall.

'Be calm,' it reads. 'And listen to the sound of pine needles growing.'

A karesansui (dry Zen garden)

Top **Hitomi Kishi**

Bottom **Shojin ryori (a plant-based meal) at Kishi-ke**

Opposite **Pine tree at Kishi-ke**

ZEN INFLUENCES ON JAPANESE MINDFULNESS

◉ **AROUND JAPAN**

Long before mindfulness became a vogue term in the global travel industry, Japanese monks, priests, poets and scholars spent lifetimes trying to avoid the incessant chatter of their inner monologues. They often took themselves deep into the forests, where the silence was so complete they could hear the hum of a mosquito or the splash of a single frog as it leapt from a pond. They thought of time not in hours or days, or even in accordance with the lunar calendar, but only acknowledged its presence in the slow passing of the seasons.

When we think about Japan's traditional approach to mindfulness, it is defined by a sensitivity to such ephemera and a belief that the world's imperfections are its truest source of true beauty. We see this in the tea ceremony, ikebana (flower arrangements), Japanese garden design, calligraphy and ink painting, and swordsmanship and bushido (the way of the warrior). These arts are concerned with focusing the mind, being at one with your environment and attaining higher levels of perception. They are pure and immediate experiences of reality,

Though the influence of Taoism and Confucianism should not be overlooked, Zen Buddhism is the underlying current. In 1958, the eminent scholar Daisetsu T Suzuki averred that Zen had entered internally into every phase of Japanese cultural life.

Think of the tea ceremony, the purpose of which is to create a harmonious balance between the participant and their environment, or ikebana, which forces the viewer to consider the beauty of a solitary sprig of blossoms rising from a rustic earthenware pot. You might not associate the martial arts with a spiritual philosophy that denounces violence, but you'll find the imprints of Zen there, too. Japanese warriors – at least those whose teachings are still used today – never charged into battle mindlessly. After all, what is the legendary swordsmith Miyamoto Musashi's *The Book of Five Rings* if not a strategy guide to using the mind effectively?

Though we may view these artforms as products of a bygone era, Japanese mindfulness is experiencing a minor renaissance. Craft collectives are being established in rural Japan to protect and preserve traditional arts. Tea ceremony schools are attracting new apprentices from across the globe. Prestigious temples are offering zazen meditation classes in foreign languages. Japanese mindfulness techniques have even found their way into the worlds of business and leadership.

The practical application for all this is obvious: in a modern world, where the stream of endless smartphone notifications and infinite-scroll apps has caused societies to become increasingly plugged in, of course people are searching for new sources of calm, of methods for disconnecting from the virtual world.

'Zen' means meditation, so in theory, by experiencing Zen-influenced Japanese arts, one is striving for a meditative state, where all anxieties are tranquilised and nothing becomes more important than the moment itself.

Japanese mindfulness techniques have become popular internationally

Opposite **Ikebana encourages reflection**

BUDDHISM THROUGH THE EYES OF THE MONK IN MASCARA

◎ TOKYO

When I first meet Kodo Nishimura, there is absolutely nothing to suggest his stardom. He slides open the *fusuma* door, steps onto the tatami, smiles and hands me a sticker of two praying hands surrounded by a white circle in the middle of a pride flag.

'This is a rainbow sticker I co-created with the Japan Buddhist Federation,' he says. I'm struck by his calming presence, the genuine kindness that comes through in the timbre of his voice. 'They were very forward-thinking and wanted to create something that supports LGBTQ rights.'

This setting, in the family temple where he grew up, and his dark robes and golden *igiboso* (a stole worn by the ordained) betray his vocation as a Buddhist monk. But Nishimura is also the Monk in Mascara, the Monk Who Wears Heels, and he has long led a double life. When not reading sutras, meditating or carrying out services in the temple, he might be attending fashion events in Paris, modelling for brands like Ralph Lauren, applying makeup at the Miss Universe contest, giving talks to the United Nations or Harvard University or as was the case in 2019, teaming up with the Fab Five for *Queer Eye: We're in Japan!* He even turned his unlikely story into a book, *This Monk Wears Heels,* which subsequently

became a TV program aired by Japan's public broadcaster NHK.

As a homosexual man, who had much more in common with his female peers, neither socially conservative Japan nor the monkhood felt like a good fit. Had Nishimura divined the tea leaves as a child, he would never have believed this would be where he'd end up.

'I loathed the idea of becoming a Buddhist monk,' he says. 'I thought, "How is it possible for Amida Buddha to guide us to the Pure Land, *scientifically*, and why do people seriously believe in something that sounds like a fairytale?"'

But after a period of revaluation and some sage, if slightly cryptic, advice from his mother – who told him you can't criticise Mozart unless you fundamentally understand the music – he changed his mind. 'I wanted to know how they teach Buddhism and what was the role of a Buddhist monk,' he says. 'I also wanted to fortify my identity as a Japanese person.'

During his training, Nishimura began to frame things in terms of colour. If boys were blue and girls were pink, he felt he was purple. But sometimes he also felt yellow.

'In Pure Land Buddhism, there's supposed to be a Pure Land, or heaven, that we go to after we pass away. And in that Pure Land there is a pond of lotus flowers that are blossoming in different colours,' he says. 'In the sutra, it says that a blue lotus flower shines in blue, yellow lotus shines in yellow, red lotus shines in red and white lotus shines in white. My master told me that this means every person should shine in their own colour. That was very liberating for me.'

He then tells me something that rings like a mantra: 'If you really dare to bare your vulnerability and insecurities, you can grab the hearts of people who are watching.'

Nishimura began applying some of the 850-year-old teachings to his everyday life, trying not to give in to frustration and searching for meaning in mundane and trivial moments. He's also used them to reconcile the conflict between Buddhism as a study of the mind and makeup and fashion as expressions of physicality.

'Makeup helps me feel empowered and helps me to spread my message,' he says. 'Guan Yin, the Buddhist Motherly figure of Compassion and Mercy, says, "If you're wearing something shabby, how will people listen to you and respect you?" I think it correlates because the world also exists of things that you can see and feel.'

Though we may associate Buddhism with asceticism and esoterica, with lonely mountain hermitages and endless sessions of rhythmic chanting, Nishimura thinks monks, by and large, are a liberal bunch, and the religion they practise is increasingly modern. Buddhism teaches not to discriminate against behavioural choices or immutable characteristics, and for Nishimura, it's about striving to live each day with meaning and finishing it knowing that you prioritised what – and who – was important.

'Buddhism is alive and keeps evolving with the times,' he says. 'I would like to show people that Buddhism is not only minimalism, it's not only about funerals; it can be for people who need the courage to be themselves.'

🌐 kodonishimura.com

Top and bottom
Kodo Nishimura, the monk who wears heels

ZAZEN: SEEKING ENLIGHTENMENT IN TAKAYAMA

⊙ GIFU

The *whomp* of the sliding van door startles me awake. I step, gingerly, into the shrivelling cold.

'Where are we?'

'Zennoji Temple, near Takayama,' says Hisako-san, my interpreter and a doting mother hen figure who's rarely left my side for the past week. 'We are going to do zazen.'

Zazen is a form of seated meditation, a study of the self. 'To study the Buddha Way is to study the self,' said the priest Dogen. 'To study the self is to forget the self, and to forget the self is to be enlightened by the 10 thousand things.'

Forgetting myself, I imply that I'm in no mood for meditation.

Hisako-san smiles. 'We shouldn't make Nakai-sensei wait.'

Nakai-sensei, Zennoji's head monk, stands at the temple entrance watching us approach, unperturbed as thawing snow drips from the eaves. He could not look more like a monk: his head is shaved, his posture is vertical, his hands are clasped upon his core and he has a warm, if infrequently used, smile.

He invites us in and bids us to sit at a low table, where bowls of roasted tea and lemon-flavoured *wagashi* (traditional sweets) await.

'Please, take your time,' he says. His voice is measured, unhurried. 'Then we will commence.'

Chinmoku, or silence, is an important aspect of zazen meditation. In this solemn temple precinct on the outskirts of Takayama, external silence is a given. But today is about the silence within.

'When something does not have a physical quality, like your mind, it is difficult to explain and understand,' says Nakai-sensei as we enter the meditation room. 'View the mind as a river of thoughts. You must not embrace those thoughts or interact with them. Just let them wash by.'

I place my meditation pillow on the raised platform, assume the lotus position as best I can and begin to meditate.

My mind is a river. It is torrential and growing in size. It is now a flash flood, the dams have burst and the map of my brain is being redrawn. It's not just that there is no silence; there is cacophony, waves of thought heaving and swelling between my ears.

I force myself not to think. Of course, this doesn't work. In fact, I realise I'm writing these very words in my head as I'm telling myself not to think. The distance between me and forgetting the self is cosmic. The only thing I can be sure of at this moment in time is the *self*.

Sensations of pain begin to arise elsewhere. My knees are not used to being

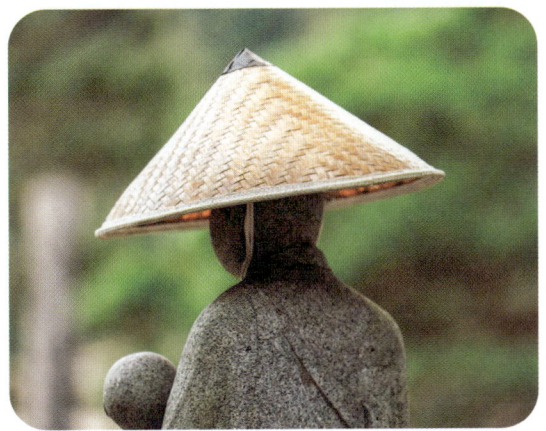

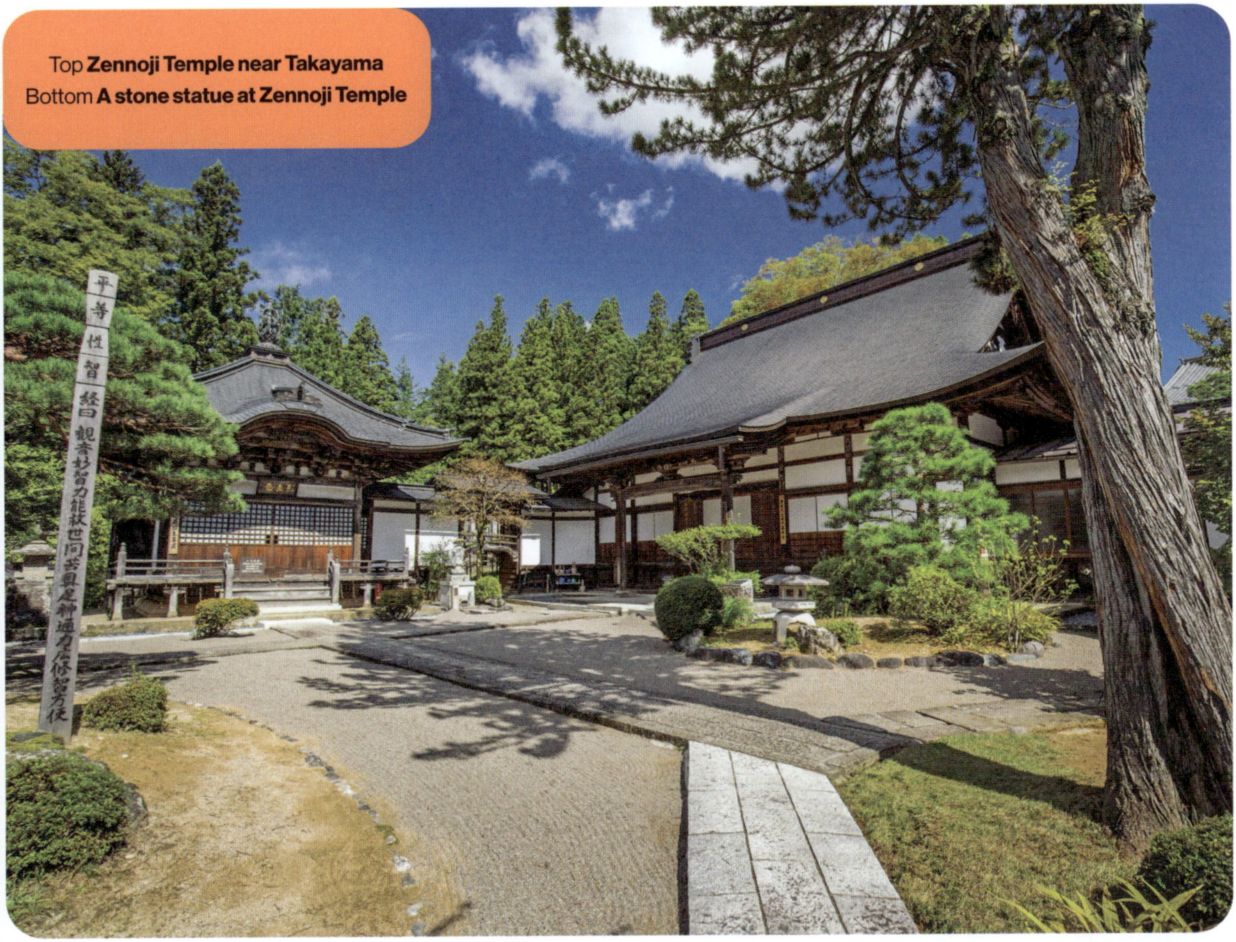

Top **Zennoji Temple near Takayama**
Bottom **A stone statue at Zennoji Temple**

in this position. The pillow feels like it's made of broken glass. Muscles I didn't know existed are on fire.

I focus, instead, on my breathing, filling my lungs with the icy mountain atmosphere and expelling it back into the cold, dark room.

Then, slowly, the flood begins to abate, the pain starts to subside. The floodwater has found somewhere else to go and a kind of clarity forms. The sun shines, birds chirp, there is a breeze, but it is a gentle one.

'That's time,' Nakai-sensei says, guiding us back to reality. 'How do you feel? Enlightened?'

'My mind,' I tell him, 'is a river.'

Eiheiji, Fukui Prefecture

TEMPLES WHERE YOU CAN PRACTISE MEDITATION

✳ **Eiheiji, Fukui Prefecture** The monks at Eiheiji are disciples of Dogen, founder of the Soto sect of Zen Buddhism. The temple's Sanzen program is quite intensive, featuring an overnight stay, four or five 40-minute meditation sessions, shojin-style vegetarian meals and participation in the 5.30am morning service. 🔗 **daihonzan-eiheiji.com/en**

✳ **Shoganji, Oita Prefecture** A small, rural temple in Oita Prefecture, Shoganji started running homestay experiences in 2004, hoping that visitors would gain a greater understanding of Japanese Buddhist culture. Guests at Shoganji practice meditation techniques, study Zen teachings or simply sit and admire the surrounding bamboo forest. The temple usually takes only four guests at a time. 🔗 **zenretreat.com**

✳ **Shunkoin, Kyoto City** Zazen experiences at Shunkoin teach guests how to incorporate Zen philosophy into their lives. Available only to private groups, guests can request other Zen arts to be incorporated into the program, including calligraphy classes, a shojin ryori meal, a tea ceremony or a koto (stringed zither instrument) performance. 🔗 **shunkoin.com/en**

✳ **Dairyuji, Oga Peninsula** A good option for beginners. Dairyuji, the Temple of the Big Dragon, holds weekend mindfulness retreats with structured meditation sessions, Dharma talks, mandala activities and free periods to explore the temple's Water Garden and the Oga Peninsula. 🔗 **dairyuji-oga.com**

✳ **Rengejoin Temple, Wakayama** A temple lodging on sacred Mount Koya, Rengejoin is a great place to experience shukubo, 'sleeping with the monks'. Alongside participating in the daily services, guests can learn how to copy sutras and begin their tutelage in ajikan meditation, which differs slightly from its zazen cousin. 🔗 **rengejoin.jp/en**

WALKING THE SHIKOKU HENRO PILGRIMAGE

⊙ **SHIKOKU**

Here's a remarkable thing about Shikoku: the entire island is a Buddhist mandala, an 18,800 sq km (7259 sq mile) diagram of eternal spiritual truths. The 88 shrines within its confines aren't organised like a traditional mandala – there is no obvious configuration or geometry – but then again, Japanese aesthetic ideals have never been comfortable with symmetrical design.

Driving along Shikoku's coastal highways and mountain roads today, you still see scores of henro (pilgrims), clad in white hakui robes and conical straw hats, searching for the mandala's secrets and, perhaps, a pathway to the Pure Land.

It all started with Kukai, known posthumously as Kobo Daishi, a monk, poet, epigraphist and calligrapher who founded the Shingon sect of Buddhism in the early ninth century. Though Kukai supposedly attained enlightenment in a cave in Muroto, a coastal region in Kochi Prefecture, he never walked the now-famous Shikoku Pilgrimage himself. His legacy looms large over the 1200km (746-mile) trail, nonetheless, because he sought spiritual succour in Shikoku's central mountains and commissioned several of the 88 temples. After his death, pilgrims came to follow in Kukai's footsteps and a circular(ish) walking route soon emerged.

Not all sections of the Shikoku Pilgrimage are created equal – some are known as *henro-korogashi*, 'places where pilgrims fall over' – but this is by design: the pilgrimage is an arduous physical journey mapped on top of a spiritual one.

In the Tokushima, or 'Awakening', section, pilgrims climb deep into the mountains, including a 15km (9-mile) slog over undulating terrain between Fujidera (temple 11) and Shozanji (temple 12). In Kochi ('Ascetic Training') the road is long and sparse, with only 16 temples in the island's largest prefecture. Ehime ('Enlightenment') has the most temples, 26, but requires pilgrims to brave challenging hikes, like the long ascent to Yokomineji (temple 60). Kagawa ('Nirvana'), the most urban of Shikoku's prefectures, is regarded as the easiest stretch, until the climb towards Okubuji (temple 88) poses one final test of mettle.

The last time I was in Shikoku, I visited a few of the temples to nose around, hopefully accost some weary walkers and question them as to the whole point of this endeavour. At Iwamotoji in Kochi, an unassuming temple with a mildly Tibetan air, I chatted with an American pilgrim. I asked him why he came, what he had gleaned from the experience.

'It's the kindness of the people. The culture of *o-settai* (generosity towards pilgrims),' he said. Sometimes people would stop to give him oranges and apples, maybe some water or even a few hundred yen. 'I know it sounds kinda silly, but it has reaffirmed my faith in humanity.'

This stuck with me because the old rationale for walking the pilgrimage is – much like Shingon itself – esoteric. Any discussion on it inevitably devolves into the naming of Buddhas and Wisdom Kings, realms of spiritual experience or otherworldly rewards that makes for tough listening unless you're well versed in East Asian spiritual discourse.

So people have found new reasons. They walk the pilgrimage as a means of escape, they want to reconnect with nature, experience life at a more measured cadence or find inner peace in the chanting of mantras. And some do it, simply, because it is there.

🌐 henro.org/shikoku-pilgrimage

Walking the Shikoku steps

INDEX

ABOUT THE AUTHOR

David McElhinney is a Northern Irish writer, journalist and editor who moved to Tokyo in 2018. Over the past seven years, he has blended reporting and social commentary with extensive travel throughout the country to publish stories on travel, arts and culture, politics and current affairs, and sports in Japan. *Intrepid Japan* is his first book, but his work has also appeared in a range of national and international publications online and in print, including *Tokyo Weekender*, *The Japan Times*, *Al Jazeera*, *The Belfast Telegraph*, *The Independent*, *The Irish Independent*, *Lonely Planet*, and *CNN*. He now splits his time between Tokyo and Belfast.

Photo credits

Published in 2025 by Hardie Grant Explore,
an imprint of Hardie Grant Publishing

Hardie Grant Explore (Melbourne)
Wurundjeri Country
Level 11, 36 Wellington Street
Collingwood VIC 3066

Hardie Grant Explore (Sydney)
Gadigal Country
Level 7, 45 Jones Street
Ultimo, NSW 2007

hardiegrant.com/explore

The maps in this publication incorporate data from the
following sources:
Global Map Japan © Geospatial Information Authority
of Japan (https://www.gsi.go.jp/kankyochiri/gm_japan_e.
html), © Michinoku Trail Club, © Ministry of the
Environment, Government of Japan - Biodiversity
Center of Japan

Data from OpenStreetMap www.openstreetmap.org/
copyright, OpenStreetMap is open data, licensed under
the Open Data Commons Open Database License
(ODbL) by the OpenStreetMap Foundation (OSMF).
https://opendatacommons.org/licenses/odbl/1-0/

Any rights in individual contents of the database are
licensed under the Database Contents License:
https://opendatacommons.org/licenses/dbcl/1-0/

Data extracts via Geofabrik GmbH
https://www.geofabrik.de

Made with Natural Earth. Free vector and raster map
data @ naturalearthdata.com.

A catalogue record for this
book is available from the
National Library of Australia

NATIONAL
LIBRARY
OF AUSTRALIA

Hardie Grant acknowledges the Traditional Owners of
the Country on which we work, the Wurundjeri People
of the Kulin Nation and the Gadigal People of the Eora
Nation, and recognises their continuing connection to
the land, waters and culture. We pay our respects to
their Elders past and present.

Intrepid Japan
ISBN 9781741179323

10 9 8 7 6 5 4 3 2 1

Publisher
Megan Cuthbert

Editor
Monique Choy

Editorial assistance
Siena O'Kelly

Proofreader
Lyric Dodson

Cartographer
Emily Maffei

Design
George Saad Studio

Typesetting
Megan Ellis

Index
Max McMaster

Production manager
Simone Wall

Colour reproduction and pre-press by Megan Ellis
and Splitting Image Colour Studio

Printed and bound in China by LEO Paper Products LTD.

FSC
www.fsc.org
MIX
Paper | Supporting
responsible forestry
FSC® C020056

The paper this book is printed on
is certified against the Forest
Stewardship Council® Standards
and other sources. FSC® promotes
environmentally responsible, socially
beneficial and economically viable
management of the world's forests.